A WOLF AT THE
SCHOOLHOUSE DOOR

A WOLF AT THE SCHOOLHOUSE DOOR

THE DISMANTLING OF PUBLIC EDUCATION AND THE FUTURE OF SCHOOL

Jack Schneider and
Jennifer Berkshire

NEW YORK
LONDON

Requests for permission to reproduce selections from this book should be made through our website: https://thenewpress.com/contact.

Published in the United States by The New Press, New York, 2020
Distributed by Two Rivers Distribution

ISBN 978-1-62097-494-0 (hc)
ISBN 978-1-62097-495-7 (ebook)
CIP data is available

The New Press publishes books that promote and enrich public discussion and understanding of the issues vital to our democracy and to a more equitable world. These books are made possible by the enthusiasm of our readers; the support of a committed group of donors, large and small; the collaboration of our many partners in the independent media and the not-for-profit sector; booksellers, who often hand-sell New Press books; librarians; and above all by our authors.

www.thenewpress.com

Book design and composition by Bookbright Media
This book was set in Sabon and Avenir

Printed in the United States of America

10 9 8 7 6 5 4 3 2 1

Education is our only political safety. Outside of this ark all is deluge.

—*Horace Mann*

CONTENTS

Introduction   *xiii*

1. Private Values   1

2. Faith in Markets   14

3. The Cost-Cutting Crusade   27

4. The War on Labor   44

5. Neo-Vouchers   62

6. The Pursuit of Profit   79

7. Virtual Learning   100

8. The End of Regulation   118

9. Don't Forget to Leave Us a Review   138

10. Selling School   154

11. Teaching Gigs   174

12. Education, à la Carte   190

Conclusion   *207*
Acknowledgments   *217*
Notes   *219*
Index   *251*

A WOLF AT THE
SCHOOLHOUSE DOOR

INTRODUCTION

When Secretary of Education Betsy DeVos was asked in an interview whether she saw the coronavirus pandemic as an opportunity to advance the cause of private school choice, she responded without hesitation. "Yes, absolutely."[1]

As schools across the country confronted the crisis and its unprecedented financial consequences, DeVos remained single-mindedly focused on the agenda that made her Donald Trump's most controversial cabinet pick. In the weeks after schools shut down, DeVos encouraged states to use federal funds to help parents pay private school tuition, and demanded that school districts share millions of aid dollars with wealthy private schools.

Initially, DeVos was treated as more of a joke than a threat—an impression solidified by a series of clumsy media appearances. Yet DeVos was no political naïf. Upon taking office, she immediately made clear her disinterest in the public schools—though they are attended by the vast majority of American children—using her policy perch to advocate for breaking up what she derisively calls "the system."

Close observers have been struck by DeVos's radical agenda. But as we argue in this book, the agenda is not hers alone. While DeVos has been the most prominent public face of the recent push to dismantle public education, she is not its architect. The movement has been steadily gaining power and notching progress for decades—building financial support, erecting a policy infrastructure, and constructing a finely honed public message.

In recent years, bestsellers like *Dark Money* by journalist Jane Mayer and *Democracy in Chains* by historian Nancy MacLean have examined efforts by the radical right to fundamentally alter the American political system. Yet these works have largely overlooked public education in their accounts. The billionaires populating the pages of these books—the Bradleys, the DeVoses, the Kochs—have long been fixated upon the nation's system of public schools, and have slowly laid the groundwork for its unraveling. Now, in our post–*Citizens United* era, conservative elites are increasingly able to translate their animus against public education into state-level policy.

When the Koch network held its annual retreat in 2018 at a resort outside of Palm Springs, the seven hundred attendees—among the richest people in America—were instructed to go "all in" on efforts to transform the education system. "We can change the trajectory of the country," Charles Koch told donors during a cocktail reception.[2] Among the network's priorities: replacing brick-and-mortar schools with a voucher program that would allow parents to purchase education products for their children in an Amazon-like marketplace.

That K-12 education is in the sights of conservative plutocrats shouldn't come as a surprise. Public schools are the biggest ticket item in many state budgets, making them a prime target for anti-tax crusaders. Then there's the fact that the country's teaching force, some 3 million strong, remains overwhelmingly unionized—the single largest body of union members in the country. But there is something more fundamental at stake here beyond just an ideological commitment to small government or a deep-seated loathing of unions. As political economist Gordon Lafer notes, "education is the one remaining public good to which most Americans still believe we are entitled to by right of citizenship."[3]

Back to the Future

This book began in response to a puzzling question: Why had conservative policy ideas, hatched decades ago and once languishing due to a lack of public and political support, suddenly roared back to life in the last five or so years? Take, for example, the idea of private school vouchers, the ignominious origins of which can be traced to the backlash against court-ordered desegregation—when state and local governments across the South paid for white citizens to send their children to private schools. With the exception of a brief and ill-fated push by the Reagan administration, vouchers had slowly faded from the conservative policy agenda. So what explained their return as a "disruptive innovation"?

In the spring of 2019, DeVos unveiled an ambitious new school choice initiative. At the center of the effort was a proposed $5 billion fund, providing individuals and corporate donors with a dollar-for-dollar tax credit for giving to scholarship programs that help families pay for tuition at private schools, homeschooling expenses, and other education services. But while the hashtag #educationfreedom was new, the rest of DeVos's agenda was a ripped-from-the-eighties retread. More than three decades earlier, her predecessor, Ronald Reagan's controversial secretary of education William Bennett, also pitched tax-credit scholarships, along with school vouchers for low-income parents. Even education savings accounts, which let parents spend state education dollars on an array of what DeVos terms "education options," date back to the Reagan era.

As we began to explore other policies favored by conservative hard-liners—market-based school choice, for-profit schools, virtual schooling, and the rollback of regulations—we noticed a similar pattern. Schemes that had first emerged as policy pipe dreams had been carefully stripped of their ideological underpinnings. Repackaged as new ideas, and accompanied by high-minded rhetoric, they've taken on new life. The ideological origins of these proposals have been largely forgotten, as have the battles fought over them. Meanwhile, the true believers have been building donor networks, cultivating political alliances, developing policy infrastructure, and crafting road-ready legislation.

Today's target is the "system," a catchall intended to conjure up waste, red tape, and soul-crushing bureaucracy. Yet the aim goes much deeper—striking at the core principles animating taxpayer-supported education. Indeed, the very idea of public education as a common good is depicted as an impingement on the freedom of individual students and their parents. "You can't have a one-size-fits-all system for every child's particular needs," said Mary Fallin, the former governor of Oklahoma, in a promotional video for the conservative Heritage Foundation touting education savings accounts.[4] We need to "break down the system so each kid is treated as a unique entity," pronounced Frank Edelblut, New Hampshire's education commissioner.[5]

Lawmakers, state officials, think tanks, and advocacy groups endlessly repeat such claims about the shortcomings of the existing system, hiding their radically conservative vision of schooling beneath banally familiar language. Listen closely, though, and the sharp ideological edge is hard to miss. At a 2017 appearance before the American Legislative Exchange Council, Betsy DeVos gleefully repurposed Margaret Thatcher's infamous claim that "there is no such thing as society." There is no education "system," DeVos told the corporate lobby group. "This is about individual parents, students, and families."[6]

The current sales pitch for pulling apart public schools even comes with an invented history. Schools, we are told, were modeled on factories, which trained students to work on the assembly line. Even as the U.S. economy has transformed, schools have continued to "batch process" students for jobs that no longer exist. None of this is really true, of course. Schools were not modeled on factories; student experiences in school are not uniform; and most of today's jobs will, according to predictions, still exist a generation from now.[7] But the conservatives' aim here isn't to offer a history lesson. Instead, this fabricated version of the past is designed to leverage anxiety among parents about the economic prospects of their children. Falling wages, fears of automation, the so-called skills gap—all of this can be used to make the case for a radical overhaul of public education, driven by a conservative agenda.

The Reagan-era push to implement school vouchers produced an avalanche of backlash. Democrats, and even many Republicans, argued that making education funding "portable"—even if the program were limited to low-income families—would devastate public schools. Teachers' unions, which held considerable sway within the Democratic Party, warned of privatization. And the public was decidedly cool to the idea of sending taxpayer funds to private religious schools. The proposal was dead on arrival.

Fast forward to the present, and Reagan's vision has not only come back to life, but its original radicalism is far harder to detect. Instead, it is rooted in the standard school-bashing that has become commonplace on both sides of the aisle. Innovation, no matter how dubious, is touted as a panacea for the ostensible shortcomings of public education.

This Time It's Different

The tradition of trashing public education has deep roots. Claims that schools were failing and required drastic intervention date back to the 1820s, with complaints from school reformers about poor teachers, low standards, and incompetent school boards.[8] Policy elites have long made their case for change by slamming the status quo.

During the past several decades, however, the rhetorical assault on America's public schools has intensified. The 1983 publication of the *A Nation at Risk* report, with its dire talk of a "rising tide of mediocrity," is credited by scholars and policy makers as a watershed moment, ushering in a newly strident discourse about public education. Since then, a national discussion about "failing schools"—increasing in intensity, but abstract in focus—has shaped public understanding about the state of education in the United States. As polling has documented, Americans have developed more and more negative views of the nation's schools, even while continuing to feel positively about the education their own children are receiving.[9]

Of course, even the fiercest critics have generally found *something* redeemable in the broad contours of American public education. Consider, for example, the free-market economist Milton Friedman, who first proposed the idea of taxpayer-funded school vouchers. Even as Friedman made the case for an approach that, as he argued, would gradually replace public schools with private ones, he still insisted on the idea of public education as a public good. "The gain from the education of a child accrues not only to the child or to his parents but other members of society," wrote Friedman in his seminal 1955 article about vouchers. "A stable and democratic society is impossible without widespread acceptance of some common set of values and without a minimum degree of literacy and knowledge on the part of most citizens."[10]

Likewise, the unlikely assemblage of billionaire philanthropists, charter school proponents, big-city mayors, and civil rights groups—a coalition instrumental in shaping the discourse about what's wrong with public schools—remains committed to public education in *some* form. While "education reform" is a baggy, ill-defined concept that means both everything and nothing, it mostly focuses on transforming the governance structures of schools. Market advocates and their close cousins, the neoliberals, push for privately run schools with merit pay for teachers because they maintain that the private sector is a more efficient delivery mechanism. The Silicon Valley–style "disruptors" want to move education online and free it from what they call "friction"—the myriad rules and regulations that govern schooling. Meanwhile, the successors of a long tradition of progressive reform believe that making schools more democratic can empower both teachers and students.

But as we argue in the chapters that follow, the present assault on public education represents a fundamentally new threat, driven by a new kind of pressure group. Put simply, the overarching vision entails unmaking public education as an institution. An increasingly potent network of conservative state and federal elected officials, advocacy groups, and think tanks, all backed by deep-pocketed funders, has aligned behind a vision of a radical reinvention.

As DeVos proclaimed during her 2018 "Rethink School" tour: "There's no more time for tinkering around the edges."[11]

What exactly does the agenda look like? There are four main principles:

1. **Education is a personal good, not a collective one.** It is more like private property than like a public park. Consumers should be able to shop for education as they do any other product.

2. **Schools belong in the domain of the free market, not the government.** They should be under the purview of personal preference and choice, not regulation and oversight. The role of the state should be as minimal as possible.

3. **To the extent that they are able, "consumers" of education should pay for it themselves.** The cost of schooling should not be distributed across society, except to provide a rudimentary education for those in poverty.

4. **Unions and other forms of collective power are economically inefficient and politically problematic.** They represent an ideological and practical obstacle to a radical free-market agenda. Their power should be limited or challenged, and when possible, they should be prevented from forming in the first place.

In state after state, these principles are being enacted into law and policy, often behind closed doors and away from public scrutiny. Some degree of secrecy or opacity is key, because Americans have consistently supported public education over the decades. Even in the wild west of Arizona, where the dismantling agenda has taken deep hold, the public has proved unwilling to give up the idea of locally controlled, taxpayer-supported, open-access schools. After the Republican-dominated legislature passed a law in April 2017 making all 1.1 million of Arizona's public schoolchildren eligible for private school vouchers, a parent group managed to collect more than one hundred thousand signatures in a matter of weeks, forcing the issue onto the ballot as a referendum measure, where it went down to overwhelming defeat.[12] Similarly, public sympathy for striking teachers—first in "red" states where deep cuts to school spending and the expansion of school choice have imperiled public schools, then in "blue" cities where the growth of charter schools has meant less money for students and teachers in traditional district schools—has demonstrated the deep support for public education that still exists.

The Battles to Come

A wolf is lurking at the door of America's public schools—prowling, biding its time, and waiting for the pack to assemble. Support for public education may be strong, but it is fragmented, variable, and voluntary—challenges familiar to any true grassroots affair. Those seeking to dismantle the system, meanwhile, are unified, patient, and well resourced.

In the battles to come, supporters of public schools will need three kinds of knowledge, and this book is organized accordingly. In the first section, we examine the dogma that underlies the dismantling agenda. Public consideration demands a clear presentation of aims and objectives. Yet the drive to unmake public education has been masked by linguistic feints and purposeful abstraction, designed to hide the principles at its core. In service of reasoned debate and deliberation, then, we trace these ideas from their roots, clarifying the ideology at the heart of this movement.

The second part of this book looks closely at the changes already in motion. Being broadly familiar with the animating spirit and aims of this movement is one thing; knowing how it takes form in public policy and the law is another. In order to advance public understanding of the dismantling agenda, the center section of the book examines the core policies of the dismantlers' effort.

In the third and final section of the book, we explore possible futures. A prospective view is essential for evaluating present policy, as policy is inherently the work of future-making. Following these efforts to their logical conclusion, we survey the landscape of a system dismantled.

Our intention in writing this book is not a subtle one. We are sounding an alarm. The diagnosis we issue is not in service of our own policy aims; we are not peddling a treatment. Our goal, instead, is to incite a public reckoning—on behalf of the millions of families presently served by the American educational system, and the many more who stand to suffer from its unmaking.

After all, what does it take to frighten away a wolf? Shouting, making noise, and standing tall.

1

Private Values

Private school. The very words evoke distinction—elegant, ivy-covered buildings dotted among quiet woodlands and lush green playing fields. Scenes like these speak to our most romantic notions about education. And when one glances at the colleges attended by graduates of America's top private schools—prestigious institutions that so often capture the popular imagination—it can be easy to conclude that public education is a pitiable alternative.

When Americans think of private schools, they often envision a place like Phillips Academy in Andover, Massachusetts, which has a billion-dollar endowment and annual tuition of close to $50,000. They picture public schools, but better—stronger students, statelier facilities, and superior academics. The more representative image, however, might be a small school run out of the basement of a church or occupying a strip-mall storefront.[1]

As for the Dead Poets Society–style depiction of a distinguished educator engaging his blazer-clad charges in a mansion-like setting? Well, that's mostly the stuff of Hollywood. Since private schools don't require their teachers to be certified, they are largely untrained. And because private school finances are constrained by tuition revenue—an amount that families pay on top of their property taxes that are already funding public education—most private schools are cash-strapped and plain-featured. In fact, the fastest-growing segment of the private school market is decidedly down-market: fly-by-night Christian schools that accept publicly funded vouchers.[2]

Nor is there much truth to the popular conception that private schools are "better" than their public counterparts. Some private schools do produce impressive lists of college acceptances, and many boast impressive average test scores. But the achievement of students at elite schools generally indicates more about the families and neighborhoods of the students than it does about schools. The private schools with the most extraordinary results are usually those with students from extraordinary privilege—young people who are likely to succeed academically wherever they are enrolled in school. In fact, according to research, when family background characteristics like wealth are taken into account, public schools may even outperform their private counterparts.[3]

Yet most Americans are convinced that "private" is a mark of distinction. According to polling by Gallup, roughly three-quarters of Americans believe that private schools provide a "good" or "excellent" education. By contrast, less than half of respondents expressed such positive views of public schools.[4]

Some of this perceptual divide certainly owes to marketing, which private schools use to their advantage, and which public schools generally don't engage in at all. Public perceptions, additionally, can be attributed to the markers that some private schools cultivate in their brochures in an effort to send the right signals—investments in facilities, for instance, or technology, that may do little to strengthen academic programming but which easily grab parents' attention.

Still, consumer psychology may be the most useful way of understanding what's happening here. As the marketing industry well understands, people disproportionately value products that they perceive to be scarce.[5] Consider a must-have celebrity accessory: the Birkin bag. Made by the French designer Hermès, this high-end handbag can cost as much as $300,000. And though top-grade leather and other luxury materials are certainly part of the product's makeup, what really makes it synonymous with wealth is its exclusivity—Birkin bags are produced and distributed on an extremely limited basis. In other words, scarcity drives the perception of quality.

While schools obviously differ from luxury leather goods, the perception of scarcity is a big part of why Americans prize private schools. Anyone can send their child to a public school, but only a minority of parents—roughly 10 percent—send their children to private schools. Therefore, parents who opt out of the public system are not only choosing to invest their own dollars in private education but also joining a small and select group. No wonder people view private school enrollment as a status symbol.

Those favorable opinions about private school education, however untethered from reality they may be, mean that policy proposals to extend the "benefit" of private schooling to everyone are generally popular. Only about half of public school parents would stick with a public school if they were offered public funds to send their child to a private school. Whether they believe the hype, or want their child instructed in a particular religion or worldview, many parents would be happy to enroll their children in a school that charges tuition, if only tuition were free.

Private Aims vs. Public Goods

When Betsy DeVos visited a pair of private Jewish schools in New York City in the spring of 2018, she raised more than a few eyebrows.[6] The ultra-orthodox schools, known as yeshivas, are controversial because they emphasize religious studies, often at the expense of teaching students basic skills in English, math, history, and science. The city launched an official investigation in 2015 after a community group alleged that students at many of the yeshivas were being denied a basic education, and were leaving school without the skills needed to function outside their religious communities.[7] But DeVos was unconcerned. "Great that you're learning such important things," she told a classroom of third graders, boys who were learning the correct order in which to say their prayers before eating, at an all-male yeshiva in Far Rockaway.[8]

Since No Child Left Behind was signed into law in 2002, our national debate about what makes a "good" school has focused overwhelmingly on standardized test scores in math and English. The signature education policy of George W. Bush's presidency, NCLB and the high-stakes metrics of its testing regimen were at the center of the vision championed by Barack Obama and his education chief, Arne Duncan—a vocal proponent of using standardized test scores to evaluate teachers and shutter schools. After a decade and a half of high-stakes accountability and "college for all" rhetoric, tempered enthusiasm for testing and accountability would make sense. But DeVos's decision to showcase private religious schools that generally discourage college-going, as in the case of the yeshivas she visited, can be hard to process.

DeVos is often painted as an anti-reformer by her critics, undoing the policy overreaches of her predecessors. Yet that view is misguided. Despite their pronouncements about "local control," DeVos and her allies are not particularly interested in returning authority to states and districts, nor are they especially concerned about curricular narrowing or an overemphasis on test prep. Instead, they'd like to junk the whole system, replacing public schools with private ones. And their vision has very little to do with school quality.

To understand what's behind this push, we need to consider the broader ideology of personal freedom. As the libertarian right sees it, Americans are restricted and restrained at every turn by big government and group sensibilities. In all walks of life, they believe, individuals should be free to decide for themselves what's best. And this is particularly true when it comes to education.

Freedom, of course, can be interpreted a number of different ways. One useful, if reductive, way of understanding such differences is to divide the concept between "freedom *to*" and "freedom *from*." Many personal liberties involve the freedom *to*—freedom to speak one's mind, for instance, or to worship as one sees fit. Other liberties, however, are framed around freedom *from*—freedom from the threat of violence, for example, or from environmental pollution. Whereas the first kind of freedom, to act as an individual, requires checks on government power, the second kind of freedom requires the opposite. Freedom from hazards usually demands collective action, usually at the direction of government, and it often requires limits to individual autonomy.

Because these two kinds of freedom exist in tension with each other, navigating the limits of freedom requires case-by-case evaluation and constant balancing. How much individual liberty should be sacrificed in the name of collective well-being? Different people have different answers in different contexts. Free-market crusaders, however, do not. Like other ideologues, they navigate such tensions by adhering to a narrow set of values. For them, government is a source of tyranny—a constraint on the freedoms that all individuals were born with. When Betsy DeVos says that she doesn't believe in the public education "system," this is what she means. She is referring to the entire package of principles and practices.

Public education has long offended such sensibilities, perhaps first and foremost because it is presented as a "public good." Unlike a private good, which benefits only those who consume it, public education benefits all members of the local, state, and national community, whether or not they have children.[9] When students graduate and enter the labor force and public life, their economic and civic productivity benefits everyone. Neighborhood residents benefit when young people become involved in the community and reinvest their success locally. And at the state and national level, returns to the common good accrue in the form of economic strength and civic competence. Like clean air, a well-educated populace is something with wide-reaching benefits. That's why we treat public education more like a park than a country club. We tax ourselves to pay for it, and we open it to everyone.

The fact that Americans are entitled to attend taxpayer-funded schools, merely by virtue of living here, makes public education even more offensive to free-market ideologues. We may not have a right to health care, housing, food, or even clean water, but universal free education is still part of the deal. In fact, the Supreme Court has ruled that even non-citizen children are entitled to a free K-12 public education—a source of outrage among anti-immigrant forces.[10] That makes public education the most pervasive and deeply rooted entitlement program among the under-65 set—a public service that can be utilized by anyone.

Our "public" treatment of schools doesn't end with the issue of access. Because public schools are a resource for the entire community, they are governed through a set of democratic processes. Consider elected school boards: imperfect though they are, the democratic process allows voters to hold them accountable for the success of the local schools. Such governance structures inhibit the freedom and autonomy of individuals to do as they wish, but they do so in service of the common good, as defined and enacted by ordinary citizens.

When DeVos and others on the radical right disparage the education "system," they're referring to all of this: the taxes that pay for public education, the democratic structures by which it's governed, and indeed the very idea of a public good. Their preference for private schools takes aim at all of these.

Public Schools as Socialism

In a commencement speech she delivered at Ave Maria University, a small Catholic school in Naples, Florida, established by the founder of Domino's Pizza, Betsy DeVos bemoaned what she described as the pernicious effects of government expansion. "Too many have abdicated responsibility for one another," DeVos told the class of 2018. "Ever-growing government has inserted itself into relationships, making folks less connected and more insulated from the needs of others."[11]

The criticism of "ever-growing government" dates back nearly a century, to the advent of the New Deal and the framework of laws and regulations that emerged in response to the Great Depression. The New Deal order reflected a belief that had steadily taken hold over several generations—that government had an essential role to play in mitigating the inequities of our capitalist economic system. Most Americans, of course, don't typically think of schools as being part of government. But those who aim to dismantle them do. When Donald Trump invoked the specter of "government schools" in his 2020 State of the Union Address, he was equating public schools "with all the negative connotations government conjures—waste, bureaucracy and liberty-crushing control," argues education law expert Derek Black. Indeed, Trump went even further, painting government schools as the enemy of his administration's signature education cause: education freedom.[12]

The argument that public schools have supplanted private institutions, namely churches, and the family is also a response to the expanding role that we expect schools to play in caring for children. According to Census data, roughly 18 percent of U.S. students live in poverty, and roughly 50 percent live in households earning less than twice the designated federal poverty threshold.[13] And as the needs of students have increased, the efforts of schools to meet those needs have likewise expanded. When school districts across the country shut down during the 2019–20 coronavirus pandemic, the reality that more than 20 million students rely on public schools for meals was thrown into stark relief.[14]

And it isn't just essential nutrition that schools provide. Increasingly, they have offered "wraparound services"—an approach that treats the school as the delivery site for a vast range of supports that children and their families require to overcome the hurdles erected by economic and social inequality. Advocates maintain that since out-of-school factors weigh so heavily in determining student achievement, using the school to address what's happening in the home and the neighborhood makes sense. But critics of "government overreach" see something very different happening. They see an ominous scenario in which the welfare state and its tentacles has expanded to encircle children. As DeVos warned: "The school building replaces the home, the child becomes a constituent and the state replaces the family."[15]

Worse yet, the entire enterprise smacks of socialism, with the state redistributing wealth to the poor through the public schools.

"Elementary and secondary education in the U.S. is the country's last remaining socialist enterprise," declared Joseph Bast, CEO of the libertarian Heartland Institute, in a 2002 blog post.[16] Bast was explaining his distaste for public education while making the case for so-called universal private school vouchers, which conservatives view as a way station en route to whole-sale privatization.

How to get there? It starts by shifting the work of public organizations, like schools, into the private domain. "We need to do something that was done about 25 years ago in the former Soviet Union and eastern bloc: sell off the existing buildings, equipment and real estate to those in the private sector," Ohio lawmaker Andrew Brenner wrote in a blog post.[17] Such sentiments sound like the rantings of a Red Scare–era kook, but Brenner happens to be the former chair of the Education and Career Readiness Committee for the Ohio House of Representatives. His goal, it seems, is to divest the state of its powers and responsibilities in public education.

Then there is the perennial complaint that the content of what public schools teach fails to instill in students an adequate appreciation for free-market capitalism. As historian Kim Phillips-Fein details in *Invisible Hands: The Businessmen's Crusade against the New Deal*, her history of business conservatism, this lament grew louder in response to the New Deal. If we fast forward to the present, we find our current captains of industry just as focused on the schools as their forebears were. The Koch brothers, for instance, spent years, not to mention a small fortune, trying to shape the K-12 social studies curriculum to be more friendly to free enterprise.[18]

But with polls consistently showing sinking support for capitalism among the nation's youth, more extreme measures may be called for. In a fund-raising pitch after the 2016 election, Larry Arnn, the president of Hillsdale College and a contender to serve as Donald Trump's secretary of education, announced that it was time to rescue students from failing schools. "Failure" in this case referred not to test score performance or achievement gaps, but to so-called progressive ideology. Arnn even cited data to prove his point: the millions of young adults who turned out to vote for Bernie Sanders. The schools, in other words, are turning the kids into socialists. The solution: privatize everything.

Freedom to Choose

The favored policy prescription to this many-headed critique of the public education system is to move students out of "government schools" and into just about any alternative: religious schools, home schools, charter schools, virtual schools, or something that isn't a school at all—an array of education "options" selected by families themselves. Proponents of this radical shift rely heavily on appeals to personal freedom, as well as the familiar language of the free market—the subject of our next chapter. According to this logic, families should be free to make whatever decisions they want with regard to the education of their children, just like they do with shoes, cars, or cell phones.

But beneath the case for empowering parents as consumers lurks a much older debate regarding who should be in charge of education: parents or the state. Since 1852, when Massachusetts passed a law making school attendance compulsory, authority has sided squarely with the latter. That means that the primary responsibility for educating children is *not* the province of the family, but of the public schools—or in the minds of detractors, "government schools." The heated debate over school choice in recent years has largely centered on what kinds of schools students should attend, the degree to which those schools should be regulated by the state, and whether students should be compelled to attend schools in their own neighborhoods. Now that is shifting.

A 2000 article from *Practical Homeschooling*, "The Meaning of Educational Freedom," succinctly captures the spirit of this shift: "We can go to the mall and buy whatever we want. . . . But when it comes to education, suddenly we are confronted with compulsory school attendance laws, compulsory property taxes to pay for the government schools, compulsory testing, compulsory inoculations, forced busing, restrictions against prayer, forced sex ed, death ed, and drug ed."[19] In 2012, the U.S. Department of Education reported that roughly 2 million students were being schooled at home, up from 850,000 in 1999.[20] While motives vary widely, a core rationale is people's active opposition to impingements on individual and parental freedom. As a 2016 column in the *National Review* put it, "Don't lose sight of a simple, liberating fact: You do not need to send your kids to government school. You can homeschool."[21]

While arguments like these have long percolated in libertarian circles, today they are considered practically mainstream. That the sort of individual freedom prized in the private sector should be advanced in education is a claim put forward by both school choice advocates on the political right and Democratic education reformers who advocate for more charter schools. But what is gaining traction is the even more radical notion that parents, not the state, should control their children's education. The insistence that the history of public education in the United States is one of government overreach is no longer relegated to the libertarian fringe; it is now shaping education policy in a growing number of states.

In Arizona, for example, where one of the country's most ambitious experiments in dismantling public education is currently under way, a freshman GOP lawmaker made headlines when he announced his goal of repealing the state's compulsory education requirement. In an interview with the *Arizona Capitol Times*, Representative Paul Mosley argued that the state had taken away the responsibility of parents to educate and provide basic care for their children: "So now schools are not only tasked with educating our children, but also feeding our children. What happened to the personal responsibility of a parent to feed and educate their kids?"[22]

Arizona's compulsory education law remains on the books for now, but Mosley's sentiment—that bureaucrats have displaced parents—is a standard political talking point these days. In *The Vanishing American Adult*, Ben Sasse's memoir and ode to self-reliance, the Nebraska senator makes essentially the same argument. Sasse paints a bleak portrait of parents doing battle with a public education system that seeks to "homogenize" children. In his view, the lengthy tendrils of the welfare state are choking the character out of young people. To fight back, Sasse, who is an avowed admirer of Betsy DeVos, encourages parents to homeschool their children.

Even the nation's largest corporations have lined up behind the cause of "educational freedom." The American Legislative Exchange Council, or ALEC—a powerful organization that advances pro-business policies and legislation at the statehouse and whose membership includes one-quarter of all state lawmakers—recently took a position in favor of "homeschooling freedom." The model resolution, which ALEC's legislative members have been encouraged to pass at the state level, begins with the following assertion: "It is the fundamental right of a parent to direct the upbringing, education and care of his or her child."[23]

The migration of a concept like educational freedom from the political fringe parallels the mainstreaming of right-wing libertarianism more generally. As writer Jane Mayer chronicles in *Dark Money*, her history of the radical right, the Kochs and other wealthy donors have created intellectual "beachheads" within university economics departments to groom the next generation of libertarian scholars.[24] Bryan Caplan, an economist at George Mason University's Mercatus Center—an anti-regulatory outfit funded by the Kochs—embodies this new breed of scholarship and the respectability now granted to ideas once dismissed as marginal. Caplan's recent book, *The Case Against Education: Why the Education System Is a Waste of Time and Money*, was published by Princeton University Press, excerpted in *The Atlantic*, and declared "bold" and "provocative" in book reviews. Among Caplan's contentions: "Government should stop using tax dollars to fund education of any kind."[25] All schools, from K-12 through colleges and universities, he argues, should be funded solely by tuition and private charity.

2

Faith in Markets

Betsy DeVos was in her element delivering a keynote address at the Arizona State University / Global Silicon Valley Summit in 2017. Speaking to an audience of self-proclaimed innovators and entrepreneurs, DeVos rattled off a list of technological changes that have transformed industry after industry, thanks to the wonders of the free market. Video rental chains, she observed, had been "disrupted" by on-demand streaming services. The taxi and hotel industries were being shaken up by Uber and Airbnb. But education remained stuck in a rut. "So much has changed and our lives are better because of it," declared DeVos. "So why is our education system so far behind the curve?"[1]

Listening to this pitch, most of the audience was likely unaware of the fact that DeVos's proposed disruption—private school choice—originated in the era of black-and-white TVs and rotary phones. For more than seventy-five years, free-market adherents have been peddling tuition vouchers, in the hope of weaning the nation off "government schools" and the taxes that pay for them. But if the crowd at the summit was unfamiliar with this history, DeVos herself certainly wasn't. Her family made its first big push for private school vouchers in her home state of Michigan when she was just ten years old.

Now here she was, a true Silicon Valley–style evangelist, presenting this old idea as a revolutionary new technology. "The time for simply tinkering around the edges," she concluded, "is over."

A Choice Is a Choice

An unquestioned faith in markets is at the very heart of the push to unmake public education. Just as consumers choose from a vast array of products in the marketplace, market ideologues argue, parents should be able to choose where and how their children are educated. In his 2012 address to the Republican National Convention, former Florida governor Jeb Bush used the analogy of the grocery-store dairy aisle to make this point. The dairy aisle overflows with milk choices, Bush told the delegates: whole milk, 2 percent, low-fat, skim, organic, milk with extra Vitamin D, flavored milks that don't taste like milk. "They even make milk for people who can't drink milk," Bush told the crowd. "Shouldn't parents have that kind of choice in schools?"[2]

Just as the free market responds to consumer demand by providing desired products and showing the proverbial exit to whatever has fallen out of favor (powdered milk, anyone?), so too will the market work its magic on public education. Give consumers the freedom to choose where and how to educate their children, and the woes of our public schools will finally be fixed. Or so the argument goes. "Bad" schools will be forced to close as consumers flee them, while "good" schools will proliferate to meet burgeoning consumer demand. Best of all, in the minds of market ideologues, the choice of what education "product" to consume will be up to parents themselves, not bumbling bureaucrats inside the public school "monopoly."

Depending on the argument being made, the particulars of these market analogies can change. Sometimes the emphasis is on market capture and anti-competitiveness. At other times, excessive regulation and red tape are the bogeymen. In still other cases, an incompetent, innovation-stifling government is the enemy. Always, however, the individual is presented as a beleaguered consumer who simply wants to operate with the same freedom in the education sector that he or she ordinarily exercises elsewhere. As a blogger on the conservative Heritage Foundation website opined: "Would it make sense to give a Burger King the power to decide whether or not a McDonald's may open next door? How about if we allowed the New York Mets to pay their players based solely on how many years they've been in the Big Leagues? As strange as it sounds, the current educational establishment employs similar faulty business practices. And the results have been disastrous."[3]

Unlike the public education bureaucracy, the market is seen as a paragon of efficiency. Rather than being directed by some central power, individuals in the market need only seek their own benefit. Their self-interested actions, in turn, are broadly beneficial—because, in aggregate, they meet the needs and desires of society at large. Thus, as Adam Smith wrote in *The Wealth of Nations*, "it is not from the benevolence of the butcher, the brewer, or the baker that we expect our dinner, but from their regard to their own interest."[4] Through the invisible hand of the market, enough food is produced.

Unlike bread or beer or even milk, education is not merely produced for the individual who consumes it, but for the social, civic, and economic benefit of the broader public. Consequently, education is governed through a public system designed to promote broad aims like democratic competence and general principles like equity. Yet for adherents of market philosophy, what is true for the production of food is generalizable to other commodities—even to goods like education. In their view, the common good is only the amassed interests of individuals. A contributor to the free-market magazine *Reason* put it this way: "The freed market is a political-legal setting in which people are at liberty to peacefully pursue their chosen plans. This activity generates, unintentionally, an undesigned order that facilitates cooperation and coordination among even distant strangers, making each person's pursuit more effective and efficient than otherwise. . . . And it does this work without compulsion or authoritarian central direction."[5]

In this view, markets are a form of natural democracy—one in which individuals express their preferences and those preferences shape outcomes. Consumers vote with dollars, and the aggregation of those individual votes produces a collective decision. It doesn't matter that choice is expressed in the form of a purchase rather than in the form of a ballot, because a choice is a choice. And, even better than a winner-take-all electoral system, in which the majority rules, the market often segments to serve the various needs and desires of minority groups. Thus, there is milk for those who can drink it, as well as for those who can't.

If market efficiency is a rule across contexts, then any "system" in public education is not just misguided, but oppressive. In the minds of market ideologues, maintaining a public education system is like turning over bread production to communist apparatchiks. As libertarian economist Milton Friedman put it: "Top-down organization works no better in the United States than it did in the Soviet Union of East Germany."[6] In a market system, individuals will make their own decisions about what they want and in what quantity. If they are dissatisfied, they will make new decisions—about how and when to switch.

A Brief History of an Old Idea

The idea that the market model should be applied to education was first outlined three-quarters of a century ago by Milton Friedman. In an academic essay titled "The Role of Government in Education," Friedman argued that it was time to "denationalize" schools in the United States. Rather than providing educational services directly, he argued, the government could give parents vouchers redeemable at an "institution of their own choice." A few years later, he elaborated on this idea, arguing that vouchers and other market mechanisms would not just advance individual freedom but also "produce and distribute goods and services of higher quality at lower costs than government does."[7] Still, the inherent superiority of the market remained secondary for Friedman. His argument, as encapsulated by the Cato Institute's Andrew Coulson, was that "state-run schooling is unjustifiable in a free society and that education is best delivered through the private sector."[8]

Friedman's initial school voucher proposal gained little traction. Just one generation removed from the Great Depression, the "free market" was still associated in the minds of many Americans with stock market crashes and economic desperation. While the number of parents choosing to send their children to private schools was indeed on the rise, that increase had less to do with market principles than with the explosive issue of school desegregation.[9] "The Role of Government in Education" appeared in 1955, just a year after the Supreme Court's landmark decision in *Brown v. Board of Education*, which outlawed the intentional segregation of public schools. In response, conservative elites in several Southern states seized on the idea of private school vouchers as a way of avoiding court-ordered desegregation.[10] Given this context, very few voucher advocates were interested in making the case that market competition would spur improvement. Instead, they were generally concerned with maintaining taxpayer support for segregated schooling.

This is not to say that vouchers held no appeal to market-oriented conservatives. But those conservatives were not yet in power. Barry Goldwater's crushing loss to Lyndon Johnson in the 1964 presidential election delayed the arrival of market ideology in the halls of power in Washington. And subsequent administrations pursued fairly traditional approaches to education policy. Even Richard Nixon, who expressed support for parochial education, did so out of preference for "a dimension of spiritual value" and "to promote diversity in education."[11] Market efficiency was not yet a part of Republican education doctrine.

Then came Reagan.

As the Hoover Institution's Terry Moe put it: "When Ronald Reagan became president, attitudes toward markets, choice, and competition became much more favorable."[12] Reagan had gained national prominence by throwing his support to Goldwater in 1964 with a stirring speech that warned of government overreach and creeping collectivism. A former supporter of Franklin D. Roosevelt, Reagan had undergone an ideological transformation mirroring the rise of a new conservative movement in the United States. By the time he arrived at the White House seventeen years later, those broad themes were backed by a specific policy agenda and an impressive network of advisors and organizations dedicated to making that agenda a reality. Milton Friedman advised Reagan in the White House, as he had advised Goldwater on the campaign trail. Meanwhile, organizations like the American Legislative Exchange Council (ALEC), which had formed in response to Goldwater's loss, had also joined the Reagan bandwagon. ALEC co-founder Lou Barnett served as national policy director for Reagan's political action committee. Another ALEC co-founder, Paul Weyrich, who also co-founded the Heritage Foundation, joined the Reagan team as well.

During a campaign focused on national security and the country's economic woes, education barely registered as an issue. Once in office, however, Reagan's team soon began planning for a school voucher program. A 1983 report, for instance, co-authored by Chester Finn Jr., who in 1985 would be named assistant secretary of education for research and improvement, argued in favor of a series of statewide voucher plans. Sponsored by the National Institute of Education at the U.S. Department of Education, the report asserted that "higher quality education is more apt to result from a 'decentralized' system in which parents select the schools they want for their children and in which schools actively seek to attract students, than from a centralized bureaucracy."[13] All other relationships in the field of education are characterized by "a voluntary coming together of provider and client," the report stressed. The nation's education system should be restructured along similar lines.

Reagan's first attempt to get a school voucher bill passed went nowhere; a proposal for a voluntary program died in Congress without ever coming up for a vote. Other school choice measures, including a proposal for education savings accounts for parents, and tuition tax credits for parents who sent their children to private schools, fared no better.

After Reagan's landslide reelection, the White House made another big push. Secretary of Education William Bennett announced a proposal to give low-income families vouchers worth $600 per student to attend the school of their choice, as part of a broader effort by the Reagan administration to replace government-provided services with private enterprise.[14] The plan would have made a dramatic change to the way the federal government aided low-income students via so-called Title I funds. Instead of money going to local school districts, as it had since the passage of the Elementary and Secondary Education Act in 1965, now it would go directly to parents who could choose how to spend it.

Despite the relatively small dollar amount of the voucher and the explicit focus on low-income families—the Reagan administration's previous school choice initiatives had come under fire for subsidizing affluent families—the plan met with intense resistance. "If this is allowed to pass," wrote the League of Women Voters' Eleanor Byman in the *Chicago Tribune*, "it would encourage the administration to meddle further and dismantle other educational programs."[15]

Meanwhile, at the state level, voucher programs weren't faring much better. When voters got to weigh in on whether they approved of sending taxpayer funds to private religious schools, they rejected voucher plans by a roughly 2-to-1 margin.[16]

A Tactical Shift

Unable to win on vouchers, market-oriented thinkers embraced the idea of charter schools. First outlined in Minnesota by policy entrepreneur Ted Kolderie, charters were a means of opening school districts to market-style competition without directing funds to private schools. Kolderie speculated that much of the public's aversion to vouchers was rooted in opposition to subsidies for affluent families or for religious education, so he took pains to emphasize the public nature of charter schools. He even avoided the word "voucher," stressing that his solution was a "contract" system that allowed schools to trade regulations for results.[17] Supporters argued that rather than destroying the public education system, charters would strengthen it, advancing equity in the process.

The message was a hit. The local press ate up the argument that Minnesota's schools required urgent change, and that "chartering" was the way to attain it. The combination of an entrepreneurial vision and traditional liberal goals—like advancing opportunity for historically underserved populations—broadened the appeal of the charter school concept. As the author of one law review article put it, "The market theory appeals to conservatives and capitalists, while the equity theory appeals to liberals and integrationists; naturally, each is at odds with each other."[18] Yet while charters were largely free of the overtly ideological patina of voucher programs, they were still very much about markets. In 1990 Kolderie authored a report that argued for "the withdrawal of local districts' exclusive franchise to own and operate public schools." In that report, he acknowledged that "some of the proposals that fly under the banner of choice may not hold firmly to the ideas of the common school, of equity and of public purpose."[19]

Market-oriented think tanks and philanthropies quickly began pushing charter schools. A report commissioned by the libertarian Reason Foundation, for instance, pronounced charters "a middle ground between the existing public-school system and a full school-choice program that allows the flow of public funds to private schools."[20] The Democratic Party, or at least one influential faction of it, also leapt to embrace the concept. The Democratic Leadership Council (DLC), formed in 1985 in an effort to propel the party toward the ideological center, proclaimed that "public school choice is a progressive approach to our nation's education."[21] When the DLC unveiled its official agenda at a 1991 gathering in Cleveland, its head, a rising young Southern governor named Bill Clinton, gave school choice a full-throated endorsement. "We are living in a world when all of us want more choices," Clinton reminded his audience, "All of us want fifty or sixty channels on cable television."[22] Why shouldn't there be more choice in public education?

Meanwhile, the right was also pushing a new approach to school choice. In 1990, conservative scholars John Chubb and Terry Moe proposed "a new system of public education that eliminates most political and bureaucratic control over the schools and relies instead on indirect control through markets and parental choice."[23] Supported in part by two conservative foundations—the Olin Foundation and Bradley Foundation—Chubb and Moe's book, *Politics, Markets, and America's Schools* was hailed by John J. Miller of the *National Review* as "the most influential book on K-12 education of the last generation."[24] Although Chubb and Moe rooted their arguments in data and talked about freedom and school improvement, the case for choice was again rooted entirely in market logic. "The whole point of a thoroughgoing system of choice," they argued, "is to free the schools from these disabling constraints by sweeping away the old institutions and replacing them with new ones."[25]

But even as the push to apply free-market principles to public education accelerated, proponents of traditional vouchers, which would divert public funds to private schools, had never gone away. The same year that *Politics, Markets, and America's Schools* was released, the nation's first voucher program was adopted in Milwaukee. Originally limited to one thousand students, the Milwaukee Parental Choice Program gave parents a voucher equivalent to the amount of Wisconsin's per-pupil state aid, and allowed those funds to be used for private—typically parochial—school tuition. While previous voucher efforts had emphasized religious freedom, the Milwaukee plan was framed as a social justice effort targeted at the underserved. As Terry Moe put it, "Up to that point, vouchers had always been associated with Milton Friedman and conservatives. But from then on, vouchers were about bringing equity to the poor."[26] Conservative scholar Paul Peterson was blunter still. Describing the previous voucher battles as "trench warfare" between conservatives and liberals, he argued that "there's only one force out there that's probably going to change the story, and that's black families."[27]

Black families were not simply pawns in a conservative scheme. Some, no doubt, were drawn to voucher programs because they preferred a religious education for their children. Many more, it would seem, opted in to voucher programs because they were simply concerned with the welfare of their children and sought alternatives to Milwaukee's struggling schools. Whatever their motives, the result was a window of opportunity for market advocates.

Voucher programs modeled on the Milwaukee approach soon spread beyond Wisconsin. In 1995, Ohio began offering vouchers through the Cleveland Scholarship and Tutoring Program. In 2001, the Florida legislature created the state's Tax Credit Scholarship Program, which allowed companies to earmark their tax liabilities to fund vouchers for low-income students. And in 2003, the D.C. Opportunity Scholarship Program was created, channeling federal funds to low-income students to pay for private school tuition.

Despite these victories, though, true believers in the free market weren't satisfied. Charter schools, for all of their entrepreneurial gloss, were still just a half measure. They opened schools up to competition, certainly; but they remained under state oversight. New voucher programs, meanwhile, were more truly in line with the vision of shifting education into the private market. Yet such programs also remained limited in scope, targeted as they were at low-income families. Milton Friedman dismissed such efforts as "charity vouchers."[28]

The real goal was a voucher for *every* child. As the Heartland Institute's Joseph Bast prophesied: "Pilot voucher programs for the urban poor will lead the way to statewide universal voucher plans. Soon, most government schools will be converted into private schools or simply close their doors."[29] Charters and small-scale voucher programs, in other words, were only a beachhead.

Full Circle

"They have hijacked the program," declared Annette "Polly" Williams, an African American lawmaker who championed the first-in-the-nation Parental Choice Program in Milwaukee.[30] Williams was referring to former Wisconsin governor Scott Walker's expansion of vouchers in Milwaukee to include middle-class families. It was only the start. In 2013, Walker, a free-market crusader, signed into law a measure expanding vouchers statewide, doing so after an intense and well-funded campaign by the American Federation for Children—the school choice lobbying group founded by Betsy DeVos.

Walker was far from alone in pushing to expand vouchers. The 2010 "wave" elections, which saw major gains for Republicans in statehouses across the country, were a huge opportunity for the true believers, and they moved quickly to transform an old vision into new policies. Within a few years, the number of private school choice programs soared. According to the advocacy group EdChoice, formerly known as the Friedman Foundation in honor of the libertarian economist, more than half of U.S. states now offer "educational choice options." These include traditional voucher programs as well as education savings accounts and tax-credit scholarships. These so-called neo-vouchers deliver the same old policy result, but with a twist: the state grants tax credits to companies and donors rather than directly fronting the bill for vouchers.

No longer are such programs limited to what Friedman dismissed as "charity vouchers." Indeed, as more expansive policies target middle-income and affluent parents, it's becoming harder to find the social justice rhetoric that fueled the growth of school choice programs in the 1990s. In Florida, for example, school choice advocates are pushing to expand the state's private school choice program—already the largest in the country—so it reaches into the middle class. Their hope is that the Sunshine State will become the first in the nation to offer universal choice, which entails providing vouchers for all.[31]

Other states aren't far behind. Although similarly ambitious efforts in Nevada and Arizona have been stymied by the courts, and by voters, the idea that parents should receive some portion of their state's per-pupil education funds to spend where and how they choose is now considered mainstream in GOP policy circles, and even among some Democrats. Seventy-five years after Friedman made his radical case for "denationalizing" education, the idea that markets can solve what ails our public schools has become an article of faith.

3

The Cost-Cutting Crusade

The Oklahoma teachers' strike was entering its second week with no end in sight. To protest low pay and the state's deep cuts to education spending, teachers thronged the state capitol, as they had every day since the April 2018 walkouts began. Decades of tax cutting, combined with a downturn in prices for the oil and gas that drive the state's economy, had drained the Sooner State's coffers. Schoolchildren, and the men and women tasked with teaching them, were paying the price. The state was wracked by a teacher shortage, class sizes had ballooned, and four-day school weeks had become the norm in one-quarter of Oklahoma's districts.

At the heart of the historic protests in Oklahoma was the same question that had fueled the February 2018 teacher walkouts in West Virginia before they spread across the country: Who should cover the state's K-12 education costs? In Oklahoma, a constitutional amendment requiring a two-thirds majority of the legislature in order to increase taxes had been approved by voters in

1992, spurred in part by a backlash to a previous tax hike to boost education funding.[1] The measure worked just as anti-tax proponents had hoped. In the twenty-five years since the amendment was enacted, lawmakers in this now solidly Republican state had never managed to meet the "super-majority" required to raise taxes. As a result, per-student funding in Oklahoma plummeted by a billion dollars in the past decade, the steepest drop in the country.[2]

The protests by Oklahoma's teachers garnered strong public support—the 2018 Phi Delta Kappa Poll of the Public's Attitudes Toward the Public Schools found that close to 75 percent of the American public sided with teachers in the walkouts.[3] But the teachers fell short of realizing their demands. While lawmakers agreed to hike teacher salaries, paid for by new taxes on cigarettes, diesel, and Amazon purchases, raising the capital gains tax on Oklahoma's wealthiest residents was off the table. The legacy of cost-cutting had come at a steep cost to the state's children; yet even a popular uprising wasn't enough to force more funding for the state's schools.

Out of Control

A rising chorus contends that American public schools spend too much, and produce too little in return. "Scores [are] continuing to muddle along, unremarkable," Betsy DeVos told the audience at a 2017 Reagan Institute event. "And yet look at the spending. This is not something we're going to spend our way out of."[4]

Such arguments originated several decades ago among hard-core conservatives. Today, however, they are increasingly mainstream. Six years before DeVos made her claim about out-of-control spending and unremarkable results, Bill Gates—hardly a conservative ideologue—made a nearly identical case. Speaking to the nation's governors at their annual meeting in Washington, DC, Gates encouraged them to "flip the curve on how much we spend vs. how well students do in school."[5]

Gates and DeVos aren't wrong. Spending on education *has* increased considerably over the past several decades. Even after adjusting for inflation, the cost of public education has quintupled since 1950.[6] But that doesn't mean that spending is out of control.

Much of the increase in the cost of public education is due to an expansion of special education services. In the 1960s, for instance, spending on special education was less than half of what it would be by the end of the twentieth century.[7] Because public schools weren't required to accommodate children with special needs, the task of educating students with disabilities was often left to parents. That all changed in 1975 with the passage of the Education for All Handicapped Children Act, later renamed the Individuals with Disabilities Education Act (IDEA), which required a "free and appropriate" education for all children, regardless of mental, physical, or emotional difference. But expanding access and equity has also been expensive. Special education costs roughly twice what general education costs, and millions of students have disabilities—two hundred thousand in New York City alone.[8]

Costs also increased as a result of more equitable funding for black and brown students. In 1917 in the South, for example, just 29 cents was spent on black children for every dollar spent on their white counterparts. Their school year was shorter, classes were crowded, and teachers were paid next to nothing. By 1950, things had improved, but spending on black children remained roughly 75 cents on the dollar.[9] In recent years, many states have not only evened out spending across racial groups, but have targeted additional funds to historically marginalized and economically disadvantaged students. As research has shown, it costs more to do right by these students, even if that means it raises the overall cost of public education.[10]

Demand for smaller class sizes has also caused spending to rise. Twenty-four states have imposed some forms of limits on class sizes, including Florida, where strict limits on teacher-pupil ratios were written into the state constitution in 2002. But limiting the number of students in a class—something parents strongly support—is also hugely expensive. Reducing a class from twenty-four to sixteen students requires a 50 percent increase in staffing—and all those new teachers come with a price tag. Framed another way, if every classroom in the United States grew by one student, the nation would save $12 billion a year on teacher salaries—about what the federal government spends on its largest K-12 program.[11]

Finally, as the United States has become a more unequal country, the needs of children who attend public schools have grown. As a result, schools play an increasingly expansive role, providing food, clothing, medical care, and mental health counseling, as well as after-school and summer programs. While advocates maintain that such interventions pay off in the form of healthier and higher-performing students, an array of public education critics sees something different: the school as an increasingly expensive welfare delivery system.

Unlike in other sectors, no one has figured out how to make educating children any less time-consuming—or costly. Huge increases in productivity, driven largely by technology, have pushed down the cost of many products over time. Computers, for example, are far cheaper than they once were; the first PCs cost over $4,000. But education is resistant to mechanization. Because learning is deeply rooted in relationships, it can't be farmed out to robots or time-saving devices. Technology, of course, is rapidly moving into classrooms. But just having more Chromebooks or online learning platforms hasn't allowed for faster or larger batch-processing of students.

In economics, this phenomenon, in which salaries increase even as labor productivity doesn't, is known as Baumol's Cost Disease. Economist William Baumol set out to understand why it was that musicians were earning far more in the 1960s than they did in Beethoven's day, even though it took them just as long to play a composition, and even though the quality of their performance was likely no better than performances of the past. Baumol observed that rising productivity was pushing up wages in other sectors, which then drove salary increases in other sectors—even among musicians. And just as Beethoven's String Quartet No. 14 still takes roughly forty minutes to play, young people still learn at the same pace and still need the same amount of attention, even as the cost of teachers has increased over time.

We could, of course, simply pay teachers less. Yet as education finance expert Bruce Baker points out, teacher pay must remain competitive in order to "recruit and retain a stable, quality work-force."[12] Thus, while teacher pay—the largest expenditure in public education—has gone up over time, it has remained relatively constant when compared to what college-educated non-teachers earn.

Will Teach for Food

When teachers shut down schools in states from Arizona to West Virginia in 2018, demanding higher pay, the news media was suddenly awash in stories of educators waiting tables, cleaning houses, or driving for Uber in order to make ends meet. A study released that year found that nearly 20 percent of teachers reported working a second job.[13] The average teacher salary of roughly $60,000 may not sound bad, but it is important to recall that most teachers actually earn less than that—a product of the fact that younger teachers, who earn the least, are more numerous than their experienced counterparts. Starting salaries in a majority of states are below $40,000. And overall, the wages of teachers have fallen sharply, even as the salaries of other college-educated professionals have risen. According to an analysis by the Economic Policy Institute, teacher salary had been commensurate with comparable workers in 1994; roughly a quarter of a century later, it was 18.7 percent lower.[14]

What accounts for the relatively low salaries of teachers? One explanation can be found in what sociologist Dan Lortie calls the "special but shadowed" nature of the profession. Teaching is viewed as important insofar as it produces a social benefit. Yet it is also viewed as easy, in large part because everyone has attended school. Having sat in classrooms for thirteen years, many Americans conclude that teaching simply isn't that hard—they've seen plenty of it, after all—while other professions remain a mystery.

Another explanation lies in who does the work of educating children. In the early nineteenth century, most teachers were men. But this began to change by the end of the century, as school districts and local communities intentionally hired women, who they could pay a fraction of a man's salary. As the profession became more female, gendered perceptions of teaching began to shift, particularly in accordance with students' age. The result was that teaching became an increasingly female-dominated occupation—today, women constitute roughly three-quarters of the teacher workforce, and an even larger majority in elementary grades. What does that have to do with pay? "We're not beyond having a cultural devaluation of women's work," explains Philip N. Cohen, a sociologist at the University of Maryland. "So if that job is done primarily by women, people tend to believe it has less value."[15]

Paying teachers less has long been a goal of conservatives, but the relatively low-status, female-dominated nature of the profession means that there simply isn't that much fat to trim. This presents something of a dilemma for those intent on reducing expenditures. If 80 percent of education expenditures go to teacher salaries, and there isn't much room to reduce them, how else do you cut costs? Reducing or even eliminating teacher pensions—another perennial conservative cause—remains deeply controversial, especially in the states where teachers aren't covered by Social Security. One alternative, then, is to cut funding for education in hopes of forcing creative solutions that will contain rising costs. But this strategy is not without risks. Cuts to education spending are deeply unpopular with the public, who are inclined to see school closures or ballooning class sizes as more cruel than creative.

Starve the Beast

"If you've got a kid that's extravagant, you can lecture him all you want about his extravagance," proclaimed Ronald Reagan during a presidential debate in 1980. "Or you can cut his allowance and achieve the same end much quicker."[16] Reagan left little doubt as to his preferred solution. Unlike previous generations of conservatives who had been primarily concerned with balancing budgets, Reagan sought to reduce spending by cutting the equivalent of the nation's allowance: taxes. Using a different metaphor, an official in the Reagan administration later referred to government as a beast that was "feeding off future generations."[17]

Such an ethos has been at the heart of conservative policy for the past thirty-five years. By slashing taxes, conservatives have created budget crises that seemingly demand a reduction in government spending.

Of course, the problem with trying to cut spending on education is public opposition. Unlike other government programs, which only some people benefit from, all Americans have access to public education. Approximately 90 percent of natural-born citizens have attended public schools—upwards of 200 million Americans. And in any given year, roughly 20 million families in the United States have children enrolled in the public schools.

Education also represents a mere drop in the federal spending bucket: roughly $60 billion. By comparison, just short of a trillion dollars is spent on Social Security. Another trillion is spent on the combined programs of Medicare, Medicaid, and the Children's Health Insurance Program. National defense, for its part, eats up $600–700 billion annually. While reducing the budget of the Department of Education, or threatening to eliminate the agency completely, has been a conservative goal for decades, the reality is that federal dollars make up a relatively minor part of overall spending on education. Of each dollar spent on education in the United States, just 8 cents comes from the federal government.[18] Starving this particular beast, then, requires a different approach.

The *real* spending action in education takes place at the state and local level. States pick up the tab for approximately 47 cents of each dollar spent on public education, while local communities contribute an additional 45 cents, primarily through property taxes.

In an effort to starve the beast, then, conservatives have worked at all levels of government to reduce taxation. This has been a logistical challenge, but they have pursued it through networks like the American Legislative Exchange Council and the State Policy Network. The former was originally established as the Conservative Caucus of State Legislators. The latter was founded by Thomas Roe, a trustee of the Heritage Foundation, who was encouraged by Ronald Reagan to start a group that would function like the Heritage Foundation for each of the states.[19] Other groups, like the Club for Growth and the Koch-funded Americans for Prosperity, support the anti-tax agenda through financial support for political candidates.

Despite the anti-tax efforts of such groups, spending on schools still adds up to a massive amount. In fiscal year 2017, public education was a $694 billion endeavor, not counting an additional $452 billion in outstanding debt.[20] And as education costs have risen in recent decades, conservatives have increasingly focused on state and local spending. As a report from the libertarian Cato Institute put it, "public schools are usually the most costly item in state and local budgets."[21] Thus, if the goal is to cut government by starving the beast, education spending must be pared back, even at the risk of provoking a popular backlash by pushing legislation and policies that are at odds with public preferences.

Bursting the Bubble

The hit movie *The Big Short* concludes by offering two different accounts—one fantastical and the other factual—of what happened after the stock market collapse of 2008. In the first, imaginary version, hundreds of Wall Street executives and financial industry officials are sent to jail for their criminal behavior and misdeeds. In the second version, Wall Street survives virtually unscathed; meanwhile, blame is predictably offloaded onto "immigrants and the poor, and this time even teachers."

Almost every state reduced spending on public education during the Great Recession, but some states went much further, making deep cuts to schools, while taking aim at teachers and their unions—the subject of our next chapter. Moreover, states including Arizona, Kansas, Michigan, and North Carolina also moved to permanently reduce the funds available for education by cutting the taxes that pay for schools and other public services.

In Wisconsin, Governor Scott Walker took aim at education through Act 10—what was first called the "budget repair bill." Act 10 is mostly remembered for stripping teachers and other public employees of their collective bargaining rights. But it also made $2 billion in cuts to the state's public schools. Though Wisconsin, like many states, already capped the amount by which local communities could raise property taxes to fund schools and other services, Walker and the GOP-controlled legislature imposed further limits, including restricting when and how local school districts can ask voters for additional help funding their schools. "They say that government should play less of a role, but they're also taking away local control and imposing restrictions," says Jeri McGinley, head of School Funding Reform for Wisconsin. "It's a vicious way to govern."[22]

The widespread public support for teacher walkouts in states that slashed education spending and the taxes that pay for schools speaks to the deep unpopularity of policies that result in ballooning class sizes and crumbling infrastructure. A raft of recent polls found strong backing for raising taxes in order to increase teacher pay—support that held across demographic, regional, and party lines.[23] Even in Wisconsin, the epicenter of a GOP-led experiment in tax cutting and government shrinking, public opinion has shifted dramatically in recent years. By overwhelming margins, voters have favored investment in public schools over tax cuts.[24]

So why would conservatives at the state level push an agenda that is so at odds with public preferences? Political scientists Theda Skocpol and Alexander Hertel-Fernandez point to the rising influence of increasingly powerful wealthy donors. Led by the industrialist Koch brothers, such hard-line influencers have pulled the Republican Party steadily toward an agenda of "economic extremism": providing tax cuts for the wealthy, slashing safety net programs, reducing spending on public schools, and privatizing services. The result is a huge gulf between public opinion and the ultra-free-market orthodoxy pushed by the Koch network—an archipelago of organizations, including the influential Americans for Prosperity, advocating for smaller government and lower taxes.[25]

The Kochs and their allies have a wide-ranging political agenda. But near the top of the list is rolling back public education. It simply isn't possible to significantly shrink government and enable new tax cuts for the wealthy without spending less—indeed much less—on students and the schools they attend.

Money Matters

Does money actually matter in education? When cost-cutting crusaders in Kansas handpicked a consultant to produce a school funding study released in 2018, the answer they were sure they'd get was "no." Instead, Lori Taylor, a school finance expert at Texas A&M, "blew a hole in conservative doctrine," as a Kansas newspaper put it. Taylor concluded that money most definitely matters in students' educational attainment, and that Kansas, where deep cuts to income and corporate tax rates hit public education hard, needs to spend a whole lot more if the state wants to meet its goals for student graduation and college readiness.[26]

Indeed, a growing body of research shows that when it comes to school spending, money does indeed matter, especially for low-income students.[27] In a 2016 study, researchers found that poor school districts that received more funding as a result of court-ordered spending reform saw graduation rates for low-income students rise by 10 percent. Perhaps more impressively, increases in spending also produced a 10 percent bump in the students' lifetime earnings.[28] According to another study, a 20 percent increase in school spending resulted in a 25 percent increase in student earnings, as well as a 20 percent dip in the poverty rate.[29]

Such findings should be convincing to politicians in both parties who claim to care about preparing students for college and careers, or who take an interest in racial and economic achievement gaps. Yet research alone is unlikely to settle this debate. The core question isn't just about costs and benefits—it's about the *goal* of public education.

Consider the question of class size. Smaller classes are hugely expensive. If those smaller classes are used to cultivate meaningful relationships between teachers and students, including more personalized feedback and higher levels of interpersonal trust, the benefits might outweigh the costs—but only if those outcomes are valued. If the aim of schooling is merely acquisition of content knowledge and basic skills, however, spending more on smaller classes may be a bad investment. In fact, conservatives have long made the case that class sizes should be larger—even *substantially* larger.

To the dismay and frustration of those intent on dismantling public education, the public has a broad and inclusive set of goals for the schools. They want young people to develop basic academic skills, certainly. But they also want them to develop critical thinking skills, citizenship competencies, and positive character traits. They want students to discover their talents and abilities, to engage deeply with literature, and to explore the arts. And if that weren't enough, they want young people to be socially, emotionally, and physically healthy. That's a tall order—one that requires extensive programming and the resources to pay for it, particularly if the goal is to reach all children, no matter what their out-of-school circumstances.

In the eyes of those like Betsy DeVos or Charles Koch, none of this makes sense for a taxpayer-funded system. They have very little interest in this expansive, and expensive, vision of schooling. And the broader pursuit of equity and justice through the education system? That's a utopian pipe dream unlikely to be realized by a bureaucratic entity, and likely to infringe upon personal liberty. If families want "extras" for their children, they should find a way to pay for them. What good is it to Walmart or Amazon if their employees read poetry in their spare time or understand American history? What use is it for the affluent class if lower- and middle-income earners can paint or play an instrument?

As they see it, the only permissible tax-based expenditure is on activity that reduces costs to taxpayers. In such an accounting, the goals of education are simple. Keep people off the dole. Prepare them to fill available jobs. Give them a hand up to help themselves. In short, give the public whatever minimal education is necessary, but no more.

And all of those other aims? If people want a well-rounded education for their children, they can pay for it themselves.

Return on Investment

In 2013, the Republican governor of Michigan convened a stealth committee of politicos and business leaders to examine the cost of public education. The group's primary task? To apply "concepts familiar in the private sector—getting higher value for less money." Ultimately, the group recommended a new kind of school known as a "value school."[30] Relying heavily on technology in place of teachers, these low-cost charter schools would run on a budget of just $5,000 per pupil—roughly $2,000 less than Michigan currently spends on each student in the state.

Under a voucher-like plan, students would pay for their tuition using a "Michigan Education Card" that worked like an electronic benefits transfer card used to distribute food stamps and cash assistance to the poor. If students had extra funds left on their cards, they could use them to purchase "extras": remedial courses, art, music, AP classes, even after-school sports.

The project imploded after the press, and more importantly the public, caught wind of it. In Michigan, as in other states where schools have sustained deep funding cuts, the public wants more investment in schools, not less, while parents stubbornly prefer flesh-and-blood teachers over algorithms. But the dream of stripped-down schools that deliver more value to employers at less cost to taxpayers remains very much alive.

At first blush, the array of reforms we've described here may appear to be ideologically incoherent or even contradictory. On the one hand, conservatives and their business allies bemoan the insufficient skills of citizens and workers. On the other, they propose policies that impede the sort of well-rounded education that would achieve those aims.

In their accounting, however, the end product of public education cannot be assessed without considering return on investment. Few, for instance, contest the fact that greater investment produces better outcomes. Instead, they take issue with the diminishing returns produced from each non-essential dollar. Doubling the investment in education, in other words, does not produce results that are twice as valuable to taxpayers. Consequently, each dollar spent above the bare minimum produces less value.

From this vantage, it makes perfect sense that market-oriented conservatives favor schools oriented toward career preparation—a side of public education that literally pays off. Taxpayers, of course, are still stuck with the bill. But businesses, who would otherwise have to bear the cost of training their own employees, receive a major benefit in the form of outsourced training. And, because graduates will be capable of supporting themselves, taxpayers will not only expand their ranks, but also reduce public expenditures. After all, if Americans are comprehensively prepared for work, the social safety net can be rolled up once and for all.

Tellingly, when the Trump administration revealed a controversial plan to reorganize the federal government in 2018, it included combining the Department of Education and the Department of Labor into a new hybrid: the Department of Education and the Workforce. The proposed merger, explained Virginia Foxx, chairwoman of the House Committee on Education and the Workforce, recognized "the clear relationship between education policy at every level and the needs of the growing American workforce."[31]

Schools have always played an essential role in readying students for employment. But the latest repackaging of vocational preparation is different because the rest of the educational system's mandate might be cut away. Most of what schools do, after all—the work commonly referred to as educating the "whole child"—brings no relief to taxpayers. It may create happier and healthier citizens and a more beautiful and just society, but it has no clear impact on the national bottom line. As economist Bryan Caplan put it: "From kindergarten on, students spend thousands of hours studying subjects irrelevant to the modern labor market. Why do English classes focus on literature and poetry instead of business and technical writing? Why do advanced-math classes bother with proofs almost no student can follow? When will the typical student use history? Trigonometry? Art? Music? Physics? Latin?"[32]

Radically reducing costs, however, will require more than merely narrowing and vocationalizing the curriculum. It necessitates paying teachers less and thinning their ranks. Teachers may not make all that much, but there are lots of them. As long as we have some 3.6 million teachers in classrooms, education will continue to cost hundreds of billions of dollars each year.

Replace teachers with algorithms, however, and shift schooling onto the internet, and the cost problem could be solved once and for all. Better yet, bypass "school" entirely by developing technologies that allow parents to pick and choose from a menu of education options, including private classes and tutoring—the "Amazon"-like education experience that the Koch network is now putting its political and financial resources behind.[33] As Terry Moe put it: "Technology is cheap. Labor is really expensive. Education has always been very labor intensive, so if our education system can substitute technology for labor and still provide kids with high quality education, then great!"[34]

Diminishing Expectations

For public education's conservative critics, "low cost" and "high quality" often appear to be interchangeable. What better evidence of this than the results of the American Legislative Exchange Council's 2018 *Report Card on American Education*, which ranked each state according to "how their education policies measure up to the demands that 21st-century success requires."[35] According to ALEC's metric, the top-ranked states were those that made the deepest cuts to education over the previous decade: Arizona, Oklahoma, Georgia, Florida, Wisconsin. Arizona, the sole recipient of ALEC's "A" rating, spent 13 percent less per student than it did in 2008. Only Oklahoma had a bigger gap: students in the Sooner State receive nearly 30 percent less than they did a decade before. Tellingly, ALEC's high-flyers were also the states where teacher pay had declined the most.[36]

In his survey of the influence of ALEC and other corporate lobbies on state-level politics since 2010, political economist Gordon Lafer makes the case that the dismantling of public education is also about diminishing the expectations of what Americans believe they are entitled to in a time of rising inequality: "Education is the one remaining public good to which most Americans still believe we are entitled by right of citizenship; destroying it through privatization may have far-reaching ramifications in erasing the commonsense consensus for using progressive taxation to provide universal services." Ballooning class sizes, abysmal school physical conditions, poorly trained teachers, or the replacement of teachers with technology all send a powerful signal to both parents and students, argues Lafer, about what they're worth, what they deserve, and most importantly, what they can demand.[37]

But the recent wave of teacher walkouts from California to North Carolina, and the widespread public support they attracted, indicate just how unpopular the cost-cutting crusade has become. There is simply no constituency demanding huge class sizes, four-day school weeks, or the use of uncertified educators to stanch a growing teacher shortage in states where pay has plummeted. In low-spending states like Arizona and Oklahoma, what began as teacher rebellions morphed into broad-based political movements against austerity. For those ideologically predisposed against public education, these public revolts represent a profound challenge. Starving the beast, after all, requires that the public be willing to elect politicians to cut taxes, shrink services, and dismantle public institutions. One solution: make it harder for the public to demand any kind of alternative. In our next chapter, we turn to the long-running conservative war against the teachers' unions—the loudest, most organized voice on behalf of the public schools.

4

The War on Labor

"The truth is, every fire starts with a spark," wrote West Virginia teacher Katie Endicott.[1] The state's twenty thousand teachers walked out en masse in February of 2018—but Endicott and her colleagues went first. Under the banner of "Fed Up Friday," teachers in southern West Virginia conducted a one-day work stoppage on February 2 to protest low pay and drastic cuts to benefits. That initial spark soon spread to all fifty-five counties in the Mountain State, and from there to Oklahoma, Kentucky, and Arizona.

In 2018, some 380,000 teachers and school support staff participated in work stoppages, including strikes and walkouts that forced the closure of schools in entire states. And teachers at a growing number of charter schools—a sector that is overwhelmingly non-union—were participating in their own protests. By the end of 2019, some 645,000 teachers had participated in some kind of labor action.

This upsurge in teacher protest provided a stark reminder of why the right loathes unions—indeed, any kind of teacher organizing. In states where austerity policies had cut the deepest, teachers used their collective power to swing the policy pendulum in a new direction. They demanded that the wealthy pay higher taxes to fund public education, employing a hashtag slogan—#RedforEd. For the teachers, the phrase became a rallying cry against the disinvestment from public education and the teaching profession. While the slogan, and the cause it represented, attracted widespread public support, conservative critics saw #RedforEd as something more nefarious. Leaders of Arizona's teacher protest movement, warned one Republican state representative, were using "teachers and our children to carry out their socialist movement."[2]

The unions weren't just focused on issues like teacher pay and school funding. In February 2019, teachers in West Virginia walked out again—this time over the issue of school privatization. Republicans in the state legislature were proposing the state's first-ever charter schools, along with education savings accounts that would allow parents to use public funds to pay for private religious schools. The controversial bill was backed by conservative and libertarian groups, which dispatched staffers to West Virginia's statehouse to testify in favor of the new legislation.

As legal scholar Joshua Weishart argues, if the first strike had been about addressing West Virginia's crippling teacher shortage, strike 2.0 was even more foundational. "It is about guaranteeing that quality public schools remain free and accessible to all children rather than a select few."[3] This time, says Weishart, teachers were walking the line to protect an entire system—particularly the principles at the core of it. In West Virginia, and elsewhere, the battle lines came clearly into focus: teachers and their unions versus those who seek to dismantle public education.

Teachers' Unions: A Brief History

The first organization of teachers wasn't a union at all. The National Teachers Association, organized by Susan B. Anthony and others in Philadelphia in 1857, included teachers, administrators, and even college presidents. As Dana Goldstein recounts in her book *The Teacher Wars*, associated educators adopted a "genteel" approach to advocacy—one rooted in distinctly middle-class sensibilities.

Four decades later, the newly formed Chicago Teachers Federation (CTF) took a different tack. Like their counterparts in organized labor, they advocated aggressively on behalf of teachers over issues like pay and classroom autonomy. As Goldstein notes, the CTF embraced an explicitly political, even militant, identity, "modeled after the male labor unions to which the fathers and brothers of Chicago teachers belonged."[4]

Those early organizations were the precursors of today's two nationwide unions of educators: the National Education Association (NEA) and the American Federation of Teachers (AFT). For much of its history, the NEA's membership tended to be suburban and rural, included both teachers and administrators, and eschewed collective bargaining. The AFT, by contrast, embraced the militancy of its Chicago forebears, and drew its strength from big urban locals—New York, Philadelphia, Chicago.

Yet for much of the twentieth century, neither union wielded much influence. The 1935 National Labor Relations Act (NLRA), which gave private-sector workers the right to organize and bargain collectively, didn't apply to public-sector unions like the NEA and the AFT.[5] Nor could teachers and other government workers withhold their labor in an effort to win concessions from employers. The result was that power remained highly concentrated in the hands of administrators.

For a quarter century, teachers and other public-sector workers pushed for the right to collectively bargain. In 1959, Wisconsin became the first state to allow public employees, including local government employees and teachers, to collectively bargain with their employers over wages, benefits, and working conditions. The Wisconsin law "meant as much as the NLRA had for private industry," argued one labor leader, who referred to the new legislation as "the Magna Carta for public employees."[6] Over the next year, sixteen more states enacted laws extending some form of organizing and bargaining rights to public employees. And in 1962, President John F. Kennedy signed an executive order allowing federal workers the right to bargain over some aspects of their work. The floodgates had been opened.

As the bargaining powers of public-sector employees expanded, teachers were also becoming more militant—particularly in New York City's United Federation of Teachers (UFT). The UFT was an affiliate of the AFT, which at the time had just sixty thousand members in the entire country. But in 1962, the UFT staged a successful one-day strike that forced New York City's Board of Education to agree to the very first collectively bargained contract for teachers. At the time, it was illegal for public employees in New York to strike. Yet New York teachers bet that the city couldn't possibly replace them all if they struck collectively. And they were right.

Across the country, teachers began striking in unprecedented numbers, and not just in cities. In 1968, for instance, Florida teachers walked off the job in the nation's first statewide teachers' strike. Demanding better pay and benefits, as well as more funding for public education, teachers stayed out of school for as long as three months in some districts.

Teachers' unions were winning wage increases and job protections and, as a result, experiencing explosive growth. By the end of the 1960s, AFT membership had expanded to two hundred thousand. The NEA, shrugging off its reputation as the AFT's polite sibling, pursued a similarly combative strategy, crafting more than one thousand collective bargaining agreements and growing to nearly a half-million members. By the end of the 1970s, nearly three-quarters of all public school teachers belonged to some kind of union.[7] And with greater numbers came more influence. As conservative political scientist Terry Moe later lamented, "the teachers' unions reigned supreme as the most powerful force in American education."[8]

With millions of members and hundreds of millions of dollars in resources, teachers' unions became a powerful political force. Deploying their leverage, they bargained for higher pay, as well as for job security protections. As unions grew in size and influence, however, they also became a target. As fiscal crises threatened one city after another during the 1970s, teachers' demands for higher salaries, even as residents—and jobs—were fleeing to the suburbs, seemed tone-deaf. When budget cuts forced layoffs, minority teachers were often the first to go, a casualty of strict seniority provisions that protected older white teachers at the expense of their newly hired minority colleagues. The disparity in layoffs only exacerbated a roiling racial divide between unions, which represented a largely white teaching force, and the communities where they taught.[9]

The AFT was a forceful supporter of the civil rights movement, going so far as to expel its Atlanta local when it refused to desegregate. And in 1966, the NEA merged with the American Teachers Association, which represented black teachers in segregated schools. But the unions were increasingly battling black and Latino parents and community leaders over whose rights mattered more when it came to making decisions about how schools should be run. The 1968 Ocean Hill–Brownsville strike, for instance, pitted sixty thousand overwhelmingly white teachers in New York City against communities of color demanding more control over their schools, including having a voice in selecting curriculum and hiring and firing teachers. The strike shuttered schools for two months, affecting nearly a million students, and left a bitter divide that still persists five decades later.

But no issue has proven as controversial as tenure protections for teachers. "Just cause" language for termination ensures that a teacher cannot be fired for her "political views, her friends, or the fact that she is an experienced teacher, earning a higher salary, in times of austerity and budget cuts," explains Leo Casey, executive director of the Albert Shanker Institute.[10] Such protected status dates back to the early 1900s, long before unions had the right to collectively bargain. Still, many members of the public view such protections as the spoils of union power—an unearned "job for life." The vast majority of Americans, by contrast, work in jobs that afford them no such protections; they are "at will" employees, hired and fired at the discretion of management and can be let go for any reason, or no reason at all.

"Today the ineffective tenured teacher has emerged as a feared character," writes Dana Goldstein, "a vampire type who sucks tax dollars into her bloated pension and health care plans, without much regard for the children in her care."[11] Goldstein argues that the media obsession with bad teachers, a veritable Hollywood trope, has all of the trademarks of a classic moral panic in which our national anxiety over socioeconomic inequality is projected onto a single group of people: unionized teachers in public schools.

But there is another reason why teachers' unions have emerged as particularly vulnerable to attack—a political punching bag for

Republicans and Democrats alike. At the same time that the unions were winning pay hikes, job protections, and political influence, the ranks of private-sector union membership were cratering. Today just 6.4 percent of workers in the private sector belong to unions, the lowest percentage since before the Great Depression. Teaching, meanwhile, remains the single most unionized profession in America. After a decades-long war on labor that has almost extinguished unions from the private sector, teachers' unions remain among the last standing, though without the strength in numbers they once enjoyed as part of a multi-sector union movement.

On the Attack

The Supreme Court's 2018 *Janus v. AFSCME* ruling, that public employees do not have to pay fees to unions to cover the cost of collective bargaining, was just a few hours old when MyPayMySay.org went live. "It's your paycheck. Union membership is your choice," proclaimed the website, which provided ready-to-print forms for teachers and other public-sector union members seeking to "opt out" of their unions. Created by the Mackinac Center for Public Policy, a conservative advocacy group in Michigan that has been heavily funded by Betsy DeVos and her extended family, the campaign also flooded the school email inboxes of teachers in union strongholds like New York, New Jersey, and Connecticut.[12] Meanwhile, the Freedom Foundation, an anti-union think tank funded by conservative billionaires with familiar names—DeVos, Koch, Bradley, Scaife—was recruiting paid workers to canvass door-to-door and in the workplaces of public employees, arming them with the same message: you no longer have to pay union dues.[13]

For all of its digital gloss, this latest effort to thin the ranks of public employees represents a very old cause. Helping to shepherd the *Janus* case to the Supreme Court was the National Right to Work Foundation. Dating back to 1953, the foundation was the brainchild of a North Carolina box manufacturer who sought to keep unions out of his workplace. As Moshe Marvit recounts, the appeal of so-called right-to-work laws, which allow workers not to pay dues to a union representing them, took off in the segregationist South, where employers saw unions as a threat, not just to their power, but to segregation itself.[14] More than six decades later, Justice Samuel Alito essentially channeled the group's argument when he wrote that "states and public-sector unions may no longer extract agency fees from nonconsenting employees."[15]

While the free-speech argument forming the basis of Alito's decision represents a new phase in the war on labor, the goal of weakening unions and their political influence has long been a central tenet of the conservative cause. "Unions exist, presumably to confer economic advantages on their members, not to perform political services for them. Unions should therefore be forbidden to engage in any kind of political activity."[16] So argued Barry Goldwater in *Conscience of a Conservative*, the 1960 treatise that ignited a new movement on the right wing of American politics. Four years after the book's publication, Goldwater ran as the Republican nominee for president, and lost in a landslide. But his campaign, as Heritage fellow Lee Edwards concluded, "marked the beginning of a shift to the right that would eventually end 50 years of liberal dominance in American politics."[17]

In demonizing unions, Goldwater was channeling conservative businessmen, angry since the New Deal over a legal and regulatory framework, ushered in by the Roosevelt administration, that they saw as hopelessly tilted against capital and in favor of labor. But Goldwater didn't simply rail about the evils of anticapitalism. Instead, he equated collectivism and social welfare with totalitarianism and social control. Organized labor and the New Deal, he and his disciples argued, had created a communist-style patronage machine that rewarded party loyalty with government jobs. In this deal, politicians were insulated from democracy, while unions were insulated from the market. With the Cold War as a backdrop, hard-line conservatives increasingly proclaimed their commitment to freedom and free enterprise, which they argued were as linked together as authoritarianism and socialism. It was a message with staying power.

Concerned about the growing power of the unions, conservatives and the business community formed anti-labor alliances like the Business Roundtable. Established in 1972, the organization soon became, in the words of political scientists Thomas Dye and Harmon Zeigler, "arguably the most powerful lobby in Washington."[18] Just one year later, the Conservative Caucus of State Legislators—eventually known as the American Legislative Exchange Council (ALEC)—was founded. As one of the organization's early leaders warned fellow conservatives, "Liberal state legislators are supported by a vast array of special interest groups." The group gaining "at the fastest rate," according to him, was "the radically liberal National Education Association."[19] Teachers and their leftist allies needed to be countered.

While Goldwater had cast his argument in the language of freedom and rights, his real target was political. He excoriated unions for carrying water for the Democratic Party: funding candidates, providing manpower for election-day chores, and distributing printed material. "In short," he opined, "they perform all of the functions of a regular party organization."[20] Singling out Michigan for particular opprobrium, Goldwater accused the United Auto Workers and their chief, Walter Reuther, of taking over the Democratic Party. "Underneath the Democrat label," he insisted, "there is something new, and something dangerous—born of conspiracy and violence, sired by socialists and nurtured by the general treasury of the UAW-CIO."[21]

Goldwater's solution was right-to-work laws that would ban the practice of making union membership a condition of employment—what he described as a "great blight on the contemporary American scene." Flash forward a half-century, and although the landscape may have changed—public-sector unions have replaced the private-sector organizations as the go-to villains for the right—the preferred fix remains the same. In 2012, not long after Scott Walker took on Wisconsin's public employees, ushering in our current era of scorched-earth-style politics at the state level, GOP lawmakers in Michigan rushed through their own right-to-work bill. While the Michigan law applied to all of the state's unions, including autoworkers, its real target was the state's powerful teachers' organization: the Michigan Education Association. A subsequent state law sought to inhibit unionization by making it illegal for school districts to deduct union dues from teachers' paychecks.

The scope of what unions can do for their members has also been dramatically curtailed. In Wisconsin, for example, teachers and other public employees can no longer bargain over anything but wages, while their pay increases cannot exceed the rate of inflation. Such measures were justified as an urgent fiscal necessity in the wake of the Great Recession, but their real function, argue labor scholars Bob Bruno and Steven Ashby, was to restrict the political influence of public-sector unions. Limiting what unions can negotiate over, they contend, essentially blocks "the ability of organized labor to translate workplace representation power into social and political power."[22]

In the six states that enacted right-to-work laws after 2010, all saw declines in public-sector union membership, but none as precipitous as Wisconsin's. Six years after the passage of Act 10, union rolls in the state had shrunk by 132,000 names, and Wisconsin, the state where public-employee unions were born, now ranks in the bottom third of the country in number of union members.[23] As of 2017, the state teachers' union no longer employed a lobbyist at the state capitol. Tim Phillips, the head of the Koch-funded Americans for Prosperity, recently boasted that the group has more members in Wisconsin than do the unions.[24]

A half-century after Barry Goldwater made weakening the political influence of organized labor a conservative rallying cry, his ideological descendants have finally put the vision into practice.

A Bipartisan Cause

"Big loss for the coffers of the Democrats!" Donald Trump tweeted when news of the Supreme Court's ruling in the *Janus* case broke. Trump was alluding to the game plan that conservative activists had begun openly flaunting in the months and weeks leading up to the court's ruling: by thinning the ranks of public-sector unions, they could vastly diminish the unions' resources, and hence their ability to support Democratic candidates and progressive causes.[25]

Just how reliant the Democrats have been on the electoral power of organized labor became obvious in 2016. As a team of political scientists discovered, laws curbing union power in states like Michigan sapped Democratic strength up and down the ballot. By comparing counties in states that had enacted right-to-work laws with adjacent counties in states without such laws, the researchers calculated that the anti-union measures cost Democratic candidates between two and five percentage points—several times the margin by which Hillary Clinton lost Wisconsin and Michigan.

Voter turnout dropped as campaign contributions from unions dried up and get-out-the-vote efforts withered.

Weakening unions also produced what the researchers describe as "large downstream effects" on both the candidates running for office and the policies enacted at the state level. "Fewer working class candidates serve in state legislatures and Congress," they concluded, "and state policy moves in a more conservative direction following the passage of right-to-work laws."[26]

The irony is that weakening the influence of organized labor—teachers' unions in particular—has been largely a bipartisan cause. Bill Clinton made his attack on Arkansas teachers a centerpiece of his 1983 gubernatorial campaign, burnishing his image as a new breed of Democrat who wasn't afraid to take on the party's own "special interests."[27] And during Barack Obama's eight years in the White House, tough talk against teachers' unions as protectors of the status quo emerged as party orthodoxy. "It's time to start rewarding good teachers, stop making excuses for bad ones," Obama proclaimed in a 2009 speech in which he praised the idea of merit pay for teachers, long a favorite policy tool of Republicans.[28]

As the Great Recession led to deep cuts in school spending, the Obama administration offered a reprieve in the form of its $4.35 billion Race to the Top program, overseen by Secretary of Education Arne Duncan. States that adopted favored policy prescriptions, including expanding privately run charter schools and weakening teacher tenure by tying teacher evaluation and pay to student test scores, could win hundreds of millions of dollars. Forty states applied to compete in the contest, with eighteen and the District of Columbia eventually receiving grants ranging from $17 to $700 million.

A 2015 study found that Race to the Top was astonishingly

successful in getting states to change their education policies as they rushed to enact laws that met the contest guidelines. As University of Chicago scholar William Howe concluded, the initiative "massively increas[ed] the public profile of a controversial set of education policies," including the use of standardized test scores for the purpose of evaluating teachers.[29] Suddenly the debate over how best to punish ineffective teachers was everywhere.

Weakening tenure and other job projections also emerged as a newly bipartisan cause. The right had long been critical of the "thickly woven" legal procedures that protected teachers.[30] As a Hoover Institution report proclaimed in 1999, "For the unions, apparently no apple is so bad that it need be tossed from the barrel."[31] A decade later, the same charge began to be leveled by self-styled Democratic school reformers like Washington, DC, schools chief Michelle Rhee. As policy analyst Richard Kahlenberg put it, "Conservatives have long attacked policies such as tenure that constrain the ability of managers to fire whomever they want, but the latest assaults on tenure have invoked liberal egalitarian ideals."[32]

When a Los Angeles judge threw out several state statutes giving job protections to teachers in the 2014 *Vergara v. California* case, the ruling was quickly hailed as a victory for civil rights. The deep-pocketed Silicon Valley group that brought the suit had argued that seniority protections for educators meant that low-income students in the state were disproportionately likely to end up with bad teachers who couldn't be fired. In his ruling, Judge Rolf Treu emphatically agreed, arguing that ending tenure was necessary to ensure that poor students in California received "basic equality in public education."[33] The trial had centered on the familiar trope of terrible teachers immune from any threat of being fired.

But as skeptics of the *Vergara* ruling pointed out, poor students are far more likely to attend schools with the least-experienced teachers and higher staff turnover than their wealthier peers. A California appeals court agreed, ruling unanimously that the plaintiffs had failed to show that state statutes protecting teachers harmed some students more than others. Similar cases filed in Minnesota, New York, and New Jersey foundered as well. The high-profile legal challenge to tenure, once championed by such Democratic Party luminaries as David Boies, who had represented Al Gore before the Supreme Court in *Bush v. Gore*, "turned into a frivolous theory that is now sinking like a rock to the bottom of the ocean, likely to never be seen again," in the words of legal scholar Derek Black.[34]

The Obama era of education reform left in its wake a decidedly mixed legacy. The administration eliminated the most punitive aspects of the No Child Left Behind law, channeled badly needed funds into schools during the recession, and took significant steps to protect the rights of historically marginalized students. But the administration's overwhelming reliance on high-stakes testing as a measure of student, school, and teacher performance spawned public backlash. And states that rushed to embrace the administration's favored policies, including adopting the Common Core standards and tying teacher evaluations to test scores, have since backed away from them.

The most lasting legacy of Obama's education policies is likely the dramatic expansion of charter schools, primed by the aid of federal funds. The share of students attending charter schools doubled from 3 to 6 percent during his two terms, while charter enrollment soared in urban districts. Charters, whose teachers only rarely belong to unions, have played a significant role in thinning the ranks of organized labor. In Philadelphia, for example, where more than 30 percent of students now attend charter schools, the Philadelphia Federation of Teachers has "withered," writes journalist

Emmanuel Felton. As public schools in the city were shuttered and charter schools expanded, union membership dropped from 21,000 to 11,000. As Felton notes, in a battleground state where union members have long been called upon to help elect Democratic candidates, Democratic policies in the Obama era meant that there were now vastly fewer union members to call upon.[35]

Nor is Philadelphia an outlier. In cities like Detroit, Indianapolis, and Cleveland—all Democratic bastions in "red" states—state laws passed by conservatives aimed at circumscribing unions intersected with Obama-era policies favoring charter schools and weakening job protections for teachers. In Detroit, the once powerful Detroit Federation of Teachers is down to just three thousand members from more than nine thousand a decade ago, while fully half of the teachers in the city don't belong to a union.

For decades, the right has sought to undermine the political influence of unions as a means of undercutting the progressive causes that unions support: higher wages that benefit all workers, social benefits along with the taxes needed to pay for them, and in education, greater school spending. Now they've nearly succeeded, with aid from unlikely allies.

Teachers Strike Back

When in January 2019 United Teachers Los Angeles (UTLA) announced the end to a six-day strike by thirty thousand of the city's educators, the mood was celebratory. Not only had the strike forced the Los Angeles Unified School District to meet the union's demand for smaller class sizes, and to explore the possibility of a cap on the number of charter schools in L.A., it also forced a debate on the city's commitment to the very idea of public education. Now the success of L.A.'s teachers was certain to inspire other educators to engage in similar actions across the country.

But just hours after the strike wrapped up, a Los Angeles teacher filed a class-action lawsuit against the union, demanding that UTLA stop collecting her dues and refund the money she had paid into their coffers. The lawsuit was part of a wave of litigation filed by conservative legal groups seeking to capitalize on the Supreme Court's *Janus* decision. Organizations including the Freedom Foundation and the National Right to Work Legal Defense Foundation, which brought the L.A. suit, began demanding that unions pay back what the groups call "forced union fees" to former members—a strategy aimed at bankrupting the unions.

Meanwhile, teachers who walked out of their schools in 2018 in West Virginia, Oklahoma, and Arizona have been targeted by Republican legislators, eager to make such collective action harder to pull off in the future. In Arizona, proposed legislation would prohibit public schools from shutting down except during approved holidays, while in Oklahoma lawmakers want to permanently revoke the certification of teachers who participate in strikes or walkouts, making sure they never teach in the Sooner State again.[36]

Somewhat surprisingly, these efforts to target teachers' unions may be triggering new waves of teacher activism. According to the Bureau of Labor Statistics, 2018 saw more workers involved in strikes and walkouts than in the previous thirty years, with teachers leading the charge.[37] Labor experts still believe that the *Janus* decision will lead to a drop in the number of union members, but the predicted mass exodus has not yet occurred. And while *Janus* was the culmination of a decades-long push to weaken organized labor in blue states by depriving unions of resources and making organizing more difficult, some of the most potent teacher uprisings occurred in states where unions were the weakest. Indeed, as unions grow weaker in states like New York and California, where they've long been a dominant presence, the consequence may be more grassroots labor activism, not less. As unions grow weaker as institutions, they are less able to tell members what they can and can't do.

Perhaps most consequentially, public opinion has shifted dramatically in favor of organized labor, and now stands at a fifteen-year high.[38] Approval of collective action by teachers is even stronger. A poll conducted in the aftermath of the 2018 teacher walkouts found that two-thirds of Americans believe that teachers have the right to strike for higher pay, better school funding, and stronger benefits.[39] A 2019 survey of adults in the six states that had seen recent teacher strikes found strong support for teachers, their unions, and even for future labor action.[40]

Meanwhile, demographic data suggest that a generational shift in attitudes toward unions is under way. Nearly 70 percent of Americans ages eighteen to twenty-nine hold a positive view of unions, compared with only about half of those fifty and older. No wonder the fiercest partisans in the decades-long crusade against unions are now sounding so alarmed. As conservative philanthropist Art Pope warned in 2018, "The younger generation is less sympathetic and less understanding of limited government conservatism."[41]

But while a pendulum swing may be under way, the war on labor will continue, and teachers' unions will remain a central target. As the seemingly endless wave of teacher strikes and walkouts has made abundantly clear, teachers are using their collective might to fight for better pay and benefits, limits on private school choice, stricter regulations on charter schools, and more funding, even if that means higher taxes. Nor are their demands confined to these traditional issues. In North Carolina, for example, teachers rallied for more school nurses and counselors, as well as an expansion of Medicaid to benefit parents and students. And in Chicago, teachers who struck in 2019 demanded not just smaller class sizes and higher pay but city action on affordable housing.

If unions represent a vehicle for demanding a more equitable distribution of social resources, they also stand in the way of particular education policy objectives that are a priority for free-market advocates. In the next chapters, we explore some specific policy goals: vouchers and voucher-like programs, for-profit education, virtual learning, and the rollback of the regulations that govern K-12 education. Much to the consternation of conservative reformers, teachers and their unions stand in the way of realizing all of these policy aims.

5

Neo-Vouchers

"College and heaven," promised the Catholic school in South Florida that Betsy DeVos dropped by on one of her first official school tours as secretary of education.[1] The visit was the first of many to the Sunshine State, which DeVos often lauds as a model for her particular brand of school choice—one that rewards private, almost exclusively religious schools, with taxpayer-funded largesse, accompanied by little to no oversight.

Private schools in Florida now rake in close to $1 billion a year in public money. The explosive growth of the state's private school choice program over the past twenty years is all the more remarkable considering that the Florida constitution prohibits public money from funding religious institutions. But as in a growing number of states, school choice advocates in Florida developed a workaround for this problem. Called tax-credit scholarships, or "neo-vouchers," these complex instruments incentivize wealthy donors and companies to direct their tax dollars to religious schools via nonprofit organizations. It's a little bit like money laundering, and it is increasingly prevalent.

Baby Blaines

As detailed in chapter 2, the conservative dream of funding private school vouchers with public tax dollars began to take shape during the Reagan years. Proponents maintained that vouchers would empower parents and introduce market logic to education, substituting consumer choice for the heavy hand of government. Educating students in private schools, they argued, would also cost less. And, as students shifted from public schools to private ones—resulting in the closure of the former and the expansion of the latter—organized labor would be undermined.

But voucher proponents had a problem. The vast majority of private schools are religious in nature. Any private school voucher program, then, would likely channel public funds to sectarian education. And while the U.S. Constitution doesn't outlaw vouchers, at least according to a 2002 Supreme Court ruling, most state constitutions contain provisions that are far more hostile to vouchers.

What this means is that even when voucher promoters have won political victories, they've often been turned back by the courts. The Colorado Supreme Court, for example, ruled against voucher programs in 2004, and again in 2015, on the grounds that they channel public funds to religious schools. And in 2006, the Florida Supreme Court struck down that state's voucher program, ruling that the state constitution bars the use of taxpayer money to finance private alternatives to the public education system. To better understand these laws, we need to take a brief trip back to the nineteenth century and examine the rise of so-called Blaine amendments, named for the U.S. congressman who first pushed for them.

American politics in the late nineteenth century were charged with race-baiting and nativism—not unlike politics in the Trump era. Back then, the growing population of Catholic immigrants was the target, as politicians angled to align themselves with the cultural majority. Among those politicians was Congressman James G. Blaine of Maine. Seeking to pave his way for a presidential bid in 1876, he proposed an amendment to the Constitution that would bar Catholic schools from ever receiving public funds. The 1875 text of his amendment read:

> No State shall make any law respecting an establishment of religion, or prohibiting the free exercise thereof; and no money raised by taxation in any State for the support of public schools, or derived from any public fund therefor, nor any public lands devoted thereto, shall ever be under the control of any religious sect; nor shall any money so raised or lands so devoted be divided between religious sects or denominations.

The amendment had significant popular support, particularly among Protestants who viewed themselves as an increasingly embattled majority and who were strongly opposed to religious sectarianism in public education. But to Catholics, the supposed secular education of the public system looked an awful lot like Protestantism in disguise; in addition to instruction in basic academic subjects, the typical nineteenth-century school day also included scripture reading and hymn singing. Catholics in places like New York withdrew their children from public schools and enrolled them in church-run schools. As they saw it, schools for Protestant students were tax-supported, while Catholic schools were not. With the support of clergy, Catholic parents began to agitate for their share of public revenue.

Blaine's amendment, which overtly pandered to the Protestant majority, passed in the House but failed in the Senate. That, however, did not prevent states from taking action to block public funding for religious schools. In relatively rapid succession, a majority of states adopted what became known as "baby Blaine" amendments to their own constitutions.

Over the next several decades, some in the cultural majority continued to agitate for an outright ban on sectarian education—a project chiefly aimed at Catholic schools. But the rights of parents to educate their children in accordance with their own faith consistently won out, including at the Supreme Court.[2]

Still, the controversy led to serious and generally successful efforts to remove religion from public schools. One observer, writing in 1912, argued that religious instruction had by that date been "either entirely eliminated or else reduced to the barest and most formal elements."[3] Legal efforts across the next half-century completed the secularization of public education by removing the last of those formal elements—school prayer, Bible study, and the posting of the Ten Commandments.

For many years, Blaine amendments remained on the books without any real need to implement them. According to a 2003 article in the *Fordham Law Review*, "the State Blaines have simply lacked occasion for robust application."[4] Neo-voucher programs changed that.

As the dismantling agenda began to take shape in the 1980s, many conservatives viewed vouchers as a natural policy tool. But most private schools, being religious in nature, could not receive public funds. Coupled with low levels of public support for policies that would reduce funding for public schools, it seemed that vouchers were at an impasse.[5] For conservatives, then, it was time to get creative.

A Laundromat for Tax Dollars

An inventive solution emerged in Barry Goldwater's home state of Arizona, which in 1997 passed the nation's very first tax-credit scholarship program. A school voucher in all but name, the program was, in the words of conservative congressman Trent Franks, "easier to pass and easier to uphold."[6]

The tax-credit scholarship program relied on a clever work-around. Instead of the state paying the tab, individuals would donate to nonprofit organizations, which would then provide private school scholarships to students. The individuals making the donations would then receive a dollar-for-dollar state tax credit, effectively reimbursing them for their "gifts." While the state wasn't sending money directly to private schools, the impact on the treasury was the same: funds were diverted from tax collection and sent to private schools.

The end result was a transaction that had more in common with money laundering than with charitable giving, as the program was set up to conceal the fact that money was coming from the state. But because revenue was never collected in the first place, the state stepped neatly around any constitutional prohibitions on support for private or sectarian education. When challenged legally, the program was upheld not only by the Arizona Supreme Court, but also by the U.S. Supreme Court, which ruled that because tax-credit funds had not "come into the tax collector's hands," they could not be viewed as "public money."[7]

Such "neo-vouchers" are complex by design. Just explaining the funding arrangements behind them requires a football-play style diagram. As Kevin Welner, co-founder of the National Education Policy Center, has observed: "People's eyes get bleary and they tune out when people start talking about tax credits. That help to avoid a situation where they respond to it the same way they respond to a voucher proposal."[8] Polls indicate that this strategy is effective. Americans are more likely to say they approve of "tax credit–funded scholarships" than "universal vouchers."[9]

By obscuring the funding of neo-voucher programs and burying their purpose—using public money for private religious schooling while reducing the funding available for public education—proponents have steadily advanced their core ideological aims, largely without inciting public confrontation. Quietly flying under the radar, they have created tax-credit programs in state after state, typically limiting vouchers to specific populations at first—foster children, students with special needs, victims of bullying—then pushing relentlessly for expansion toward their ultimate goal: vouchers for all.

A Legal Loophole

During the past decade, tax-credit scholarships have emerged as the most popular solution for voucher proponents. Eighteen states now run twenty-three of these programs, including Illinois, which enacted a massive version in 2017. Modeled on the same idea that was pioneered in Arizona, these scholarship programs never directly transfer public monies to private schools. Instead, wealthy taxpayers and corporations receive hefty tax credits—usually dollar-for-dollar credits against any state tax liability they would have incurred—in exchange for donating to nonprofit scholarship organizations.

This is entirely legal, but it is also unquestionably a loophole. In most states with Blaine amendments, a dollar cannot legally flow directly from the state to a private school. But a dollar *can* go from an individual or corporation to a nonprofit organization, and then from that organization to a private school. Walmart, then, might give $1 million to 123TaxCredit.com, a certified School Tuition Organization in Arizona. After covering its own costs, 123TaxCredit.com would then use those funds to pay private school tuition for students enrolled in its program. Meanwhile, the Arizona Department of Revenue would subtract $1 million from Walmart's end-of-year state tax bill.

When it was first created in 1997, Arizona's tax-credit scholarship program was forecast to cost $4.5 million a year. Currently, it tops $140 million annually—a figure far smaller than the $3 billion that the state contributes to public schools, but which has nevertheless undergone a thirty-fold increase. Additionally, it appears that much of that money has gone to families with children who were already enrolled in private schools, despite rhetoric focused on empowering public school families with choice. While supporters of the program like to cite freedom and markets, critics like former state senator Steve Farley have pointed out that Arizona's program has also demonstrated "how you strip a budget bare."[10] By draining funds from public education, tax-credit scholarships are also a vehicle for "starving the beast."

In Florida, the story is much the same. Corporations receive dollar-for-dollar tax credits for their donations to private school scholarship organizations. With little to no state oversight, the program has ballooned to nearly a billion dollars a year. And while participation was initially limited to low-income students enrolled in the public schools, the program is now open to middle-class families who have never enrolled their children in public schools—essentially reimbursing them for the private school tuition they were already paying.

Schools Without Rules

In 2018, the *Orlando Sentinel* published the results of an extensive investigation into Florida's neo-voucher program. Many of the eye-popping details pertained to the lack of state oversight and the weak enforcement of the few existing rules. The three-part series described a system "so weakly regulated that some schools hire teachers without college degrees, hold classes in aging strip malls and falsify fire-safety and health records."[11]

But for proponents of private school choice, the absence of oversight is a feature, not a bug. Unregulated by design, these programs are intended to undermine the apparatus of the state, not expand it. In Florida, for instance, the state is only allowed to pay ten visits a year to schools receiving tax-credit scholarship funds—a tiny fraction of participating schools. The vast majority of private schools aren't accredited, and the schools are exempt from the state's accountability system. Conservatives argue that oversight and accountability is provided by parents themselves, through the choices they make. As Foundation for Excellence in Education CEO Patricia Levesque, who also served as an education official under former Florida governor Jeb Bush, put it: "The goals of choice are not to turn private schools into public schools."[12] Reality, however, paints a more complex picture.

Freedom from "red tape" allows private schools to skirt any number of laws and regulations, including those pertaining to civil rights, anti-discrimination, and the rights of children with special needs. Even as they accept public funds, voucher schools enjoy wide latitude over who they serve and who they don't. The *Sentinel*'s investigation found eighty-three schools that accept taxpayer-funded scholarships but refuse to admit gay students. Additional schools refused to educate students with gay parents, or to hire teachers or school staff who are gay. "Students don't need to go to that school if they feel that is going to be a problem for their families and their lifestyles," an advocate for the scholarship program told reporters.[13]

One religious school in Florida that Betsy DeVos visited during her school choice tour stated openly on its website that students with special needs need not apply. Parents who find a private school that accepts special education students are often shocked to find that the protections that federal law requires under the Individuals with Disabilities Education Act don't extend to private schools. Meanwhile, parents who end up at odds with their private school on the provision of necessary accommodations are left with little to no recourse.

When the parent of a special needs student was told by a Florida private school that her daughter was no longer welcome at the school, the parent first complained to the nonprofit group through which she'd received the tax-credit scholarship—to no avail. Investigating such complaints was beyond the group's charge as a scholarship-granting organization, a spokesman for Step Up For Students later told *Education Week*. When the parent took her complaint to the state, she was similarly stonewalled. Private schools, a state education official responded, have complete discretion over "student regulation, dismissal, and expulsion policies." No laws or rules had been broken.[14]

A "cottage industry of fraud and chaos" is how Gus Garcia-Roberts described Florida's tax-credit scholarship program for special needs students in an award-winning investigation for the *Miami New Times*.[15] As one former investigator for the Florida Department of Education told Garcia-Roberts, the agency was unable to uncover "even a significant fraction" of wrongdoing.

The story has been similar in Arizona, where no state agency has the authority to prevent or penalize programmatic misconduct. According to Lisa Graham Keegan, Arizona's school superintendent when the tax-credit program passed, "the point was in part to ensure that these were not government-run programs."[16] Such lax oversight has allowed the powerful to use public education as a cash machine. Steve Yarbrough, the president of the State Senate, opened his own scholarship-granting organization—the Arizona Christian School Tuition Organization—and began taking an annual salary of $125,000. The organization also outsourced work to a company, HY Processing, that was also owned by Yarbrough, paying out millions of dollars over the course of a decade.

Enterprising donors in a number of states, meanwhile, have identified loopholes in the tax code that they can exploit to their advantage. In eight states, donors can take a state tax credit *and* a federal tax deduction, double-dipping their way to a profit. Donors in those states are reimbursed for their contributions with dollar-for-dollar tax credits; they are also allowed to deduct the full amount of those contributions from their federal taxable income, reducing what they owe in end-of-year taxes. As Carl Davis of the Institute on Taxation and Economic Policy has observed, a quirk in tax law makes such profits available only to high-income taxpayers. As a result, the rich "enjoy a profit" by "spending on the state's behalf."[17]

Advocates of the tax credits even highlight their profitability to potential donors. In Georgia, Whitefield Academy, which promotes itself as "a Christ-centered preparatory school," noted on its website that donors subject to the alternative minimum tax "actually stand to make money on this program." The school later removed the tax advice, one of many examples of questionable practices associated with neo-vouchers highlighted in a 2017 report by the School Superintendents Association titled *Public Loss Private*

Gain. The report characterized the tax-credit programs as "get rich schemes for shrewd taxpayers," warning that "the potential for wealthy individuals to turn a profit by claiming these credits is accelerating the diversion of critical resources away from public schools."[18]

It's not just savvy donors who have figured out how to benefit from a largely unregulated system. Neo-vouchers have also proven ripe for gaming by schools and parents. In Arizona, for example, many parents began using tax-credit scholarships to pay tuition bills at the private schools their children were already attending. Knowing that parents had previously paid tuition out of pocket, a number of schools responded by raising prices. In effect, Arizona's neo-vouchers simply subsidized private schools. Parents have gamed the system in another way: by badgering friends to "earmark" scholarship donations for their children, trading donations with other families, and collecting multiple scholarships. A 2009 investigation of the program concluded that, far from making private school education more accessible for Arizonans who couldn't afford it, neo-vouchers had "fostered a rigged system that keeps private education a privilege for the already privileged."[19]

Indeed, the Arizona program was so rife with abuse that even its architects seemed horrified by what they'd wrought. "This is horrible . . . this is not the program I fought for," reflected Clint Bolick, founder of the Goldwater Institute and an attorney for the tax-credit program in court, to the *East Valley Tribune*. Bolick had recently learned that leaders at his son's private Montessori school, along with a number of parents, had figured out a way to game the system. The school paired up families so they could exchange tax-credit donations to benefit each other's children. "My jaw dropped," Bolick said.[20]

What Gets Taught

In a photograph that accompanied the inaugural story in the *Orlando Sentinel*'s "Schools Without Rules" series, six students from TDR Learning Academy sit tucked in a row of cubicles, hunched over worksheets. The picture neatly captures an unregulated education in action. The school's principal, who bends down to assist a young charge, lacks a college degree. The worksheets come courtesy of Accelerated Christian Education, a popular Christian curriculum based on a literal interpretation of the Bible. The curriculum instructs students that humans and dinosaurs once lived side by side, that homosexuality is a sin, and that slaves who "knew Christ" were better off than free men who weren't Christian.[21]

In a review of seven thousand schools across the country that accept public money via traditional school vouchers or neo-vouchers, reporter Rebecca Klein determined that a third of them were using a curriculum provided by one of three popular—and ideologically extreme—Christian textbook companies: Accelerated Christian Education, Abeka, and Bob Jones University. "The ideas in these textbooks often flout widely accepted science and historical fact," wrote Klein. "That means there are thousands of kids receiving an extremist and ultra-conservative education at the expense of taxpayers."[22]

With no power to regulate the curricula of private schools, states with tax-credit scholarship programs are channeling funds to schools like Florida's Clearwater Academy International, which uses learning materials based on the ideas of L. Ron Hubbard, the founder of Scientology.[23] While critics of public education have made a case against the current state and national standards in math, English, and science, perhaps more troubling is the total freedom of voucher schools to teach anything at all, no matter how dubious the pedagogy and how ideological the curricula.

Another review of curricula used by voucher schools in Florida found materials steeped in religious and political opinions about such topics as gay rights, abortion, and government programs, including the Endangered Species Act, which was referred to as advancing "a radical social agenda." As the *Orlando Sentinel* investigative team concluded: "They disparage religions other than Protestant Christianity and cultures other than those descended from white Europeans"—a deeply concerning finding given that six of ten recipients of tax-credit scholarships in Florida are either black or Hispanic.[24]

Critics of constitutional prohibitions that keep public funding from going to religious schools often attribute them to nineteenth-century anti-Catholic bias. "There's hope that Blaine amendments won't be around much longer," Betsy DeVos said in a 2018 speech to an organization affiliated with the Catholic Archdiocese of New York. "These amendments should be assigned to the ash heap of history."[25] However, reviews of popular curricula used by voucher schools have, ironically, identified a profound anti-Catholic bias, including the message that "God's intervention prevented Catholics from dominating North America."[26]

How many schools accepting public funds are passing such "facts" onto students? We may never know: Florida law prohibits state education officials from even asking about what gets taught in private schools accepting tax-credit scholarships.

The Education Debit Card

Tax-credit scholarships are hardly the only neo-voucher around. Education savings accounts (ESAs) have proliferated in Arizona,

Nevada, and Florida, as well as in Mississippi, North Carolina, and Tennessee. ESAs allow parents to withdraw children from the public schools and receive money in a state-approved account, often attached to a debit card. Families can then spend the funds on private school tuition, tutoring, materials, or even save the money to spend on college down the road. Sometimes they simply pocket it.

As these programs have taken off, groups like the Friedman Foundation have pushed for a wider array of policy mechanisms to advance their agenda. And they now advocate for almost no limit on how public dollars can be spent. In *The Education Debit Card*, a 2013 Friedman Foundation publication, author Lindsey Burke writes that states "should make ESA dollars universal and available for any education-related purpose, including private school tuition, private tutoring, online learning courses, or education-related services."[27]

Arizona enacted its ESA program in 2011. And, similar to the way neo-vouchers are often introduced, participation was initially restricted to disadvantaged students—in this case, children with disabilities. Families participating in the Arizona Empowerment Scholarship Account program could withdraw their children from the public system and keep 90 percent of what the state would have spent, using the funds at their discretion for educational purposes. Eligibility was soon expanded to military families, foster children, and parents with children in low-performing schools.

Even as legislators continued to expand the ESA program, oversight remained lax and accountability minimal. A 2017 investigation found that the program was rife with fraud. Some parents withdrew scholarship funds and deposited them into 529 college savings accounts to be used down the road, then left the program and returned to their public schools. Others used their education debit cards to make purchases that they then returned for gift cards that could be spent on anything. Still others claimed the scholarship funds, but then sent their children to public schools. And in cases where money was misspent, the state lacked both the means and the authority to recover any of it.[28]

In 2017, Arizona legislators gave a stamp of approval to one of the nation's most ambitious neo-voucher programs to date, effectively making every student in the state eligible for an ESA. "All children are different, and they learn in different educational environments," declared Debbie Lesko, the former state senator who sponsored the legislation. "We shouldn't force them to be in the same educational model we've used for the last 150 years."[29] Betsy DeVos chimed in too, saluting Arizona and its Republican governor for enacting what she described as "a big win for kids." While the legislation limited initial participation to thirty thousand students, the conservative Goldwater Institute revealed that it planned to begin pushing for elimination of the cap.

In 2018, voters in Arizona overwhelmingly defeated a ballot measure that would have made every K-12 student in the state eligible for an ESA. As one columnist put it, voters didn't just say "no" to Proposition 305, "they stoned the thing, then they tossed it into the street and ran over it."[30] And yet the 2018 midterm results had barely been announced before voucher proponents in the state, allied with powerful school choice lobby groups, proclaimed their intention to fight on. Since the measure failed at the polls, Republican lawmakers have attempted to expand the program via piecemeal legislation, including a bill that would let students on Native American reservations use their voucher funds at schools out of state.[31]

When given the opportunity to vote on sending public money to private schools, voters have always responded with an emphatic thumbs-down. And yet, as part of the push to "unbundle" schooling from the institutions of public education, there is powerful political momentum behind neo-vouchers in all of their forms. In 2016, the influential American Legislative Exchange Council adopted the Education Savings Account Act as a model bill to disseminate to state legislators. A recent investigation by *USA Today*, the Center for Public Integrity, and the *Arizona Republic* found that ESA proposals had been introduced in nineteen states, copied from ALEC's fill-in-the-blank bills.[32] The Koch network has likewise committed to putting its political heft and financial might behind the expansion of ESAs—investing in "idea generation, leadership training, election campaigning and policy advocacy."[33]

Meanwhile, traditional voucher programs have come roaring back in recent years, expanding dramatically in states like Wisconsin, Indiana, and Ohio. Unlike the small-scale voucher programs of the 1990s, which came clad in the rhetoric of social justice, the most recent incarnations are targeted at more affluent families whose children have never attended public schools—the sorts of families who have taken advantage of tax-credit scholarships.

The Supreme Court has also set the table for voucher crusaders. In 2017, the court ruled on *Trinity Lutheran Church of Columbia, Inc. v. Comer*, identifying no inherent separation between government and religious organizations. In a 7–2 ruling (with Justices Sonia Sotomayor and Ruth Bader Ginsburg dissenting), the court found that the state of Missouri had violated the rights of Trinity Lutheran Church by denying it an otherwise available public benefit on account of its religious status.

Three years later, the Supreme Court took up *Espinoza v. Montana Department of Revenue*, which concerned the legality of a tax-credit scholarship used primarily for religious education in the state. In questioning, Trump appointee Brett Kavanaugh made clear the slippery slope that conservatives had worked so hard to design.

Wasn't the case simply a "straight violation" of Trinity Lutheran, he asked? Ultimately, his four conservative colleagues agreed. As Chief Justice John Roberts observed in his majority opinion, once a state decides to subsidize private education "it cannot disqualify some private schools solely because they are religious."

6

The Pursuit of Profit

David Brennan knew a thing or two about the free market. The Akron, Ohio, industrialist had made a fortune buying manufacturing companies, chopping them up and selling them off for parts to the highest bidder. What if those same market forces could be unleashed on the "government schools" that Brennan and his allies viewed with such disdain?

He found a more than receptive audience in Ohio's Republican Party. By the mid-1990s, Brennan had emerged as one of the state's most powerful and generous political operators—his lavish giving to GOP lawmakers helping to usher in Ohio's school choice movement and the lax legal landscape in which it thrived. When Governor George Voinovich wanted to create a private school voucher program, Brennan was the person he tapped. And Brennan, in turn, figured out how to tap the state treasury: the private schools he ran took in more state funding per pupil than 85 percent of Ohio's public schools.[1]

But the real profit, Brennan soon concluded, lay in schools that were publicly funded but privately managed. In 1997, the Ohio legislature allowed for the creation of new start-up charter schools in Lucas County and conversion charter schools across the state That same year, Brennan started White Hat Management—a for-profit school management company named for his trademark Texas-style accessory. At its height, White Hat was Ohio's largest charter operator, and the third-largest operator of charter schools in the country.

Brennan had indeed figured out how to subject public education to market forces and make schools profitable. Teachers and administrators at White Hat–run schools were paid a fraction of what they earned in "government schools," freeing up plenty of money to return to White Hat through building leases and management fees. And that money added up: ten former White Hat schools estimated they paid the company $90 million in management fees over three years—95 percent of the state and federal funds they had received.[2] Meanwhile, the political largesse that was channeled to influential lawmakers kept regulators from peering too closely into the company's business practices. But while Brennan proved remarkably adept at raking in taxpayer funds, White Hat's schools consistently ranked among the very worst in Ohio.

Two decades after Brennan launched his experiment in for-profit education, it sputtered to an ignominious end. By 2018, down to a single online school and ten "life skills centers" providing computer-based GED classes, White Hat announced that it was getting out of the school management business for good. "I don't do things that don't make money," Brennan declared in a 2002 interview. "I just don't think it's right."[3]

Yet the dream of mining profits from schools lives on. White Hat's remaining contracts were bought out by an assortment of

companies, including the latest large-scale player in the world of
for-profit education: ACCEL Schools.[4]

For-Profit 1.0

In 1971, the RAND Corporation issued a series of reports about a
new idea in public education—turning over part of school operations to a for-profit provider. In explaining the origins of the
concept, the RAND team concluded that "the performance contracting movement is the foster child of discontent with our educational system coupled with the governmental struggle to improve
procurement procedures."[5]

Pointing to new government contracting practices as a model,
these first-generation privatization proponents argued that schools
and districts should pay for services rather than provide them
directly. The Department of Defense didn't make its own bombs
or airplanes. Instead, it contracted the work out to companies like
Lockheed Martin. Schools, too, could contract with service providers to create curriculum or deliver classroom instruction.

In the 1970s, more than 150 districts negotiated such contracts.
But as they quickly discovered, the cost efficiencies promised by
these arrangements came at a price. In 1970, for instance, the
school district in Gilroy, California, contracted with Westinghouse Learning Corporation to run an elementary school. To
save money and boost efficiency, Westinghouse cut teachers at
the school and hired less expensive paraprofessional aides to help
run self-guided "instructional centers." Ultimately, results were
lackluster, at least as measured by student achievement. Shortly
after its Gilroy experiment, Westinghouse gave up performance
contracting.[6]

Around the same time in Texas, the Texarkana public schools

contracted with a for-profit provider to improve academic performance. As in Gilroy, student achievement did not appear to improve. Improving test scores, it turns out, is harder than it seems, as Dorsett Educational Systems recognized. In response, employees began providing students with advance copies of the standardized test and teaching them how to pass it. Needless to say, the cheating scandal tempered enthusiasm for performance contracting.[7]

Critics weren't the only ones beginning to doubt performance contracting in education. Once they recognized the limited profits, cumbersome contracts, and relatively small scale of school management work, companies lost interest as well. The brief experiment faded.

But despite these early wobbles, the private management of public education never entirely lost its allure. Outsourcing the management of schools and various education-related services was also seen as a way to break the grip of the education "monopoly." As Donald M. Levine, chair of the National Conference on Performance Contracting in Education, wrote in 1972: "Whatever its ultimate utility, performance contracting will have confirmed the fact that education need not remain the preserve of the certified professional, that there are alternative methods and alternative personnel who may be, in their own ways, as effective as the trained teacher. And it will have widened the horizons of school administrators by confronting them with organizations whose survival depends on educational efficiency."[8]

The Case for Profit

In the 1980s the UK's Margaret Thatcher thrilled conservatives on this side of the Atlantic with her take-no-prisoners approach to weakening labor unions and scaling back the welfare state. Ronald Reagan instructed his Office of Policy Development to consider how government services, including Amtrak and the U.S. Post Office, could be privatized. Though the President's Commission on Privatization ended up producing little in the way of concrete achievements, it did something equally important, according to Reason Foundation co-founder Robert Poole: it "made privatization ideas respectable."[9]

Soon, a new wave of for-profit companies began rising to the occasion, picking up where the performance contracting movement left off. This time, however, would-be privatizers did so on a much larger scale. In the early 1990s, Minnesota-based Education Alternatives Inc. (EAI) took over the management of nine schools in Baltimore, Maryland, and all thirty-two public schools in Hartford, Connecticut.

Still, the public remained skeptical. As a *Christian Science Monitor* reporter observed: "'Privatization,' one of the buzzwords of the 1990s, is seen as an answer to running everything from prisons to the space shuttle. But nowhere does the idea raise more sensitivities than when applied to public education."[10] Nor did details about lucrative contracts, like the $100 million EAI netted in Hartford alone, do much to win over communities where experiments in privatization were under way. "People are skeptical of our motives and inclinations," remarked EAI chairman John Golle.

Less than two decades had passed since the performance contracting bust, but by the 1990s the political ground had shifted dramatically. Conservatives had long pushed for privatization, but now they were joined by the Democratic Party's own champions of free markets and the private sector. Led by a rising political star named Bill Clinton, these self-styled "New Democrats" mapped

out a "Third Way" of governing that represented a stark departure from the party's New Deal heritage. In fact, it echoed Ronald
Reagan's maxim that the nine most terrifying words in the English
language are "I'm from the government and I'm here to help." The
New Democrats, organized through the Democratic Leadership
Council, also took aim at "big government," pressing the model
of public/private partnerships. As the Reason Foundation's Robert Poole observed: "There was more real privatization during the
Clinton Administration than the Reagan Administration."[11]

The New Democrats also began to push for infusing the spirit
of the free market into public education. In their influential 1993
book, *Reinventing Government: How the Entrepreneurial Spirit
Is Transforming the Public Sector*, David Osborne and Ted Gaebler
made the case for what they called "entrepreneurial schools," which
would compete among each other for customers. "Why would anyone prefer monopoly? Competition in road construction, in health
care, even in public transit, seems like nothing more than common
sense," they argued. "And forcing department of administration
bureaucrats to compete for a living—what a refreshing idea!"[12]
The logic of the market, they contended, would "banish bureaucracy," thereby rendering the heavy hand of government unnecessary. As an example, Osborne and Gaebler pointed to Minnesota,
where an ambitious experiment with charter schools was shifting
the education "customer" from the school district to the family.

The New Democrats took pains to distinguish themselves from
their market-loving counterparts on the right. As Osborne and
Gaebler wrote, "Privatization is one answer, not THE answer."[13]
Nevertheless, a new consensus had emerged around business practices in education. A new generation of entrepreneurs was ready to
take another crack at making a buck.

Making Education a Business

Media entrepreneur Chris Whittle had a plan. Where other for-profit education ventures had been stymied by regulatory handicaps, not to mention the challenge of trying to wring profit out of a system limited by tax revenues, Whittle was convinced he had figured out the answer: scale.

The original idea behind the Edison Project (today known as EdisonLearning), which Whittle started in 1992, was to create a vast network of a thousand private schools, funded through government vouchers. But after the election of Bill Clinton in 1992, vouchers fell off the policy menu. Privatization was the new tool of choice, pushed as a respectable option by Democrats and Republicans alike, and Whittle embraced the moment. Edison would run all aspects of the schools it managed, and it would do so at the largest possible scale—Whittle initially sought to raise billions for the venture.

It wasn't just Whittle's ambition that separated him from previous "edupreneurs." Whereas they had avoided referring to "privatization," Whittle's strategy was to remove the stigma from the word by changing the nature of the conversation. Rather than hiding his ideology, he wore it on his sleeve. As he declared in 1992: "The biggest contribution business can make to education is to make education a business."[14]

To manage Edison, Whittle recruited a high-profile team—including the former Yale University president Benno Schmidt and Reagan White House education official Chester Finn Jr. But it was Whittle's pick of John Chubb as chief educational officer that revealed the ideological nature of the enterprise. With co-author Terry Moe, Chubb had written perhaps the most influential conservative book in the history of education: *Politics, Markets, and America's Schools*. Arguing for a "thoroughgoing system of choice," the book made the case for sweeping away the nation's existing educational infrastructure.

By 2001, Edison had 114 schools in its portfolio, serving 74,000 students in twenty-three states.[15] But while Whittle seemed to have figured out the growth part of the company's equation, he soon confronted the same challenges that had befuddled other for-profit ventures. With revenues in public education "fixed" by public tax dollars, the only way to turn a profit was to cut costs; that meant getting rid of teachers and swelling class sizes.

But Edison never did manage to post a profit. Nor did the company's other metrics fare much better. Edison schools, like previous privatization efforts, were ultimately accountable for the test scores of their students, which forced limits on the kinds of programs they could offer and opened them up to additional criticism—that they were teaching only to a narrow set of exams. Weak educational performance in cities like Baltimore and Philadelphia only stoked resentment in communities where the public was already angry about losing control of local schools. Then, in 2002, after the Securities and Exchange Commission launched an investigation into Edison's accounting practices, the value of its stock dropped by 95 percent.

The country's biggest experiment in for-profit education was a bust. And yet in its ruins lay a key lesson for advocates of school privatization. Edison's business had depended upon the company's ability to ink lucrative contracts with school districts. Such an arrangement left the education "bureaucracy"—school boards, administrators, teacher groups, and parent organizations—with tremendous power to kill off for-profit ventures. If money-making schools were to succeed, the entire system needed to be upended, with individuals and families replacing school districts as the consumers of education. For an applicable model, profit-seekers only had to look to higher education.

For-Profit Higher Education

John Sperling was a disaffected academic in the early 1970s when he started the Institute for Professional Development. After his superiors at San Jose State, where he was a humanities professor, shot down his idea for a flexible degree program for working adults, Sperling left the university. He drew up a plan, cashed out his savings, and began offering evening and weekend classes. Two years later, Sperling moved to Arizona to open the for-profit university that would upend the higher education landscape: the University of Phoenix.

For-profit colleges were nothing new—they'd done a booming business in the mid-nineteenth century, offering training in the "useful arts." But the University of Phoenix was different. It granted diplomas just like traditional colleges and universities, but with a flexible format explicitly geared toward students who lacked the time, flexibility, or resources to attend school full-time. Sperling's choice of Arizona hadn't been coincidental: the state's few regulations meant virtually no limits on expansion. Within a decade, the University of Phoenix had six thousand tuition-paying students on the rolls.

Inspired by Sperling's success and emboldened by Reagan-era deregulation, other entrepreneurs launched their own for-profit ventures. By the late 1980s, for-profit education was growing at a clip of roughly 10 percent annually, and taking in millions in federal financial aid. Soon, those millions would become billions. Whether through federally backed student loans, Pell Grants, GI Bill benefits, or Department of Defense Tuition Assistance Funds, for-profit schools were chewing through a larger and larger share of public resources.

New schools seemed to pop up constantly. Some had quasi-public sounding names, like the University of Southernmost Florida or Missouri College. Others, like Briarcliffe College or Westwood College, nodded at the liberal arts, while outfits like High-Tech Institute and ITT Technical Institute borrowed titular stature from places like Caltech and MIT. Some, like Trump University, leaned on celebrity name recognition. All sought to convince students of their legitimacy, even as questions regarding low rates of completion, skyrocketing student debt, and outright fraud were getting harder to ignore.

Journalists and policy makers began to take notice, as did the federal government, which convened an investigative commission at the behest of Secretary of Education William Bennett, who eventually went on to start his own for-profit education company, K12 Inc., in 1999. But these red flags did nothing to dissuade investors, who were bullish on for-profit schools. In 1994, Sperling launched an initial public offering of the Apollo Education Group, the parent company of the University of Phoenix. As Trace Urdan, an equity analyst for Wells Fargo Securities, observed, "Apollo was a rocket ship of a stock."[16]

And that rocket-fueled expansion was built into the company's business model. To meet investor expectations, the school was growing at an astonishing 25 percent a year. By 2000, the University of Phoenix had enrolled more than one hundred thousand students. "Every quarter, the company must meet or beat analysts' expectations, or the stock tanks," Sperling observed in his memoir.[17]

Shifting Risk

As with K-12 education, critics saw in for-profit higher education the potential for fraud and abuse. Advocates, however, made a different kind of argument—one based on cost savings. Through a process of "creative destruction," they argued that for-profits would do a better job of keeping expenditures in check. "For-profits live and die based on their ability to maximize revenue while simultaneously containing costs," argued Richard Vedder of the Koch-supported Center for College Affordability and Productivity. Nonprofits, he contended, "are more likely to have an underworked and overpaid faculty, bureaucratic administrations, and rent-seeking employee groups that resist changes in the status quo."[18]

Market-oriented conservatives applauded the fact that for-profit schools, which generated 90 percent of their revenues from tuition and fees, moved the cost of higher education out of the public sector, with its dependence on state subsidies, and onto students and families. While public colleges and universities are far more dependent on tuition and philanthropy than K-12 schools are, they still receive significant state subsidies. For-profit schools, by contrast, generate roughly 90 percent of their revenues from tuition and fees. As historian of education A.J. Angulo observed in his book *Diploma Mills*, the privatization of higher education "served as a countervailing force to ever-expanding public institutions," which conservatives saw as "complacent, bloated, and of little contemporary relevance."[19]

Of course, most of the capital flowing to for-profit schools has come from the U.S. Treasury—to the tune of tens of billions every year in the form of student aid. In fact, so dependent are for-profits on these funds that when ITT Technical Institute was banned in 2016 from enrolling new students receiving federal aid, the company promptly closed all 140 of its campuses. And for-profit schools, on average, charge more than nonprofit schools, whether public or private. If costs are kept in check, the net savings are rarely passed on to students.

Indeed, few of the arguments made in favor of for-profit higher education hold up to scrutiny. Yet the schools continue to grow. Today, hundreds of for-profit colleges and universities enroll millions of students. By one estimate, roughly 10 percent of all students in higher education attend for-profit schools. And they remain mostly profitable. The largest chains—those that are publicly traded—generate billions in pre-tax profits each year.

In 2010, for-profit colleges and universities employed 35,000 recruiters and spent $4.2 billion on marketing and recruiting— 22.7 percent of all revenue. According to a 2012 U.S. Senate report, "Investors' demand for revenue growth is satisfied by enrolling a steady stream of new student enrollees," and "hitting an enrollment quota" is often the "highest priority."[20] Relying on internal documents and interviews with former employees of for-profit schools, the report concluded that "companies used tactics that misled prospective students with regard to the cost of the program, the availability and obligations of Federal aid, the time to complete the program, the completion rates of other students, the job placement rate of other students, the transferability of the credit, or the reputation and accreditation of the school."[21]

Supporters of the for-profit sector have argued that dissatisfied students are free to leave. But when they do, they take their debt with them. And that debt can't be discharged, even in the event of bankruptcy. For-profit higher education is risky, argues sociologist Tressie McMillan Cottom, and it is a risk that is heavily borne by women of color, low-income students, veterans, and workers whose tenuous grasp on economic security requires constant re-credentialing.[22]

Indeed, the truly transformational aspect of for-profit higher education can be found in precisely this shifting of the cost of education—and its accompanying financial risk—onto individual students. Embattled as the for-profit sector may be, it serves as a beacon for the market ideologues who dream of engineering a similar shift in K-12 education.

K-12: Meet Big Pharma

If the business community was going to pry open the K-12 sector to for-profit ventures, it would need a new playbook. It was one thing for colleges and universities to operate on a for-profit basis—they weren't hamstrung by local school boards, district bureaucracy, or watchdog parent groups. But years of failure raised serious questions about whether it was possible to wring a profit from elementary and secondary schools.

Charter schools, however, offered a new opportunity for profit seekers in K-12 education. Specifically, the private governance model of charter schools might allow entrepreneurs to dodge district management and public oversight. Perhaps more importantly, school choice would allow charter operators to sell directly to parents, rather than to bureaucrats or regulators.

In selling directly to consumers, leaders of for-profit schools reinvented a model successfully employed by pharmaceutical companies. Advertising directly to parents, entrepreneurs could promise the sky and, conveniently, leave out details like the for-profit status of their schools or the performance of their students. To keep this window of opportunity from closing on them, however, they would need to take another page out of the big pharma playbook: lobbying legislators, and spending heavily on campaign donations, to beat back any attempts at regulation.

For-profit charter schools first took off in Betsy DeVos's home state of Michigan. While Minnesota's charter school law had allowed for only two forms of schools—teacher-led cooperatives and nonprofit charters authorized by a school district—Michigan's 1993 law contained no such stipulation. Two years after the law passed, billionaire and conservative powerbroker J.C. Huizenga opened his first for-profit school. His chain, National Heritage Academies—which places an emphasis on morality and character building modeled on Christian values—has since expanded to nearly a hundred schools in nine states. Shortly after NHA was up and running, the Leona Group also set up shop in Michigan, then quickly expanded to market-friendly Arizona. The organization subsequently opened schools in Ohio, Indiana, and Florida, and took over the management of entire school districts in Michigan. Today, Leona operates more than sixty schools.

As these for-profit networks have grown, so has their political sway. Huizenga, for example, is one of the top donors to Michigan Republicans, topped only by another influential Michigan family: the DeVoses. And by showering lawmakers with donations, the for-profit lobby has emerged as a forceful curb against any oversight that might slow the growth of for-profit schools or the earnings of their management companies. The result is that Michigan has the most for-profit charter schools in the United States, even as the sector remains largely unregulated. In the words of Gary Miron, a professor in the College of Education and Human Development at Western Michigan University and an expert on Michigan's charter school sector: "No state comes near us when it comes to privatization."[23]

While Betsy DeVos's home state may be the most welcoming to for-profit schools, the path to political influence is well-worn across the United States. Ron Packard, the founder and former CEO of K12 Inc.—the nation's largest for-profit chain—once referred to lobbying as a "core competency" of the company he founded.[24] In Ohio, the late David Brennan of White Hat Management is reported to have camped out near the room where Education Committee meetings were held, handing state legislators envelopes of cash as they exited.[25] And in Florida, the largest for-profit charter network in the state, Academica, is not only a major donor to conservative PACs and candidates, but also includes influential lawmakers among the ranks of its employees.[26] In fact, Florida's charter school law, with its lax regulation and oversight, was written with the aid of the founder of yet another for-profit charter network: Charter Schools USA. Started in 1997 by Jonathan Hage, an advisor to former governor Jeb Bush, the network now runs roughly fifty schools in Florida. Hage's company and its real estate arm give lavishly to pro-charter legislators, who do their part to expand funding to the charter sector and fend off regulatory efforts.[27]

"Regulatory capture" is the term used to describe what happens when the government agencies tasked with monitoring and regulating an industry abandon that responsibility, instead working to advance the interests of particular groups. In states rife with charter school fraud, the same elected officials who are supposed to protect taxpayers are awash in contributions from charter operators profiting at public expense. In Arizona, for example, a yearlong investigation by the *Arizona Republic* exposed that charter schools "have turned into cash cows through multi-million-dollar business deals between charter schools and their founders."[28] One of the most egregious examples cited by the journalists was Republican lawmaker and charter school founder Eddie Farnsworth, who leveraged the state's lax charter laws to become a millionaire. After the *Republic* series wrapped up, Farnsworth earned millions more by selling his for-profit charter school chain to a nonprofit entity created specifically to buy it.[29]

And yet the political influence of the state's charter sector has made regulating it virtually impossible. As the *Republic*'s E.J. Montini summed up the situation: "Lawmakers protect and even encourage a lack of transparency and accountability within the charter school system."[30] Recent legislation aimed at tightening oversight of Arizona's five hundred charters, including requiring more disclosure of financial information, notably exempted the state's largest—and most politically powerful—charter operators.[31]

Where watchdogs see scandal, market crusaders see a success story. Arizona recently claimed the number one spot in the *Report Card on American Education*—the state-by-state ranking compiled by corporate legislative powerhouse ALEC. Similarly, the Center for Education Reform (CER), a school choice advocacy group, gave Arizona an "A" rating in its 2018 national rankings, citing the lack of regulation for charter schools. "When educators have the ability to be flexible and tailor work to students, and schools don't have to pay all their time and money on non-education requirements, they tend to be more effective," CER's Jeanne Allen told the *Arizona Republic*.[32]

Perhaps no state offers a more vivid picture of regulatory capture than Ohio, where for-profit charter operators are among the largest contributors to the Republican Party. In 2018, the cozy relationship between the charter sector and the officials charged with oversight emerged in sharp relief with the implosion of the largest for-profit charter management company in the state. Founded in 2000 by GOP donor William Lager, the Electronic Classroom of Tomorrow

(ECOT) and Lager's other companies received more than $1 billion in taxpayer funds; meanwhile, the Republicans Lager showered with campaign contributions looked the other way. When the corruption became too blatant to deny, state officials finally cracked down on ECOT's fraudulent practice of inflating student attendance numbers to pad its bottom line, ordering the school to begin paying back state funds. Soon after, ECOT collapsed, leaving twelve thousand students without a school. Today "ECOT" and "scandal" are synonymous in Ohio, yet for years the school was touted by Republicans as a free-market education success story.

Blurred Lines

In September of 2016, Donald Trump traveled to Cleveland to deliver his first education speech as a candidate. The backdrop for Trump's address, which was mostly devoted to Hillary Clinton's emails, was Cleveland Arts and Social Sciences Academy (CASSA), which Trump praised for "doing a great job with education." But as education analysts were quick to point out, the school was failing by the measures of Ohio's school accountability system.[33] Trump, of course, may simply have been taken in by the school's website, which described CASSA as "award winning." Unlike pharmaceutical companies, whose claims are subject to verification by the Food and Drug Administration, education providers are not constrained in the claims they can make. As in Lake Wobegon, every school in the for-profit sector is "above average."

In selling their product to parents, for-profit charters are also free to downplay their tax status. Prospective "customers" of CASSA, for instance, must scour its website to learn that the school is part of ACCEL Schools, a new for-profit charter management organization created by K12 Inc. founder Ron Packard. But unless they are ready to dive into ACCEL's tax records, they won't learn much. The words "for profit" don't appear on the school's website or on the ACCEL Schools site.

Does the tax status of a charter school matter? Advocates of for-profit schools insist that it doesn't. As Charter Schools USA founder Jonathan Hage put it: parents never ask, "What's the tax status or the proprietary nature of the curriculum or the company?"[34] The for-profit network, which advertises its services extensively, sparing no expense, makes no mention of the company's tax status in its promotional materials.

Making matters more complicated is the legal gray area, often by design, that distinguishes nonprofit and for-profit schools. ECOT, the Ohio virtual school that imploded in 2018, was a nonprofit; but founder William Lager's management company, which ran the schools, was a for-profit entity. Most states require charter schools to operate on a nonprofit basis, but they often do little to impede the self-dealing that occurs through facilities leasing and contracting for services. A January 2019 report from the Ohio auditor general concluded that schools run by three "management companies" were spending more than twice as much on facilities as other charter schools were. One Cleveland charter school, for instance, was paying about $516,000 above market rate to its for-profit landlord Imagine Schools.[35]

While high-profile fraud cases like ECOT have done much to tarnish the for-profit brand, there's plenty of fiscal wrongdoing among nonprofit charter schools. Many of the cases that investigative journalists in Arizona have documented, for example, involve financial shenanigans, including sky-high salaries and "related party transactions" among nonprofit operators. The Arizona-based American Leadership Academy, whose twelve charter schools emphasize patriotism in their curriculum, is a registered nonprofit with the IRS. But the school's founder, Glenn Way, has raked in tens of millions of dollars by developing land and constructing buildings, which his schools then purchase; once constructed, the schools pay another of Way's firms to manage them.[36] Such practices are perfectly legal in Arizona's largely unregulated charter school sector. An entity need not be "for profit" to make a buck.

As proponents are quick to point out, tax status is not necessarily an accurate predictor of school performance. While for-profit virtual schools, the subject of our next chapter, are notoriously awful, networks like Michigan's for-profit National Heritage Academies include some of the state's top-performing schools as measured by test scores. And nationally, for-profit charter schools perform only slightly worse than their nonprofit counterparts.[37] Thus, defenders of for-profit schools have made the case that if we are concerned only with results, we should ignore the tax status of schools.

"It shouldn't matter where a student learns as long as they are actually learning," Betsy DeVos proclaimed in a speech to the American Federation for Children, the school choice lobby group that she founded. DeVos, of course, is a major proponent of for-profit schools, but the sentiment of her statement also has been echoed countless times by self-styled "progressive" advocates for market-based education reform. While for-profit schools may have fallen out of favor among Democratic charter school enthusiasts in the era of Trump and DeVos, decades of hearing Democrats argue that "privatization is one answer" has muddled the case against schools that are run for money. The goal, dating back to the era of Bill Clinton and the rise of the "New Democrats," has been to remake public education along free-market lines. So what precisely *is* the case against profit, the most free-market principle of all?

Profit and Loss

In research that would win him a Nobel Prize in Economics in 2016, Oliver Hart laid out the high cost of privatizing essential services. Privatization increases pressure to cut labor costs—worker pay, as well as funding for training—which, as he put it, "can lead to a substantial deterioration of quality."[38] Although Hart's research was focused specifically on private prisons, it has implications for any publicly funded good, including public education, because in both cases a similar dynamic is at play: when revenues are fixed, operators are incentivized to slash costs. And because the schools' funding is distributed on a per-pupil basis, profit must come from spending less, either on students or on teachers.

The dream of running K-12 schools for profit is now entering its fifth decade, and by at least one measure the experiment appears to have been a success: roughly one in five charter school students attends a school that is operated on a for-profit basis. Yet the same challenge that plagued the first generation of performance contractors in the 1970s persists today: it simply isn't that easy to make money by running schools. As funding for public education emerges as a potent political issue, a model based on shifting money from the classroom into private pockets appears more vulnerable than ever. Meanwhile, the steady drip of investigative reports into unsavory or even fraudulent practices has meant increased regulation and calls for outright bans on for-profit schools.

Some of the early pioneers in for-profit schools, like Chris Whittle, have given up hope of turning a profit in public education. After the Edison Project flamed out, Whittle returned to his original vision: a network of for-profit private schools. While Edison had stressed ruthless cost-cutting in cities like Baltimore and Philadelphia, Whittle's latest venture, Avenues: The World School, promised luxury, with tuition running upwards of $50,000 a year. Avenues, which has attracted investors to the tune of $700 million, is targeted at the global elite, with campuses slated to open in major cities around the world.

But for plenty of other "edupreneurs," the quest to make a profit in public education looks more promising than ever. In our next chapter we explore the rise of education technology, including virtual schools, and the age-old pursuit of a "teaching machine" that can drastically lower the cost of labor in public education by minimizing the role of teachers—or even rendering them unnecessary. Thanks to education technology, and the vast sums of capital behind it, the dream of replacing public education with an amalgam of consumable products and services is now within reach.

7

Virtual Learning

"The U.S. education system currently operates as an 8-track tape in an iPod world," Jeb Bush proclaimed in 2011. But there was one state that Bush, then serving as chairman of the Foundation for Excellence in Education and co-chair of Digital Learning Now! singled out for praise: Ohio. Thanks to the Buckeye State's bold political leadership, more students would have "the opportunity to achieve their God-given potential." As Bush concluded: "Ohio is on a path to transform education for the 21st century and give more students access to a customized education through digital learning."[1]

It would be seven more years before the Electronic Classroom of Tomorrow, or ECOT—Ohio's virtual school behemoth—would implode, leaving its twelve thousand students scrambling to find a new school. But even as Bush, who gave the commencement address at ECOT in 2010, fawned over the state's digital future, signs of real problems in the virtual sector were mounting. ECOT's test scores were one red flag—only 14 of Ohio's 609 school districts performed worse. Also, education officials had been sounding a steady stream of alarms about the school's enrollment and accounting practices since its opening in 2006.[2]

But where critics and regulators saw warning signs, Bush and other online education evangelists saw endless possibilities. Virtual schools like ECOT were a mechanism for achieving what had long been only a dream for conservatives: to privatize education, cut costs, undermine the power of organized labor, and promote a competitive market free from the grip of bureaucrats. And while ECOT was tanking on the metrics that were supposed to matter, the school and its related businesses were enriching founder William Lager. Indeed, Lager had managed to solve the puzzle that had for so long confounded entrepreneurs: how to make education profitable.

Today, virtual schools account for less than 1 percent of total elementary and high school enrollment. Yet the sector is growing rapidly, and has been cheered on by the likes of Harvard Business School guru Clayton Christensen. Approximately 300,000 students are enrolled full-time in virtual schools, with an additional 130,000 enrolled in so-called blended learning programs that rely at least in part on computer-based instruction. More significantly, the sector has largely shifted out of the hands of state and school district officials and into the private sector.[3] Today, more than half of students who are receiving a virtual education are enrolled in for-profit schools. Staying a step ahead of regulators, virtual schools have realized many of the dismantlers' greatest ambitions.

From Correspondence Schools to Distance Learning

Historically, education has been a place-based enterprise. To run a school, communities need a sufficiently large pool of students and a sufficiently qualified pool of local teachers. Yet for much of the nineteenth and early twentieth century, many communities struggled with one or both of these requirements. The Northwest Ordinance, for instance, which expanded U.S. territory to include Ohio, Indiana, Michigan, Illinois, and Wisconsin, required settlers to support education by setting aside a section of each township for a public school. As historian Carl Kaestle observes, "not all communities had . . . available schoolteachers, or sufficient population to support a school."[4] One solution was learning via correspondence. By the late nineteenth century, the U.S. Post Office was handling nearly 8 billion pieces of mail a year, distributing them across 140,000 miles of rail lines.[5] The emergence of this vast new communications network connected small and isolated communities to the rest of the country.

Social reformers saw distance education programs as an opportunity to promote the advancement of rural people, immigrants, and women. The Society to Encourage Studies at Home, founded in Boston in 1873 by Anna Eliot Ticknor and local philanthropists, offered roughly two dozen correspondence courses to New England wives and mothers. Organized like a college, the society was divided into "departments," including French, English, science, history, and art. Students were encouraged to select the equivalent of a major, and then read and review the selected materials that arrived by mail.[6]

For their part, entrepreneurs saw a business opportunity in distance education, and that drove expansion at far faster rates than the spirit of benevolence had. By the turn of the twentieth century, the International Correspondence School in Scranton, Pennsylvania—the largest of the learn-by-mail companies—was enrolling one hundred thousand new students a year.[7] The school's courses, in areas like sales management and building superintendence, were heavily marketed to potential students as a way to get ahead professionally. A mail-based program marketed to coal miners, for example, promised the engineering knowledge needed for promotions. A 1905 advertisement asked miners, "On which side of the desk are you?" An accompanying pamphlet boasted of "1,001 Success Stories."[8]

Elementary and high schools also adopted correspondence courses, but mostly as a means of expanding the variety of courses and depth of the curriculum. Districts that lacked the personnel to provide courses in subjects like foreign languages could access instruction from afar, through the mail or over the airwaves. In the 1920s, the Federal Communications Commission granted radio broadcast licenses to colleges and universities. And by the early 1930s, Wisconsin was offering instruction over the radio on music and other subjects. Television soon displaced radio, and by the early 1950s the FCC had reserved one-quarter of the television broadcast spectrum for educational purposes. Such "extension" work by colleges and universities was generally perceived as a public service rather than as a money-maker.

Of course, early communication technologies had some major shortcomings. Rail transportation may have revolutionized mail delivery, but postal intervals made the exchange of materials and feedback a lengthy and cumbersome process. And while the expectation that students would work on their own gave the programs flexibility, students were largely unsupervised. Distance also meant the absence of face-to-face contact, severely limiting relationships between students and teachers. Perhaps not surprisingly, the drop-out rates were massive.

Technology was beginning to address some of these deficiencies, particularly the time delay of correspondence by mail. By the late twentieth century, advances in satellite communication had even begun to allow for two-way video—bringing teachers into the same room with faraway students. In 1989, programs in Maine and Oregon began using two-way video to reach schools in the sparsely populated parts of their states. And soon, schools and districts began to experiment with the internet as a way of connecting teachers with students in remote areas.

You've Got Mail

In 1991, America Online began offering internet services. By then, the internet had already been around for roughly two decades, largely as the preserve of government, the military, and research universities. It wasn't until the early 1990s that the internet was common enough, and fast enough, to be a tool for distance education.

The aim, in early online programs, was to expand student access to courses their schools might otherwise not be able to offer. Virtual classes could supplement the school curriculum, making it possible to offer Advanced Placement courses and specialized electives in far-flung parts of states like Utah and Hawaii. One early report, from 2001, observed that virtual schools were "expanding curricular options and extended teaching resources" for existing schools.[9] And, in many cases, a school could have students take one virtual course each semester without losing any of its per-pupil funding.

Much like the correspondence schools of the previous century, the early virtual schools saw their role as complementing the existing system rather than competing with it. "We don't replace the local school," observed a leader of the Illinois Virtual High School. "Rather, we partner with them to supplement the curriculum at the local school."[10] With seed money from the federal government, states began to build systems that would bring distance education into the twenty-first century. In 1994, Utah created the Electronic High School. Two years later the Hawaii E-School program launched, offering online instruction to any student in the state.

In 1997, Florida authorized the first statewide, internet-based public high school. The initial mission of the school was fairly similar to that of other virtual education experiments: "to fill gaps and expand curriculum options rather than replace local school offerings."[11] Small schools and schools in isolated parts of the state were especially interested in the Florida Virtual School (FLVS) as a means of increasing curricular rigor for students, and especially in expanding their Advanced Placement offerings.

Before long, however, FLVS's mission began to change. In 2000, the state legislature made the school its own legal entity, freed from the oversight of Florida's Department of Education. To some, this may have seemed like an insignificant step. But prominent backers like then-governor Jeb Bush saw the new school not just as a supplement to brick-and-mortar schools, but as a potential competitor to them. Moreover, because virtual schools operated at a lower cost than traditional schools, any direct competition would invariably bring down the cost of public education. By the 2008–2009 school year, FLVS was generating $4 million in annual revenue from sales of its services outside the state.[12] The next year, Bush launched Digital Learning Now!—a project, backed by major tech companies, designed to expand online learning throughout the country.

The Cost-Cutting Crusade 2.0

Virtual schools had an obvious advantage over their brick-and-mortar counterparts: they were significantly less expensive to run. During the 2001–2002 school year, virtual schools operated at an approximate cost of $300 per course per semester—roughly $3,000 a year to educate each student.[13] By contrast, the average per-pupil expenditure in brick-and-mortar schools that year was $8,259—a figure drawn from the range of per-pupil expenditures between Utah on the low end ($5,294) and Washington, DC ($14,557), on the high end.[14]

By eliminating the in-person expenses of education, virtual schools achieved the cost-cutting goal that conservatives had long pursued. The case that advocates made was that students would benefit from exposure to new technology, but states were equally motivated to use virtual education to cut costs. Michigan, for instance, enacted a controversial law in 2006 requiring students to take at least one online course in order to graduate, causing enrollments in the Michigan Virtual School to more than double over the next five years.[15] Other states, including Florida, Arkansas, Virginia, and Alabama, adopted similar laws.

As discussed in chapter 3, schools are stubbornly resistant to labor-saving devices. A string quartet might benefit from the aid of a digital tuning device, but it still requires four players to perform; similarly, education has been largely unable to displace teachers with technology. Additionally, schools resist economies of scale. Paper and pencils may be less expensive in bulk, but all other costs in education rise in line with school size. More students means more teachers, more textbooks, more heating fuel, and more school lunches.

Consider, by contrast, a computer application. The cost of initial software development is the same, whether the final product is purchased by 10 people or 10 million. But the initial cost of development becomes negligible if it is used by enough people. Therefore, virtual schools in the early 2000s held the potential to make schools less like string quartets and more like software companies, particularly if the technology could be used to raise class sizes. As the author of one report concluded: "There is the potential for significant cost efficiencies."[16]

Teacher and administrator salaries account for roughly 80 percent of costs in education. Consequently, conservatives seeking to reduce costs had long been pushing for larger class sizes, only to see classes grow smaller year after year. In the late nineteenth and early twentieth century, class size hovered near forty. By the mid-twentieth century, however, the pupil-teacher ratio had dropped to roughly 25-to-1. Over the next several decades, class sizes crept further downward, as mandatory reductions were enacted by voters from California to Florida.

In places like Arizona, however, conservatives had succeeded in reversing historical trends. Even as class sizes were shrinking elsewhere, they ballooned in Arizona—the legacy of the state's low per-pupil spending. Parents may have lamented overcrowding and rising teacher-to-student ratios, but anti-tax crusaders saw the cost-saving impact. As Justin Olson of the Arizona Tax Research Association observed: "Per unit, if you want to look at it from a purely business perspective, we are efficient."[17]

The most audacious advocates of larger class sizes argued that such a move would actually *improve* outcomes. By firing the lowest performers, schools could retain their best teachers, who would be well suited to handle larger classes.[18] The value-added movement, which sought to measure teacher effectiveness through student standardized test scores, was in no small part driven by this ethos. Seeking to use student test scores as a means of gauging teacher effectiveness, advocates of the method believed that it would trim the fat from teaching staffs and realize cost savings in the process.

That said, if parents were resistant to larger class sizes, machines could simply compensate for the curtailed workforce, instructing students for part of the day. As the Hoover Institution's Terry Moe put it, "We have ways for computers to do a fantastic job of teaching kids. . . . What that means is that we can use a lot fewer teachers to educate kids."[19] Students might spend most of the day in face-to-face instruction, in typical classrooms, but also spend two hours completing virtual learning modules, thereby allowing schools to trim their teaching staffs by a third.

Proponents of virtual schools also maintained that increasing competition would bring down costs. When brick-and-mortar schools were the only option, competition had been difficult to foster because of the constraints of geography. Distance from home was consistently among the top factors behind parental choice of schools—particularly among families without cars. And the start-up cost for a physical school was a massive barrier for those seeking to enter the market. But if geographic distance was no longer an issue, providers might be able to compete with each other in earnest. In doing so, they would not only realize the conservative aim of a competitive market but also drive down prices. As a 2017 report on virtual schools observed, "The promise of lower costs—primarily for instructional personnel and facilities—makes virtual schools financially appealing to both policymakers and for-profit providers."[20]

The Profitability Formula

If virtual schools had the capacity to cut costs, they also had the potential to realize profits. Not surprisingly, they drew investors like "junk bond king" Michael Milken, who made a $10 million investment in K12 Inc.—the for-profit virtual schooling company co-founded in 2000 by the secretary of education under Ronald Reagan, William Bennett.[21]

Virtual schools were less expensive than brick-and-mortar schools because they did not have facilities costs, and because their teachers were paid considerably less than their public school counterparts. In some programs—those offering students "credit recovery," for instance—instruction did not need to be delivered by a licensed teacher, which could further lower costs.

But the real key to profitability was in larger class sizes. Parents, of course, had long fussed about that issue. Yet virtual schools had a distinct advantage over their place-based counterparts: no one could see behind the screen. By leveraging technology, virtual schools could expand the number of students that each teacher "taught," with no limit to the number of students tuning in to a prerecorded lecture. As one 2018 study determined, teachers in virtual schools are responsible for three times as many students as their peers in brick-and-mortar schools—45 compared to 16.[22] And as a 2015 report by Stanford University researchers found, the average virtual high school class size was 71; the largest was 180.[23]

In addition to larger class sizes, algorithms could be used to render most teachers unnecessary. "Personalized" assignments, determined by student performance on computer-rated multiple choice assessments, could be endlessly deployed without the need for human intervention. Of course, many students would still need to be supervised. Yet, in cases where this task could not be offloaded onto parents, virtual schools could establish "learning centers" staffed by lower-paid paraprofessionals. Thus, while virtual schools might not be able to eliminate *all* teachers, they could certainly get by with far fewer of them, and even those jobs could be redefined. A Michigan law, for example, requires "mentors" at virtual schools to touch base with students just once a week by email.[24]

Initially, virtual schools attracted licensed teachers who were interested in working from home or earning additional income. Over the years, however, class sizes expanded while pay remained unchanged. According to a 2011 investigation by the *New York*

Times, many teachers at virtual schools run by K12 Inc. "said the job had become less desirable as the company increased enrollment, particularly because pay at many K12 schools starts in the low 30s."[25] Other teachers reported being asked to take on additional students at a rate of $1 per student per day, and also complained of unwieldy class sizes.

While huge class sizes and poorly paid teachers made virtual schools far less expensive to operate than their place-based counterparts, states often paid operators as though they were running brick-and-mortar schools. When Michigan Connections Academy and Michigan Virtual Charter Academy opened in 2010–2011, both were eligible for the state's standard per-pupil funding formula. That netted each a minimum of $7,162 per student, despite significantly lower costs for delivering instruction. In the state's 2016 education budget, Governor Rick Snyder proposed scaling back per-pupil funding for virtual schools—to 80 percent of what brick-and-mortars receive. The legislature, however, which had been strongly lobbied by for-profit providers, rejected the governor's proposal. The same has been true in other states. As Virginia state senator George Barker remarked in 2011, "It's a really screwed up system. Here's something that is clearly cheaper. You have a larger number of kids per teacher. There's very little overhead. And yet, we're paying more."[26]

The extensive lobbying operations of the virtual sector's biggest players have swamped efforts to subject the schools to additional oversight, or to scale back their funding. According to the National Institute on Money in State Politics, the two largest virtual school management companies, K12 Inc. and Connections Education, have spent more than $14.5 million on lobbying since 2000. K12 Inc. has employed hundreds of lobbyists, working chiefly at the state level to ensure that virtual schools escape unfriendly regulation.

The combination of profitability and lobbying has proven to be a combustible mix in states with lax virtual school oversight. Nationwide, virtual schools have captured less than 1 percent of public school students. But in states like California, Ohio, and Pennsylvania, virtual schooling is an industry with annual revenues in the hundreds of millions of dollars.[27] In Pennsylvania, virtual schools have exploded in number even while posting dismal results and being wracked by scandal. Fewer than half of the students who attend one of the state's fourteen cyber charters graduate, and none of the schools receives a passing grade under the state's accountability system.[28] The founder of the Pennsylvania Cyber Charter School, Nick Trombetta, was sentenced to prison in 2018 for embezzling more than $8 million from the school to purchase luxury goods and a private plane.[29] Meanwhile, the profits that are so enriching the cyber industry flow disproportionately from Pennsylvania's poorest school districts. One recent study found that communities that struggle economically are far more likely to send students to cyber charters than affluent communities.[30]

But the red flags and calls for tighter regulations, even by charter school advocates, haven't slowed the political juggernaut behind virtual schools. Their expansion has long been at the center of the education agenda of the American Legislative Exchange Council (ALEC) and backed by deep-pocketed donors including the DeVoses and the Koch network. "Virtual schooling and digital learning, in general, fit into our broader vision of where we would really like to see the education system go," ALEC's director of the Education and Workforce Development Task Force, Inez Stepman, said in an interview. "Technology is just a piece of a much more broad effort to individualize the education system and create more pathways for students and their unique needs."[31]

Over the past decade, ALEC's "model" virtual schooling law, known as the Virtual Public Schools Act (2005), which was created in partnership with for-profit K12 Inc., has popped up in state after state. When Tennessee passed a law authorizing virtual schools in 2011, it looked like a cut-and-paste of ALEC's model legislation.

Virtually Union Free

Replacing teachers with technology is also key to another long-standing conservative goal: weakening labor unions. Teachers in virtual charters do not belong to unions, which means that they lack the ability to negotiate with their employers as a group over pay, benefits, and working conditions. And because they have little or no face-to-face contact with their fellow teachers, their work-places are likely to remain union free. While union organizing among charter school teachers has picked up in recent years, the virtual school sector remains almost entirely non-union.

As opponents of teachers' unions have recognized, virtual teachers lack the power of unionized teachers. In their paean to virtual schools, John Chubb and Terry Moe write: "Teachers will be less geographically concentrated in districts, considerably more dispersed, and much more difficult for unions to organize." But, as the authors also point out, the impact extends beyond virtual teachers, because the presence of virtual schools will make it more difficult for union members to exert political influence: "The teaching profession will become much more diversified and less conducive to sameness and solidarity. There will be many new schools and a dramatic increase in choice and competition. All these developments, operating together in mutually reinforcing ways, will work to sap the organizational strength of the teachers unions, [and] undermine their political power."[32]

The teacher strikes in 2018–19 vividly demonstrated the power of withholding labor. In four of the five states where teachers walked off the job in 2018, including Arizona and West Virginia, it is illegal for teachers to strike. Yet as these teachers well understood, replacing thousands of them is next to impossible in the best of times, let alone during times of acute teacher shortages.

Virtual schools, however, have two advantages that their brick-and-mortar counterparts do not. The first is that virtual students who spend their days at home are supervised by a committed and unpaid labor force: parents. The second is that virtual schools can import talent from anywhere in the United States. And once teachers are no longer required to be licensed to work at virtual schools, far cheaper talent from around the world can be imported. To that end, K12 Inc. has already experimented with outsourcing parts of its teachers' jobs, including having student essays graded in India.

Results

When Betsy DeVos was pressed by Democratic lawmakers to defend her support of virtual schools as part of her confirmation process, she was quick to sing their praises. "High quality virtual charter schools provide valuable options to families, particularly those who live in rural areas where brick-and-mortar schools might not have the capacity to provide the range of courses or other educational experiences for students," wrote DeVos, pointing to virtual academies in Ohio, Nevada, and Oklahoma. As she claimed, such schools boasted graduation rates approaching 100 percent. An education researcher, however, quickly checked her claims by comparing DeVos's figures with data from the schools' state education departments. The schools' performance, in reality, was abysmal.[33]

According to a 2015 study by Stanford University and two other research partners, online charter schools were significantly weaker academically than their brick-and-mortar counterparts. Examining two hundred online schools and their students, who altogether total two hundred thousand, the researchers found that online students had significantly less contact with teachers, struggled with engagement, and performed far worse academically than students attending traditional schools. Just how bad are the schools? The researchers estimated that attending an online charter "would equate to a student losing 72 days of learning in reading and 180 days of learning in math, based on a 180-day school year."[34] To underscore that finding: it would be like students had never been taught math at all.

Not all online schools are equally weak. But according to a 2018 report by the National Education Policy Center, the worst performing virtual schools were those with the largest enrollments and the largest student-to-teacher ratios—the very ingredients that make these schools so profitable.[35]

In state after state, virtual schools rank at the very bottom of school performance indicators. Such measures, based chiefly on student standardized test scores, are obviously limited. Yet the results are stunning. Michigan Virtual Charter Academy, which is operated by K12 Inc., recently scored in the third percentile in academic performance—meaning 97 percent of schools in the state performed better. A recent study found that Indiana students who transferred to virtual schools fell further behind, findings that researchers attributed to students not having a physical classroom.[36] At Ohio's defunct ECOT, which became the poster school for virtual dropout factories, federal data show that more students dropped out or failed to complete high school than at any other school in the United States.[37] Such results are particularly striking when paired with insights into the operations of these corporate entities. A *New York Times* inquiry into K12 Inc., for instance, portrayed "a company that tries to squeeze profits from public school dollars by raising enrollment, increasing teacher workload and lowering standards"—a description that could be applied to any number of virtual schools.[38]

For all of the damaging headlines, the profit potential of these schools remains enormous. Between its founding in 2000 and its collapse in 2018, ECOT took in more than $1 billion in state funding, and an additional $130 million in federal money, much of which enriched founder William Lager and the affiliated companies he set up to sell products and services to the school.[39] A damning state audit into officials at two Indiana virtual schools found that they had been breathtakingly successful at defrauding taxpayers by fudging enrollment figures, then funneling the proceeds through a dizzying array of related companies. The auditors concluded that the officials "focused on maximizing profits and revenues by exploiting perceived vulnerabilities" at every level of state and local governance.[40] K12 Inc., the subject of intense media scrutiny in recent years, had more than a billion dollars in revenue in 2019.[41]

The good news for investors: the untapped market for virtual school students is far larger. Nearly a decade has passed since Rupert Murdoch announced News Corp's move into online education, describing K-12 education as "a $500 billion sector in the U.S. alone that is waiting desperately to be transformed by big breakthroughs."[42] While the big breakthroughs have never arrived, the rush of investors certainly has. Today, the education technology marketplace is exploding, growing not just in the number of online schools but in the vast array of products and services flooding into public schools.

Seeing potential for enormous profit, companies have raced to build their market share, raising concerns about the concentration of power in private hands. Just as Facebook dominates social media and Google dominates internet search, so do companies like K12 Inc. seek to dominate the online education industry, running both virtual schools and providing online curriculum and programs to brick-and-mortar schools. Currently, K12 Inc. schools account for nearly one-third of all virtual school enrollments. Connections Academy, the second largest, accounts for nearly 20 percent. EdisonLearning—a reincarnation of Chris Whittle's Edison Project—has also recently entered the virtual schooling market.

Crackdown

When ECOT, the Ohio virtual school giant, suddenly closed down in 2018, it sent shockwaves through the state. Lax oversight of Ohio's virtual school industry even became a potent campaign issue as candidates in the 2018 midterms sought to pin blame for the scandal on their opponents. While state regulators sought to "claw back" some of the profits that ECOT's founder had pocketed, media outlets began digging into the politically connected industry of virtual schooling.

In light of such abuses, calls for more oversight and regulation— to rein in the Wild West of virtual schooling—have grown louder. As the authors of a 2018 report for the National Education Policy Center put it: "Since so many of the virtual schools are driven by profit, one option is to limit private owners and operators. Another option is to create and implement safeguards regarding private EMOs." The authors recommended creating regulatory oversight boards, mandating transparency regarding financing and student performance, and establishing accountability mechanisms.[43]

In California, virtual schools are the target of a new law banning the for-profit management of charter schools in the state. The law, which prohibits companies from running or managing charters, was prompted in part by a 2016 *Mercury News* investigation into K12 Inc., which turned up dismal graduation numbers as well as reports of grade inflation and exaggerated enrollment. The probe revealed that students could be logged onto K12's software for as little as one minute and still count as "present" and thus figure into calculations for how much taxpayer money the company would receive from the state.[44]

In light of these setbacks, virtual schools have doubled down on their investments. Financed by the deep pockets of large corporations, virtual schools have lobbied would-be regulators to go easy on them. In Ohio, for instance, the ECOT scandal went unaddressed for years as campaign funds filled the coffers of the officials tasked with overseeing the school. Virtual schools have also invested heavily in public relations, churning out "edvertising" aimed at attracting new customers—the subject of chapter 10.

Scandal-plagued as they may be, virtual schools continue to grow because they maintain a powerful ideological allure for those intent on unmaking public education. Moving school online promises to cut costs, while undermining the political force of organized labor. And although virtual schools may have fallen short of the education panacea that Jeb Bush and others have been selling for more than a decade, they've delivered something even more important to their supporters: a way to profit from public education.

8

The End of Regulation

When Betsy DeVos became the nation's top education official, she made no secret about her twin goals: to advance school choice and eliminate the "red tape" she believed was stifling America's schools. But while the first aim has generated countless news stories and protests, her anti-regulatory zeal has attracted far less scrutiny. Ultimately, though, it might do far more to transform public education.

For conservatives, the federal government's retreat from oversight and the push to dismantle regulatory structures represents the realization of a decades-long effort to curb the excesses of what they see as a nanny-state run amok. To mark the end of his first year in office, Donald Trump celebrated his administration's victory in the war against government bureaucracy by posing next to a tower of documents and scissoring through a red ribbon.

The position of the libertarian Cato Institute is characteristic of this larger movement. "Today, there is no greater impediment to American prosperity than the immense body of regulations chronicled in the Federal Register," the organization declares on its website. In place of those regulations, Cato envisions "a market-oriented vision of 'regulatory rollback' that relies on the incentive forces of private property rights to create competitive markets."[1]

When Betsy DeVos proclaims that "bureaucratic red tape should never get in the way of helping students," she has a particular end in mind. She isn't suggesting a careful sorting-through of regulations, many of which do help students by defending the vulnerable or protecting the public interest. Instead, she believes that parents are the only regulators needed.

For those seeking to dismantle public education, regulation is the last battlefield. It's all that stands between them and their ultimate policy aims.

An Era of Progress

In the early years of the twentieth century, writer Edwin Markham shocked middle-class readers of *Cosmopolitan* magazine with his vivid and brutal descriptions of child laborers. His depiction of children who "know no rest, no play, no learning, nothing but the grim grind of existence," helped to propel a broad-based movement demanding the regulation of labor.[2] The resulting prohibition against child labor was part of a vast legal framework that emerged during the Progressive Era, often in response to corporate abuses detailed by muckraking journalists who wanted to protect consumers and the public interest.

A quick review of federal regulations indicates the spirit of the age. In 1906, the Pure Food and Drug Act and the Federal Meat Inspection Act established regulations targeting adulterated and mislabeled products. The National Conservation Commission of

1909 was charged with preserving natural resources, and seven years later the Organic Act created the National Park Service to "promote and regulate" federal protected land. In 1914, the Federal Trade Commission was created to protect consumers and combat anticompetitive practices; that same year, the Clayton Act updated and strengthened the Sherman Antitrust Act. In 1916, the Keating-Owen Child Labor Act established regulation of employment, as did the 1916 Adamson Act, which limited the workday for railroad employees. To help pay for these reforms, Congress passed the Revenue Act of 1913, establishing a federal income tax; and three years later, the estate tax was enacted.

Because the federal government had no constitutional authority over schools, there were no national efforts to regulate education. But beginning in the Progressive Era, states increasingly exerted themselves in the area of public education—which until then had remained mostly a local matter.[3] States were chiefly concerned with student absenteeism, and they established compulsory attendance laws that placed new obligations on schools and parents. As historian of education Nancy Beadie has argued, the enforcement of such laws typified "an increasing willingness on the part of state legislatures, state courts, and state departments of education to assert public power over children and households through the agency of schools, to use state financial leverage to strengthen state supervision of teachers and standardization of curriculum and operations, and to broaden the purview of schools as official state agencies in matters of public health, labor regulation, child welfare, immigration, and 'juvenile delinquency.'"[4]

Leaders at the state level also began to express concern about the quality of education delivered to young people—a concern that led directly to regulation of the teaching profession. As one law review article notes, credentialing requirements exemplified "the state's interest in ensuring that students in *all* localities achieve a certain level of academic prowess through their exposure to teachers with adequate credentials."[5] By the 1920s, most teachers were required to earn licenses.

The rise of regulation in public education, then, mirrored the wider phenomenon reshaping American political and economic life. The age was defined by a carrot-and-stick ethos, which historians of education David Tyack and Thomas James sum up this way: "States learned to use their common school funds as stimuli to local communities to build schools and as levers to secure compliance with state regulations. In order to receive state funds, local districts typically had to comply with certain minimal requirements, such as keeping schools open for a certain term, hiring only certified teachers, and submitting records to the state superintendent."[6]

Brewing Backlash

Almost as soon as regulatory structures began to emerge in the late nineteenth and early twentieth century, corporate interests began complaining that they were costly and burdensome. As one lawyer argued in 1917: "The total cost to the taxpayers of the country of the regulation of business by direct legislation and by commissions is stupendous; but, in addition to this more or less common burden imposed on the taxpayers of all classes, there is further imposed upon the businesses regulated an enormous expense in complying with statutory and administrative regulations sometimes of no practical benefit to any one, and frequently a hindrance to business."[7] Though it would certainly become more intense over the decades, the theme of this critique would remain relatively constant over time.

The presidential candidacy of Barry Goldwater represented a

coming-to-consciousness for many opponents of regulation. But as Rick Perlstein chronicles in *Before the Storm,* his history of Goldwater's rise to prominence, anti-regulatory fervor had been brewing for years. By the time Goldwater launched his crusade against what he called centralized government control, a veritable army of put-upon industrialists, anti-tax advocates, and partisans of small government were waiting. "History teaches that [regulation] seldom achieves the intended objectives," Milton Friedman wrote in the *New York Times* in 1964. "It generally only weakens the capacity of the ordinary man to provide for his own needs."[8]

Goldwater was crushed by Lyndon Johnson in the 1964 election. But in the wake of that defeat, his acolytes began building policy capacity for their favored causes, with deregulation high on the list. As they did, their cause was strengthened by even stronger regulatory interventions. In the 1960s and early 1970s, federal regulations imposed stiffer penalties and made enforcement easier through what neoconservative Robert Kagan called "unambiguous numerical standards and fixed deadlines."[9] Laws like the Occupational Safety and Health Act of 1970, the Clean Air Act Amendments of 1970, and the Clean Water Act of 1972 ramped up inspections and opened doors to public lawsuits.

Critics of regulation became even more vehement. Rules constraining the activity of public and private actors, they maintained, were more expensive and intrusive than ever. Worse, regulatory agencies were protecting industries from competition. In fields from hairdressing to classroom teaching, regulated professions had insulated themselves to their advantage. The result was greater expense to the public and, potentially, lower quality. As a 1985 Brookings Institution report asserted, government agencies "had sheltered the regulated industries from competition and fostered very costly inefficiencies."[10]

Among those who agreed with this assessment was Ronald Reagan. "Government is not the solution to our problems," Reagan told the nation upon his inauguration. "Government," he insisted, "is the problem."

As he had with so many policy positions, Reagan assumed Goldwater's stance on deregulation. But deregulation was particularly important to Reagan, who quickly adopted it as the defining feature of his administration. As one scholar observed in 1982: "Recent political discussion, particularly that emanating from the Reagan administration, has dwelt on little else."[11] In a 1983 radio address about deregulating the natural gas industry, Reagan described his position as "one that believes in trusting the wisdom of the people rather than taking power away from them and concentrating it in the other hands."[12]

Reagan masterfully communicated his anti-regulatory agenda as commonsense politics. As a result, deregulation moved from the margins to the mainstream. In the span of a decade, even Democrats were denouncing government intervention. When Bill Clinton proclaimed in his 1996 State of the Union speech that the "era of big government is over," he wasn't entirely parroting Reagan. A Democrat, Clinton did add that America could not "go back to the time when our citizens were left to fend for themselves." Yet whatever his caveat, it was clear that deregulation's time had come. A cause that had once lingered on the political fringes was now supported by both major parties.

License to Teach

By the 1980s, regulation in public education had expanded dramatically past compulsory education. Student rights were established across a wide range of issues including disciplinary matters.

Teachers, in addition to being protected from competition by certification, won legal guarantees against discriminatory practices in compensation, evaluation, and dismissal. Class sizes were often limited. Textbook adoptions were controlled by state and local rules, and accountability mechanisms were erected in a majority of states.[13]

Still, the regulation that tended to rankle conservatives the most was an old one: teacher licensure.

The first problem with licensing teachers, as many conservatives saw it, was the matter of "regulatory capture." State certification requirements, in their view, restricted the labor market in a manner beneficial to those already in it. Just as a good hairstylist can be determined by customers, they argued, so might good teachers be determined by students, families, and school administrators. Yet savvy insiders, conservatives argued, had established professional licensing requirements mandating training. These requirements, in their view, limited the pool of potential applicants, artificially driving up their salaries by creating scarcity.

By limiting the pool of potential teachers, licensure also did something else that infuriated conservatives: it gave teachers more bargaining power. Unlike ordinary wage workers, teachers could not be easily replaced. When teachers withheld their labor by striking, they had far more power than they would have if state laws didn't require them to be licensed. With teacher training institutions controlling the volume of teachers produced each year, the market for labor was anything but free in the eyes of conservatives.

Third was the matter of cost. By requiring special credentials, teacher licensure also raised the cost of entry into the profession. Would-be teachers faced not only the cost of a licensure program, but also the opportunity cost of not working during the period of training. That, in turn, raised wage expectations among prospective teachers.

Finally, conservatives tended to view the emphasis on teacher preparation as mostly leftist propaganda. Critics of all political persuasions had long lambasted university-based training for focusing more on theory than practice. And Americans broadly believe that anyone can teach—a belief rooted in the gendered nature of the profession, its parallel with child-rearing, and the fact that people have the firsthand experience of observing teaching for more than a decade during their own schooling.[14] But what particularly outraged conservatives was an emphasis on issues like school diversity and social justice rather than on skill-related training. Scholar Ken Zeichner summed it up this way: "The prevailing view among deregulation advocates is that teacher education courses at colleges and universities add little value to a teacher's effectiveness and that which needs to be learned about how to teach can be learned on the job."[15]

Given all this, it should come as no surprise that early efforts to dismantle the regulatory infrastructure of public education began with efforts to eliminate training requirements for teachers. By the late 1980s, conservatives and neoliberal Democrats aligned behind alternative certification efforts, many of which involved moving teacher preparation out of universities. Perhaps most visible among such efforts was Teach For America, which was founded in 1989 to channel high-achieving graduates from elite colleges into teaching after only five weeks of training.[16]

Small victories in watering down teacher training requirements, however, were not enough for anti-regulatory crusaders. The American Legislative Exchange Council, for instance, continued to push its "Alternative Certification Act" model legislation, which seeks to open the teaching profession to "well-educated, qualified, and mature individuals"—no teaching degree required. Versions of this bill have been introduced in Michigan, New Mexico, Wisconsin, West Virginia, and Kansas, which used model ALEC language to roll back teacher licensure requirements. The conservative Kansas Policy Institute, meanwhile, argues that the Sunflower State should go still further, junking teacher certification entirely.

As teaching shortages have taken hold in many of the same states where ALEC's influence is strongest, the response from conservative legislators has been to loosen licensure requirements. Arizona, for example, has responded to a dire teacher shortfall by issuing so-called emergency teaching certificates. Applicants must have a bachelor's degree, but can otherwise sidestep state certification. Between 2015 and 2018, the number of licenses the Arizona Department of Education issued to untrained teachers soared by more than 400 percent. And, according to a recent examination of state data, Arizona has issued more than 7,200 licenses to untrained teachers since 2015.[17]

But even such loosened regulations don't satisfy the most ardent believers in a market-oriented vision for education. Doug Tuthill, president of a group administering Florida's school voucher program, wonders why teachers even need bachelor's degrees, and maintains that private schools receiving taxpayer-funded vouchers should be free to hire whomever they want. "I've seen no scientific or anecdotal evidence showing that all college degreed teachers are better than all non-college degreed teachers," writes Tuthill. "Bill Gates does not have a college degree but I'm confident he's more capable of teaching coding and business management than many degreed teachers."[18]

A Charter Is a Contract

For many conservatives, much of the initial allure of charter schools owed to their relative freedom from regulation. Rather than being governed within the nested hierarchy of state agencies and district central offices, charter schools are legally independent entities. Responsible for outcomes detailed in their agreements with the state, charter schools have a number of autonomies that traditional public schools do not—including, in some states, the ability to hire unlicensed teachers. But while the steady stream of news reports involving charter school fraud can give the appearance that charters operate without any oversight, the reality is that they have never been the regulation-free zones that conservatives envisioned.

First, there is the fact that charter schools cannot simply open and start teaching students immediately; instead, as their name implies, they must first be issued a charter—a process controlled by state and local agencies. Roughly half of chartering is done by local districts, and about a third is done by state education agencies and independent boards; the remainder—roughly 15 percent—is done by higher education institutions, nonprofits, and municipalities.

Then there is the application process to open a charter school, which groups like the American Enterprise Institute have lamented as a "paperwork pileup" of regulations. As the group claimed in a 2015 report, charter school authorizers routinely require "unnecessarily extensive, time-consuming applications." The report, which featured a cartoon of a school and its leader collapsing beneath a mountain of paperwork, concluded that an overly burdensome application process "severely compromises operators' ability to innovate."[19] Betsy DeVos has offered a similar critique, arguing that rules intended to safeguard charter school quality ensnare schools in red tape.

Regulation also constrains the charter sector through limits on the number, and even the kinds, of schools that can open. Today, roughly two dozen states have caps on the number of charters they will allow. Massachusetts, along with limiting the number of charters that can open in the Bay State, limits the percentage of local funds that can flow to charter schools. An additional policy provision in Massachusetts favors charter operators that have a successful track record of operating schools in the state—a requirement that the Pioneer Institute, a free-market think tank, characterizes as an innovation-buster.

As the number of charter schools has exploded in urban areas—in a growing number of urban school districts, the percentage of students attending charter schools now tops 30 percent—the call for more regulation has accelerated. In Washington, DC, where nearly half of students attend charters, parents and education advocates want charters to be subject to many of the same rules that govern traditional public schools, including open meeting and public record laws. California recently imposed sweeping new regulations on charter schools, including requiring that all teachers at charter schools hold a state teaching credential, and granting local school boards more power to block or expand charters.[20]

Dramatic news stories of sudden school closures, as well as fraud perpetrated at the expense of teachers and students, are also fueling calls for more charter oversight. In Philadelphia, which has been rocked by a series of high-profile charter school scandals, new rules instituted in 2018 govern the terms under which charters can make changes to curriculum, facilities, and enrollment. In response, the pro-charter advocacy group Excellent Schools PA filed a lawsuit to try to block the measure's enforcement, insisting that it would limit charter schools' "independence" and "restrict their ability to serve children."[21]

In response to the push for more oversight, school choice advocates have stepped up their complaints that charter schools are stifled by regulatory creep. In a recent op-ed, Jeanne Allen and Patrick Korten of the Center for Education Reform, a school choice advocacy organization, warned of an explosion of laws governing charter schools. From curriculum to teacher licensing and discipline, they argued, charter schools are increasingly pushed to act like the public schools they were intended to "supplement or replace." Allen and Korten laid the blame squarely at the feet of policy makers who "seem no longer able to tell the difference between policies that advance the cause of effective charter schools and those that strangle them."[22]

Ardent free-marketeers maintain that parents are the only regulators that schools need. A statement in the *National Review* by representatives of conservative groups—including the Heritage Foundation, the Friedman Foundation, and the Hoover Institution—neatly sums up this view: "True accountability comes not from top-down regulations but from parents financially empowered to exit schools that fail to meet their child's needs."[23] Seen through this lens, the real education reform success stories, then, are not the "portfolio" districts—systems of charter schools in cities like Denver and New Orleans in which schools are opened, shuttered, or expanded on the basis of standardized test scores. Instead, the triumphs are in those places where schools are easily opened and run with minimal regulation.

Civil Rights Enforcement

Early civil rights regulations for students addressed issues of segregation and discrimination, largely through state constitutional provisions. The first school desegregation ruling was handed down in 1931, when the Superior Court of San Diego County ruled that a local school board was violating California law by segregating Mexican American students. A federal court in California reached a similar conclusion in the 1947 *Mendez v. Westminster* decision, ruling that remedial schools for Mexican American students in Orange County violated equal protection under the state's laws governing public education. But such broad rights were difficult to enforce at the local level, particularly without clear and consistent legal controls. Even the Supreme Court's landmark decision in *Brown v. Board* created only limited protections for students. After all, parents could avoid integration simply by moving to a new school in a different neighborhood.

But regulations against racial discrimination kept coming, and had significant implications for students and schools. Title VI of the Civil Rights Act of 1964, for instance, prohibited racial and ethnic discrimination in any program or activity receiving federal funds—including most public schools. Like much federal legislation, it established a general prohibition, offering little in the way of detail. Still, it allowed the Justice Department, or affected individuals themselves, to file suit. A year later, Title I of the Elementary and Secondary Education Act established even stronger regulations in an effort to clarify what was required of schools.

The growing framework of laws and regulations established rights for other marginalized groups. The Equal Educational Opportunities Act of 1974, for instance, required districts to take affirmative steps toward helping non-native English speakers overcome barriers. In 1975, the Education for All Handicapped Children Act—later renamed the Individuals with Disabilities Education Act—established a clear regulatory mechanism for enforcing the rights of students with disabilities. And gender discrimination was addressed in Title IX of the 1972 reauthorization of the Higher Education Act. Originally used to establish parity in athletics programs, Title IX stated that "no person in the United States shall, on the basis of sex, be excluded from participation in, be denied the benefits of, or be subjected to discrimination under any education program or activity receiving Federal financial assistance." A generation later, it would serve as an important policy tool in combating sexual assault on college campuses.

As the regulations began to pile up, complaints from critics about red tape and the distortion of organizational priorities grew louder. As policy scholar Paul Hill wrote in a 1979 Brookings report: "The rules governing Title I now resemble a complex code of statutory law, and like a code of law they place a heavy burden on the user to find the relevant provisions and decide what all of them mean in combination."[24] But the chief complaint among conservatives was related to the price tag associated with all this regulation. Rules created compliance costs for organizations and enforcement costs for government—costs ultimately borne by taxpayers.

Because federal civil rights regulations apply to all schools receiving appropriations, the U.S. Department of Education has in many ways functioned as a civil rights agency. But upon assuming office, Betsy DeVos immediately set to work scaling back this role. She revoked Obama-era guidance about protecting transgender students, proposed a delay in another Obama-era rule aimed at addressing the disproportionate identification of students of color for special education, curtailed protections for victims of sexual assault under Title IX, and withdrew policy guidance focused on limiting racial disparities in discipline. Most tellingly, the Department of Education's Office for Civil Rights instructed its investigators to limit systematic investigations of discrimination complaints. An analysis done in 2018 found that under DeVos's leadership, more than 1,200 civil rights investigations, begun under the Obama administration, had been "scuttled," and that the department had "tilt[ed] away from systemic issues to complaints by individuals."[25]

DeVos also moved quickly to halt the enforcement of regulations on the for-profit college sector. In 2017 she paused the Borrower Defense to Repayment rule, established in 1994 to protect students from colleges' fraudulent recruitment practices; when she eventually reinstituted the program eighteen months later, she changed the rules to prevent students from receiving full debt relief. Similarly, DeVos halted the Obama-era Gainful Employment regulations, which required colleges to show that students could repay their loans on the basis of their anticipated income after graduation.[26] A letter to the Department of Education, co-signed by twenty-one higher education organizations and authored by the senior vice president of the American Council on Education, protested that the overturned rule, "while not perfect, addressed a serious existing problem and was targeted at where the problems occurred and where the Department had clear statutory authority to act."[27]

For DeVos and other ardent advocates of the free market, the priority is not to promote discrimination. Instead, it is to protect the freedom of individuals to act as they wish. Market freedoms, they insist, are the most important freedoms of all. And if deregulation means that rights are infringed on, that's a price they're willing to pay.[28]

The Finances of Regulation and the Regulation of Finances

Regulation increases costs. Perhaps most significantly, this occurs as a result of the open-ended obligations that schools face in response to equity commitments. Mandates that students have "equal educational opportunity," receive an "appropriate educa-tion," and are taught in the "least restrictive" environment estab-lish ambitious goals. And, in so doing, they burden schools with potentially exorbitant costs.

Poor children are far more expensive to educate than their more affluent peers, at least if the aim is to produce relatively equal outcomes. Educational research has shown that economically disadvantaged students benefit from costly programs like early childhood education, smaller classes, and wraparound program-ming that extends beyond the school environment. Were it not for legal requirements, schools could refuse to provide these services, cutting their costs dramatically. Even still, districts and states have been repeatedly sued on the grounds of failing to live up to these obligations.

Non-native speakers are also expensive to educate, benefiting as they do from trained teachers and specialized classes. Once more, the regulatory framework requires schools to act in a manner that allows for equal participation. When the Bilingual Education Act was passed in 1968, funding for programs increased from $7.5 mil-lion to $68 million. In 1974, the Equal Educational Opportunities Act was passed, requiring school districts to overcome barriers lim-iting equal participation by students. That same year, the Supreme Court's decision in Lau v. Nichols ruled that "there is no equal-ity of treatment merely by providing students with the same facili-ties, textbooks, teachers, and curriculum." Program funding, in one year, doubled—from $68 million to $135 million, and steadily expanded thereafter.[29]

A third group of students whose education comes with a cost are those with physical and intellectual disabilities. Often twice as expensive to educate as their mainstream peers, students with disabilities can file civil suits if their needs are not being met or if they are not being educated in the "least restrictive environment" possible. And the ensuing cost of meeting their needs has vexed cost-cutters to no end. As the libertarian Reason Foundation complained, the regulatory state has "created ample provisions to protect and serve children with disabilities" without establishing "a cost-control provision in the law to protect the schools."[30]

Market-oriented conservatives argue that the cost of such regulations is mostly wasted. Parents unhappy with the quality of a particular school, if provided choice, will simply move their children until they find the right fit. But what if no school chooses to spend what it takes to educate the least advantaged? In such a scenario, parents might have no particularly attractive alternatives. "Schools of choice"—charter schools and private schools—do not offer encouraging evidence that the market will provide for all young people.

Nationwide, charter schools serve fewer students with disabilities than traditional public schools. As scholar Gary Miron has observed: "There is considerable evidence that charter schools actively discourage families from enrolling disabled children and counsel them to leave when they do manage to enroll."[31] Indeed, an entire industry of advocates and lawyers has emerged to help parents get the special education accommodations from charter schools that they are entitled to under federal law.

Private schools, for their part, are free to admit (or not admit) any student they like. Regulatory protections don't apply to students who attend private schools, even when the schools receive public funds via voucher programs or tax credits. One Catholic high school in Indianapolis, for instance—an institution participating in Indiana's taxpayer-funded voucher program and that DeVos visited in 2017—was criticized for having zero special needs students enrolled. As the CEO responded, "The school isn't geared to provide such services and families know it."[32]

Taxpayers also stand to lose in an unregulated marketplace. Presently, regulations govern how schools can and can't spend public funds. That is, there are certain things that schools *must* do if they receive public funds, as well as a long list of things they cannot do. Such rules are often portrayed as onerous. And sometimes they are. But a look at states where the regulatory framework has been rolled back reveals the extent to which financial abuse flourishes without safeguards. School management companies, both for-profit and non-profit, are now routinely implicated in headline-grabbing financial scandals, many involving related-party transactions—wherein charter schools purchase goods or services from companies in which board members and other administrators have a financial stake.

In Arizona, long the poster state for a "hands off" approach to school regulation, charter school fraud has become so flagrant and so frequent that journalists can barely keep up with reporting on it. Damian Creamer, the founder of the Primavera online charter school, paid himself roughly $10 million in salary despite the fact that the school had the third-worst dropout rate in the state. American Leadership Academy founder Glenn Way made nearly $20 million through no-bid construction contracts he signed with the school. And state lawmaker Eddie Farnsworth made $13.9 million from his Benjamin Franklin Charter Schools—selling them to a nonprofit company that he created.[33] Eventually, Arizona lawmakers responded with new regulations. But in the Grand Canyon State, it seems, even regulation seems to need regulation. One set of rules, for instance, made it more difficult to open a new charter while also making it easier for some charters to expand. But those rules disproportionately benefited a small number of chains, which happened to have strong relationships with Governor Doug Ducey. As a member of the Phoenix Union High School Board observed: "It's very curious how the people who are connected to the governor are calling the shots on things that benefit them."[34]

Such shenanigans have led to even bolder regulatory efforts regarding financial integrity and transparency. But those efforts have often met with stiff opposition. In Utah, a push to force privately managed charter schools to disclose how they spend public funds ran into resistance organized by charter school lobbyists. The bill that finally made it to the governor's desk had been so watered down that it did little to make charter school dealings more transparent. And the lawmaker who led the charge was both personally fatigued and politically weakened by the effort. As he told reporters coving the story, the fight over the proposed legislation had been such a headache that he would never introduce a similar bill again.[35]

Driving Without a Seatbelt

Deregulation efforts in education took off in the mid-1980s. As the authors of one report put it, "Freed from barriers posed by rules about how they organize and deliver education, schools could design services that best meet the needs of their students."[36] Yet these scholars also noted that freeing schools from rules might also mean that providers "with the biggest problems, such as political corruption, are freed from ensuring students a minimal level of education."[37]

This has been the historical trade-off. Regulation can be rigid, inflexible, and burdensome. It can be disorienting and incomprehensible. But regulation also establishes a legal framework for protecting and enforcing the rights of parents and young people, as well as for preserving the integrity of public funds. At worst, regulation does exactly what its critics say, binding educators in red tape. Yet regulation, ultimately, is the product of democratic governance, and regulators work for the public. Additionally, regulations apply equally to everyone, ensuring fair treatment for historically marginalized populations.

Rather than work to find some balance in regulatory oversight, conservative policy elites have sought to remove all regulation. In pursuit of that aim, they have heaped unmitigated scorn on the process of rule-making and the very nature of governmental oversight—a strategy that has proven remarkably effective. As scholar William H. Clune observed, "A certain amount of undifferentiated social indignation is required to overcome the inertia and lethargy of the regulatory process." Yet, as he also appreciated, "if this spirit is applied full strength to government programs, the result is likely to be wreckage rather than efficiency."[38]

The push to dismantle regulations is not about carefully paring excess. Instead, it is a consequences-be-damned crusade to unmake an aspect of American life that secures collective safety by limiting individual freedoms. It's a move to cut the seatbelts out of our cars.

9

Don't Forget to
Leave Us a Review

When you leave a retail outlet, an airport, even a hospital, you're likely to encounter a Smiley Terminal. These battery-powered consumer feedback machines allow customers to rate a recent transaction with the press of a button, assigning their experience an emoji-style rating between deep frown and grinning satisfaction. Best of all, the entire exchange is fast and "frictionless," in the parlance of Silicon Valley.

Today, the idea of someone installing a Smiley Terminal inside a school is more of a joke than a threat. But consumer rating systems that once seemed unheard of in other industries have ended up reshaping them. Restaurants, retail, and ridesharing all depend heavily on internet-based rating systems that direct traffic to some businesses and away from others. And if the teaching profession is redefined as gig work—a possibility we explore in chapter 11—Uber-like rating systems will inevitably follow. In fact, such systems aren't truly that different from what already exists in education. Websites like GreatSchools.org offer ratings on a 1–10 scale of schools and include a space to leave consumer reviews. There's even a Yelp-style review site for teachers—RateMyTeachers .com—on which students have been assigning teachers a 1–5 rating for nearly two decades.

Viewed through the eyes of a free marketeer, these consumer-driven rating systems represent the ultimate empowerment of the individual. In a 2017 speech, Betsy DeVos asserted that "the entrenched status quo" in public education "has resisted models that empower individuals." After all, how does government know what an individual wants? Government is no more qualified weighing in on what kind of school you want than it is in determining where you should go on vacation, or what kind of blue jeans look best on you.

But how would an education marketplace based on individual choice actually work? Critics often contend that families don't have enough information to make informed decisions when it comes to selecting schools. The obvious remedy, of course, is to visit the schools. But that's not realistic in a marketplace with lots of options, including virtual schools or even individual courses offered by competing providers—the future envisioned by conservative policy elites. So how can families make good choices when they have only a limited ability to sample the products?

To those who place their faith in markets and individuals, such questions are an insult. After all, how do people make choices about where to eat or what movie to see? It's not the task of government bureaucrats to assign people to particular restaurants or to rate films. That happens through individual choice exercised through the market.

Free-market conservatives have pushed hard for deregulation. And the logical extension of that push is to turn quality evaluation over to consumers, just as in the rest of the so-called sharing economy. In a dismantled future, crowd-sourced ratings will replace ratings by authorities, in the same way that Yelp ratings have replaced traditional restaurant reviews.

A consumer-based rating system has an ideological appeal insofar as it promises to foster a freer and more complete marketplace that includes public and private schools, virtual schools, and à la carte programs. Jonathan Beckham of the Florida school voucher group Step Up For Students, a private school tuition scholarship program in Florida, was quoted in the *Washington Post* as likening the vision of a ratings-powered marketplace to shopping on Amazon: "I can see thousands of products and services that are pre-approved for acceptable use for my program. I can click into those products and get detailed product information and availability for it. I can add it to my shopping cart and checkout using my ESA funds directly."[1] Put that way, the idea of a Smiley Terminal inside a school isn't so funny after all.

Origins of the Five-Star System

Rating systems are a relatively modern invention. Word-of-mouth marketing, of course, is as old as social interaction. But the first formal ratings of goods were devised in an effort to make markets work more efficiently. In small, face-to-face relationships, individuals can determine the quality of goods for themselves—using their own good sense. In a truly competitive marketplace, however, there are more purveyors than any single consumer can know firsthand. Consequently, as large-scale markets emerged in the late nineteenth century around goods like corn, timber, and cattle, great efforts were made to establish standard rating systems.[2]

One early rating system was devised under the supervision of the

U.S. Department of Agriculture. In 1916, the USDA began developing grading standards for cattle, along with a set of valid and reliable ratings in response to demands from the livestock market. In 1923, the department published these ratings, along with a slew of standards for cattle, veal, and lamb. Terms like "common," "canner," and "utility" were used to indicate the quality of meat until 1950, when the ratings were rebranded as "prime," "choice," and "commercial." Today, billions of pounds of meat are graded annually, and the ratings you see on packages at the local grocery store are largely the same as they were a hundred years ago.

Star ratings began to emerge around the same time. Unlike the USDA ratings, which required consumers to distinguish between the merits of prime, choice, and select beef, a star visibly conferred quality. While no one seems to know exactly who assigned the first star, one early adopter was the Michelin restaurant guide. In 1926, the French tire company began using a star to identify which restaurants served food worth driving to. Five years later, the guide adopted its current system, which awards up to three stars by anonymous "inspectors." Then, as now, winning (or losing) a star might mean instant success, or the beginning of the end.

In the July 31, 1928, edition of the *New York Daily News*, film critic Irene Thirer announced her plan to rate movies on a scale of zero to three stars. Three would indicate "excellent," two "good," one "mediocre." A zero-star review would indicate that "the picture's right bad."[3] The first film to earn a star—and it did earn just a single star—was the silent potboiler *The Port of Missing Girls*. While the film has been all but forgotten, the star rating system took off.

These early rating systems all had a key feature in common: reliance upon experts. Whether the product being assessed was ground beef, fine dining, or movies, the task of determining quality fell to a professional who assigned a rating on the basis of some kind of objective criteria. Only a USDA assessor, a Michelin inspector, or a professional film critic could be trusted with the power of dispensing judgment.

In 1979, a couple of avid restaurant-goers named Nina and Tim Zagat changed that. While living in Paris, the Zagats began a hobby of compiling a list of restaurants, including details about what they did and didn't like. When they returned to New York City, they solicited their friends' opinions about where to eat, and pitched to publishers a plan for a new kind of dining guide. After receiving a thumbs-down, the Zagats decided to fund a print run themselves. And when *New York* magazine ran a cover story about the Zagat guide, the little red book was soon selling upwards of 75,000 copies a month. By putting the power to rate restaurants in the hands of diners themselves, the Zagats permanently upended the notion that only experts could dispense stars.

Then came the internet. In 1995, Amazon began allowing customers to post reviews of products; Yelp arrived a decade later. Suddenly, almost anybody could play the role of critic, weighing in on books, movies, restaurants, hotels, and virtually anything else that could be consumed. At last count, Yelp had amassed some 171 million reviews, a collection of what *New York Times* food writer Pete Wells refers to as "mash notes and spitballs." But while ratings have been outsourced to the crowd, much of the crowd's wisdom amounts to the simple act of complaining. "When we complain, we experience something that we don't like and we say something about it," wrote Wells in a 2019 essay. That's very different from the job of a critic, who is tasked with plumbing the sources of dissatisfaction.[4]

Another key difference is that Yelp's reviews are anonymous.

While critics sign their names to their columns, Yelp and its imitators have no process for verifying whether the reviewer even ate at the establishment in question. The result is a sort of complainer's free-for-all, heavy on torchings. In fact, a study by Northwestern University researchers found that dissatisfied patrons are more likely to leave reviews than satisfied ones, and as a result, the reviews often paint a misleading picture that drives potential patrons away.[5]

Internet-based rating systems like those on Amazon and Yelp also created a new kind of market—in this case, for positive reviews. "These days it is very hard to sell anything on Amazon if you play fairly," said Tommy Noonan, who operates ReviewMeta, a website that helps consumers spot suspicious Amazon reviews. "If you want your product to be competitive, you have to somehow manufacture reviews." A 2018 *Washington Post* investigation shed light on the depth of the problem, uncovering a vast network of paid and fraudulent reviews. In fact, the reporters concluded that questionable customer reviews are now crowding out authentic ones on Amazon.[6]

Review fakery isn't the only problem with our increasing reliance upon ratings. A study of more than a million online restaurant reviews found that while so-called restaurant attributes—things like the quality of the fare, price, and service—affected ratings, "exogenous factors" also exerted a surprisingly significant influence.[7] As the researchers determined, customer reviews tended to take into account factors like the weather outside and neighborhood demographics.

If ratings for headphones on Amazon or that new neighborhood restaurant are flawed, what does that augur for assigning stars to the far more complex universe of schools?

The School-Rating Business

During the 2018 "lame duck" session at the Michigan capitol, GOP efforts to weaken the incoming Democratic governor and attorney general weren't the only measures that grabbed headlines. Republicans also passed controversial legislation requiring the state to rate schools using A-F letter grades. Early in the year, Jeb Bush visited Michigan to make the case for such a rating system. Letter grades, he told a conservative policy group in Grand Rapids, are a "simple and pretty easy way" to hold schools accountable, while giving parents the information they need to choose a school for their kids.[8]

Florida was the first state to adopt the practice of grading its schools in the manner of a student report card. In 1999, the inaugural year of Jeb Bush's two terms as governor, Florida rolled out a system that assigned grades to schools solely on the basis of student standardized test scores. Other school-quality indicators, such as student attendance, teacher training, school climate, and student discipline metrics, were intentionally left out of the mix. "An accountability formula should reflect only objective measures of academic achievement," Bush argued in a 2016 interview.[9]

Other states quickly followed Florida's lead. Today more than twenty states have implemented some version of an A-F grade scale for schools. But such grading systems, popular among conservative lawmakers, school choice groups, and the American Legislative Exchange Council, spurred a backlash. Giving A ratings to schools solely on the basis of student test scores, which closely correlate with student demography, means that the wealthiest, whitest schools earn the top grades, while high-poverty schools get Ds and Fs. "'A' is for affluent," is how the *Dallas News* summed up school letter grades in Texas. "You can't fund some schools at inadequate levels and then use the same metrics to grade them as others," argued Texas lawmaker Mary González. "If you do, you are going to hurt low-funded schools and communities of color and say that they are failures."[10]

With their appeal to "objective measures" and reliance upon the judgment of state-level bureaucrats, A-F letter grades are a direct descendant of the original five-star rating systems. But just as in other industries, education ratings have moved from the realm of experts to crowd-sourcing.

GreatSchools was founded in 1998 as a guide to schools for parents in one particular California county. Over the next four years the guide expanded across the entire state, and, with the backing of a familiar philanthropic roster—Gates, Walton, the New Schools Venture Fund—GreatSchools quickly became a nationwide ratings hub. It largely relied on existing state data; but the organization set itself apart by allowing parents to assign schools a rating of terrible, bad, average, good, or great.

The success of GreatSchools, which often ranks first in internet searches for schools, soon inspired imitators. Schooldigger.com ranks schools based on test scores, but also includes crime data, real estate data, and "everything our team hopes is useful in helping you make better school choices." Niche.com combines what it describes as "rigorous cleaning and analysis on large data sets" with millions of reviews from "real people." But what exactly does "real" mean? Online school-rating sites have no mechanism for verifying enrollment at the schools that are being reviewed. And the self-selected nature of the reviewers means that those most likely to rate schools are either the most loyal or the most disgruntled.

Even the "objective" measures used by these sites offer only a partial picture of school quality.[11] With their heavy reliance on metrics that correlate with student demography, all of the school-rating

sites send a message that the only "good" schools are in the suburbs, where the student population is wealthier and whiter. In fact,
in a recent study that looked at the cost of houses in nearly ten
thousand zip codes before and after GreatSchools began publishing school grades, the authors found that home values rose quickly
once the schools received a high rating.[12]

Online rating services like GreatSchools aren't the only ones
publicizing school-quality metrics. Newspapers routinely list the
best and worst schools in a state as measured by test scores. In
2010, the *Los Angeles Times* became the first paper to publish the
so-called value-added scores of individual teachers in the city's
public schools, using student standardized test scores to gauge
teacher effectiveness. The decision spurred outrage, particularly
among teachers who argued that the measures were incomplete at
best and inaccurate at worst.

One recent study determined that the publication of value-added
ratings in L.A. had an unintended consequence. Students who were
already high-achieving ended up being assigned to the classes of the
top-rated teachers the following year.[13] One possible explanation
for this development: parents with influence pushed to get highly
rated teachers for their children, just as affluent families have seized
on the ratings provided by GreatSchools and other school-rating
sites and are flocking to areas with highly rated schools.

Why Schools Are Different

Why *can't* schools be reviewed the way that, say, a sandwich shop
is? After all, parents crave the kind of immediate insight about
schools that the opinions of other parents can provide.

Schools differ from other kinds of goods because they take time
to understand and experience fully. Not only that, but they don't

end up making a difference to students immediately. You may be out of school for several years before you realize the impact of your schooling. A sandwich, by contrast, can be judged as soon as it's tasted. Was the bread fresh? Was the combination of ingredients tasty? Economists refer to a product or service that can be evaluated immediately as an "experience good." Education, the quality of which is far more difficult to assess, is what's known as a "credence good." It can take months, or even years, to figure out the quality of a school, and students and their families may give different ratings at different times.

Exacerbating the issue is the fact that schools are highly complex organizations. We want schools to do an incredible range of things, and we don't necessarily agree on what matters. Is the best school the one that posts the highest test scores, or the one that parents say they like the best? Is it the one that is preparing students to enter the workforce or the school that affirms cultural traditions?

Even when we agree on what matters, we don't always value those facets equally. What, then, does a five-star rating from one person mean vis-à-vis a five-star rating from another person? Could each be awarding the top score for very different reasons? Consider a simpler good than education—a car. People want cars in different sizes and designs, with different acceleration abilities, and with different carrying capacities. They place different values on fuel economy, technological gadgetry, trim, and resale value. Some even want to be able to shed the roof on a sunny day. If a car gets fantastic gas mileage but doesn't have four-wheel drive, does that make it a three-star car? What if a vehicle can accommodate a family of seven, but consistently loses drag races? Schools are even more complex in terms of performance. How, then, can we reduce them to a single rating?

Then there's the problem of attributing credit. With simple

goods, like food, attribution is simple. If the food coming out of a restaurant's kitchen is good, the cooks get the credit. But what if a student is excelling in math? What if she loves reading? What if a student is a less-than-model citizen or is distracted in class? Who deserves praise or bears the blame? Parents, friends, mentors, and community members all play a role in a child's life, and young people are strongly influenced by the safety and security of their home and neighborhood environments. How, then, can the influence of the school be separated from the many other influences in a young person's life? If a student is thriving in school, does the school get five stars, or does the family?

Another complication in treating schools like other ratable commodities is that students are, for the most part, children. Should a seven-year-old be rating schools? A ten-year-old? One potential solution is to turn the work of rating over to their families. But what do family members know? Parents do not spend their days inside schools, but instead rely on secondhand information from their children, as well as from others. Additionally, parents may be predisposed toward some school qualities—curricular rigor, for instance—while overlooking others, like the social and emotional health of students.

Further complicating matters is that education is often perceived as a positional good, meaning that its value is derived in comparison with what others are receiving. Certainly many of the benefits of education are absolute: a student learns to read or does not. But in promoting social status, education also provides relative advantage. One person's gain can only come at another person's expense. Consequently, parents can believe that a school is good because it is giving their children an edge over others—in college admissions, for instance—even if the actual quality of the schooling is no better.

Hitting the "Like" Button

"She drives the class up a wall, talks to herself in a very scary manner, and has a thing against cats," reads a student comment published on RateMyTeachers.com. "I hate her and I hope she gets fired."[14] Founded in 2001, RateMyTeachers.com was devised to give students a platform for critiquing their teachers on the basis of their classroom experiences. Alas, it quickly degenerated into a teacher-bashing site, and even spawned a subgenre: YouTube videos featuring teachers reading particularly cruel reviews.

RateMyTeachers was an early foray into what are known as online reputation systems—systems that use consumer ratings of individuals as the basis for recommendations. Such systems are integral to much of the so-called sharing economy—from Airbnb to TaskRabbit. Uber, for example, asks riders and drivers to rate each other using a five-star scale after every ride. In the gig economy, such rating systems take the place of managers or administrators, using algorithms to disperse rewards and punishments.

Anecdotes abound of Uber drivers who've been "deactivated"—Silicon Valley parlance for getting canned—after receiving low passenger ratings. Riders, too, end up banned from ridesharing apps when they receive consistently bad scores from their drivers. Proponents of these systems tend not to dwell upon the unfairness or prejudice that is baked into the algorithms that power this decision making; instead, they extol the virtue of a future powered by ratings. "On-demand companies are pointing the way to a more promising future, where people have more freedom to choose when and where they work," wrote founder and former Uber CEO Travis Kalanick, in October 2015. "The future of work is about independence and flexibility."[15]

Kalanick's homage to freedom, choice, and autonomy would be

at home in a Betsy DeVos speech. Indeed, she frequently holds up Uber as a model for her consumer-driven vision of education. In this vision, consumers might "hail" schools—or even teachers—the way they now summon a ridesharing service, handing out stars at every step of the process. But the attraction of the on-demand model isn't just about ease and convenience for consumers. Rating systems have enabled companies like Uber to manage huge numbers of workers without having to hire supervisors; every customer is now a boss. Making education similarly rating-dependent could effectively wipe out the bureaucracy—the unions, administrators, researchers, and the career teachers—whom former secretary of education and K12 Inc. co-founder Bill Bennett once referred to as "the blob."

Consider the issue of teacher evaluation. If you believe that teachers' unions use their power to protect their worst members, then consumer reviews hold an inherent appeal. Education reformers of all stripes have long argued that there are too many ineffective teachers in classrooms, and that more rigorous evaluation is needed. And yet even after states and school districts adopted recent reforms aimed at weeding out more bad apples, few teachers ended up being labeled as ineffective.[16] Why is this? Evaluating teachers is time-consuming and requires training. It's also expensive. As the stakes attached to teacher evaluations have grown steadily higher, the number of administrators needed to rate teachers has likewise ballooned.

New York City's public schools, for example, have roughly 75,000 teachers in need of annual evaluation. That requires an enormous number of professional raters, all of whom themselves need training and oversight. One option is to have successful and experienced teachers do the work of evaluating their colleagues, an approach known as Peer Assistance and Review. But while teachers may be uniquely qualified to judge other teachers, devolving evaluation away from administrators to educators and their unions is not what those who wax enthusiastic about Yelp for schools have in mind.

"Imagine if every plumber, manufactured product, cell phone provider, home builder, professor, hair stylist, accountant, attorney, golf pro, and taxi driver were rated," mused University of Chicago law professor Lior Strahilevitz, making the case for more reputation and less regulation. The proliferation of reputational rating systems, he argues, would result in a "diminished need for regulatory oversight and legal remedies because consumers would police misconduct themselves."[17]

Strahilevitz doesn't mention K-12 education, but reputational systems already play an outsized role in our understanding of school quality. If we were to take his argument to the logical next step, teachers, too, would be judged by consumers, in this case parents and students, rather than relying on Michelin-style experts to evaluate them. By shifting power in this way, schools, and even individual teachers, would be made more responsive to market forces as their "customers" voice approval or displeasure directly, immediately, and publicly.

Imagine students' phones buzzing at the end of a class with a notification to assign a thumbs-up or thumbs-down to their teacher. Perhaps rating a teacher might even be made mandatory, the equivalent of an "exit ticket" in which students must demonstrate some level of understanding in order to leave the classroom. Pinged once each week or once a day, students would quickly generate more ratings in a year than professional evaluators could produce in an entire career. The algorithm would do the rest, rewarding the top-rated teachers and "deactivating" those with the fewest stars.

RateMyTeachers.com foreshadowed this future. But the website required students to be motivated enough to seek it out, search for a teacher, and then take the time and trouble to pen an anonymous review. Young people, it turns out, are not so different from adults—given the option to fill out a survey, most won't. This is why rating systems have grown ever more simplistic. Uber passengers, for example, may rate their drivers for everything from the route taken to being excessively, or insufficiently, chatty. But that feedback takes the form of a star, not an essay-style review.

Studies do show that student surveys are a powerful source of feedback regarding the quality of teachers and schools. But a good student survey asks dozens of specific questions in order to separate out the many things that we hope teachers are doing in their classrooms. And because student experiences in classes and schools vary so widely, well-designed surveys must be able to capture the whole range of student perception. Perhaps most importantly, no student survey is currently used in the manner of an online reputation system. Some school districts do consider student survey results in teacher evaluation, but only as a single component in a system governed by human judgment. Moreover, such surveys ask students targeted questions about particular elements of teacher practice, avoiding leading questions that might open the door to misuse—such as, "How much do you like your teacher?"

Such judicious use of student feedback is not what critics of "the blob" have in mind when they rhapsodize about "an Uber for schools." Instead, they envision a system in which traditional power structures are upended, and in which students and their families are transformed not just into customers, but also into managers. As tech journalist Josh Dzieza argues, Uber-style rating systems turn "customers into unwitting and sometimes unwittingly ruthless middle managers, more efficient than any boss a company could hope to hire."[18] Even without the precariousness of gig employment, rating systems would upend power relations in schools. Teachers would be held hostage by their students, who would soon realize their power. And parents, too, would come to treat teachers as their employees.

Even though stars and smiley faces will never capture the complexity of teacher practice or school performance, such rating systems will only become more common. Behind the concerted push for Yelp-like school ratings lurks the ideological view that education is a private good to be consumed and rated like any other product. Take your education dollars and spend them in the education marketplace on whatever you like. Just don't forget to leave a review.

10

Selling School

The advertisements for schools in Indiana are as ubiquitous as soybeans these days, reflective of the state's increasingly competitive school choice marketplace. Billboards filled with the faces of beaming students try to sell parents on charter schools, or on one of the private religious schools now funded by taxpayers through the state's burgeoning voucher program. Traditional public schools have gotten in on the act, too, working to stanch the flow of "customers" to competing schools.

Meanwhile, Indiana's virtual schools are eagerly peddling the message that young Hoosiers shouldn't have to go to a physical school at all. "You know, you really don't have to spend seven and a half days of your life on the bus," says one ad, depicting a dejected-looking student on her way to school. Another e-school ad conveys a scene meant to strike fear into the hearts of parents. "Don't let this be your child's routine," it says, while a fearful-looking student is threatened by a harasser.[1]

In a speech to the American Enterprise Institute, former governor Mitch Daniels referred to what he called the "delightful sightings" of roadside billboards and direct mail pieces promoting an array of schools to Indiana families. At present, the phenomenon is confined primarily to urban areas; but Daniels imagined a future in which all schools, even those in affluent suburban districts, would feel the need to advertise. His hope was that schools would begin competing with each other more seriously for students and the dollars that come with them.[2]

Edvertising

Welcome to the world of "edvertising," a fast-growing byproduct of the push to restructure public education along free-market lines. As education is redefined as a matter of private choice, school marketing has exploded—bombarding "customers" with emotional appeals, questionable claims, and lofty promises. And unlike other products, like prescription drugs, the marketing of schools is almost completely unregulated.

Pharmaceutical ads are equally ubiquitous. But drugmakers are limited in the claims they can make, and their products include long lists of disclaimers. That's because drugs are covered by socalled truth-in-advertising rules, which are enforced by organizations like the Food and Drug Administration and the Federal Trade Commission. According to the FTC, "When consumers see or hear an advertisement, whether it's on the Internet, radio or television, or anywhere else, federal law says that ad must be truthful, not misleading, and, when appropriate, backed by scientific evidence."[3] Schools, on the other hand, are generally free from such constraints. After all, the selling of education snake oil is a relatively new phenomenon compared with the marketing of health tonics and cure-alls, which government regulators have had several generations to catch up with.

Today, edvertising is a minor element in the advertising landscape. In the future, however, it may become a common feature of American life. Already, school marketing is expanding beyond billboards, mailers, and Google ads to include more aggressive sales techniques. In modern ad-speak, some schools now "target market" through "micro-influencers." They offer gift cards to students for referring their friends, reward them for mentioning their school on social media, and incentivize them to leave reviews online.[4] At its worst, such marketing takes on a predatory aspect, with schools offering students laptops, tablets, or sneakers to enroll. And though such practices may be ethically dubious, they are not illegal.

In a school landscape already riven by inequities of race and class, edvertising threatens to open new chasms: between privately subsidized charter networks with vast budgets to devote to advertising, and traditional public schools—or even small, independent charter schools—which must now direct scarce funds toward marketing. Meanwhile, selective marketing will enable schools to target "desirable" parents, while passing over entire neighborhoods whose students would likely be a downward drag on the ultimate marketing signal: test scores.

The Brand Pioneers

Long before choice and competition fueled an explosion of school marketing, private schools were working to persuade parents to opt out of their local public schools and pay tuition. For most of the nineteenth and twentieth centuries, this was not a particularly costly proposition. But by the late twentieth century, private school tuition began to increase rapidly. Between 1988 and 2013, average independent school tuition nearly doubled (after accounting for inflation)—from an average of just under $12,000 per year to just over $23,000—driven mostly by rising spending on salaries and benefits for teachers and other personnel.[5]

In order to convince parents to shell out such a substantial sum, private schools stepped up their sales pitches. Because public education is free, many private schools marketed themselves as the educational equivalent of a luxury good. "We do not compete on price," is how one private school CFO put it.[6] The luxury on offer often relates to comfort—better cafeteria food, for instance, or well-appointed student lounges. More significantly, however, luxury is often defined by social distinction. As one study of private schools reported, "When it comes to encouraging families to enroll, school leaders overwhelmingly reported that the overall prestige, the quality of the academic experience, and the unique offerings of a school were more important to prospective families than tuition rates or financial aid policies."[7]

Elite schools use marketing to convey to prospective parents that they offer an educational experience that is superior to the local public school. Images of high-end architecture, state-of-the-art technology, and carefully manicured grounds send a powerful signal, even if they have little direct connection to teaching and learning. And just as with other edvertisements, private school marketing is often divorced from what's actually on offer.

Take the issue of small class sizes. Private schools heavily market the claim that small student-teacher ratios enable them to provide more academic and personal attention. But small class sizes are a huge expense that many private schools have been actively seeking to reduce. Consequently, many schools have worked to create some wiggle room between what they say and what they do. For instance, in a meeting of a group of private school business officers debating how best to create that wiggle room, one participant suggested "gradually increasing the student [to] faculty ratio as a child progresses from kindergarten to high school." Another suggested a mix of class sizes, "some that were small, and others that were large, depending on the subject matter being taught."[8]

Today, much of private school branding happens online. Visit any elite school's website and you will be met instantly with high-definition pictures of historic-looking buildings and modernist glass science labs, as well as by polished images of students—wearing suits and ties, engaged in creative pursuits, or showing off their athletic prowess on the tennis court or the lacrosse field. Click over to the "Fast Facts" page for a given school, and the data are likely to include the number of faculty with advanced degrees, as well as their alma maters. At prestigious Deerfield Academy in Massachusetts, for instance, the website notes that 70 percent of faculty have advanced degrees. Never mind the fact that full professional licensure for public school educators in the state requires a graduate degree, or that half of American teachers possess one. Referencing teachers' educational backgrounds is part of brand-building.[9]

Listing the top colleges attended by graduates of these elite private schools is another essential component of their brand-building. Deerfield, for instance, lists on its website the "most attended colleges" of graduates: Yale, Georgetown, Dartmouth, the University of Virginia, and Harvard. The implication is that Deerfield deserves the credit for this, not the student and his or her inherited privileges. A Deerfield rival, St. Paul's, lists many of the same schools, with the addition of Brown, Cornell, Penn, Columbia, and Princeton—in other words, the rest of the Ivy League. Such messaging conveys to parents that, in a time of rising economic anxiety, matriculating at one of these schools promises a path to a secure and prosperous future. As one private school official noted, elite institutions "have to sell to the heart, not to the head."[10]

Borrowing Prestige

In today's education marketing landscape, charter schools—especially large charter networks that operate dozens or even hundreds of schools—now far outpace private schools, both in the sophistication of their advertising efforts and in the sheer amount of resources they devote to school marketing.[11] And yet there is continuity between the techniques pioneered by elite private schools and the ways that charter schools build and sell their brands today. With no rules about what they can and can't say, charter schools have borrowed the prestige of elite private schools. And they are beating private schools at their own game.

In a lengthy interview on a popular New York City talk radio program in 2015, Eva Moskowitz, the CEO of Success Academy, the city's largest charter network, bragged to host Brian Lehrer about the number of applications that her schools receive.[12] The volume of applicants was proof of sky-high demand, she continued, making the case that the network, which today has as many students as the Empire State's sixth-largest school district, needed to continue to expand aggressively. What Moskowitz never mentioned was the expansive—and expensive—marketing that goes into producing that demand. After labor, which chews up the lion's share of most school budgets, marketing is Success Academy's biggest cost. In fact, one study found that the network was spending more than $1,000 per student on marketing alone.[13]

With its corporate-style branding and marketing, Success Academy embodies the new style of selling school. Prospective parents receive between ten and twenty direct mailers a year, some of which arrive with the school's application attached. A gear store sells laptop cases, headphones, even baby onesies, all featuring the network's distinctive "SA" logo. Success Academy has its own You-Tube channel, Twitter, and Instagram accounts, while digital ads run constantly across the internet, promoting the charter network to prospective parents, teachers, even students. Across all of these platforms, Success Academy's brand identity never wavers.

But for all of its digital-era prowess, Success Academy's sales operation is also rooted in an old approach to school marketing—that pioneered by private schools. Consider the use of the word "academy," for example. Along with its close cousin "prep," the academy name is ubiquitous in the charter school world. There is the Preparatory Charter School, or "Prep Charter," as it is known in Philadelphia; University Prep Charter in the Bronx; Veritas Preparatory Charter School in Springfield, Massachusetts, which seems to nod to the Latin mottos of Harvard and Yale; Ivy Prep Academy in Atlanta; and Ivy Academia Charter School in Los Angeles—just a small sampling. Regardless of what these schools actually provide—among urban charter schools, "academy" and "prep" are often shorthand for highly regimented schools that feature strict, "no excuses" discipline for their minority student bodies—the names connote an air of distinction and privilege.

Or take the use of school uniforms. Success Academy, like many charter schools—and a growing number of traditional public schools—requires that students wear an officially sanctioned uniform. In its official justification for mandating uniforms, Success nods to equality. "If children are dressed in [the] same or similar fashion, they aren't distracted by each other's clothing and judgments about what others are wearing. Uniforms are an equalizer," says Anne Michaud, a spokesperson for the charter network.[14] But uniforms are also a form of "prestige borrowing." Success

Academy's ensembles, which include preppy sweaters, blazers and button-down shirts for boys, jumpers and plaid skirts for girls, are virtually indistinguishable from the uniforms worn by students attending New York City's elite private schools, like St. Mark's, whose students must conform to a dress code described as "neat, clean and modest (business casual)."[15] While there is little research evidence that such uniforms make a difference in student performance, they send a strong visual signal of prestige to potential school consumers and investors.

"I'm the class of 2032," pronounces one youngster. "I'm the class of 2030," chimes another. The ad, broadcast on Success Academy's YouTube channel, features the network's youngest enrollees proclaiming the year they will be graduating from college. Viewers likely had no idea that at the time the ad was made, Success had yet to send a single student to college, or that the network's very first graduating class, in 2018, consisted of just sixteen students, down from the seventy-three that started as ninth graders.[16] Outsized claims regarding college-going rates are common throughout the charter school marketing world. The "fine print," meanwhile—that three out of four charter school graduates, on average, leave college without a degree—never appears.[17]

Another page from the private school playbook has to do with exclusivity. Private schools have long understood that turning students away is the best way to gild their brands. Consequently, elite schools work hard to recruit many more students than they can accept. *Look how many people can't get in*, is the message sent. And though charters can't engage in selective admissions—they must, instead, select students through a lottery if available slots are insufficient—they can certainly brag about the length of the waitlists. In fact the National Alliance for Public Charter Schools, in documents that have since been removed from its website, advised its members to "publicize their lotteries to demonstrate the strong popularity of charter schools."[18] When Eva Moskowitz brags about the huge number of applicants to Success Academy relative to available spots, she is simply following a marketing playbook.

In a recent book titled *Selling School: The Marketing of Public Education*, scholars Sarah Butler Jessen and Catherine DiMartino argue that by devoting substantial resources to marketing, charter management organizations convey to the public not just that there is demand for their product, but that they are offering a high-quality good. In the public mind, the demand that results from aggressive marketing is conflated with the quality of whatever is being sold. "That's how we perceive advertising campaigns, and we argue that the same is true for schools," says Jessen. "Investing in marketing and creating demand translates into perceptions of quality."[19]

Market Survival

The justification for "edvertising" is that so-called schools of choice cannot rely on place-based student enrollment like traditional public schools do. They must appeal to parents directly, and how else to do that other than through marketing? As a report from the National Charter Schools Institute instructs charter operators, "to be successful, your charter school will likely have to market itself."[20] Indeed, true school choice requires marketing, argues Maurice Flurie, the CEO of Commonwealth Charter Academy, one of the largest cyber schools in Pennsylvania: "Our schools are different. And I think the better we are with our marketing and our advertising, it starts to draw out those differences so a parent can make an informed choice on, 'What's the best one for me?'"[21]

But with more than 3 million students now attending charter

schools, totaling 6 percent of the nation's K-12 student population, school marketing has exploded, spawning a veritable industry of school sales experts, brand builders, and messaging mavens. Imagine, then, what it will be like in a deregulated marketplace governed only by the laws of supply and demand.

When the Arizona Academies of Math and Science posted an online job ad for a digital marketing specialist, the charter school network was explicit about what it was after. The "full-stack digital marketer" would excel at creating "heart-grabbing ads" aimed at helping the schools reach their ambitious goal of serving twenty thousand low-income students within five years. "We want a unicorn someone who is obsessed with storytelling and copy writing, paid media advertising, branding, A/B testing, web design, funnel building, and influencer marketing," the ad declared. The new hire would join a marketing team with a $400,000–$800,000 budget to spend on digital and traditional advertising, supporting the launch of "new campuses in neighborhoods that have never heard of us."[22]

A growing group of providers is working to meet, as well as to generate, demand for such services. Kreative Webworks, for instance, offers a "Charter School Marketing" package "to help schools get more visibility in their authorized areas to enroll more students." As the agency put it: "We've done this a lot. We know what parents search on, and what they respond to." Among the company's offerings: "the type of quality content that search engines love."[23]

High-profile charter management organizations (CMOs) like Success Academy and KIPP have already developed these services in-house. Both devote extensive resources to building and maintaining their brands, projecting consistent imagery and narratives to an audience that includes not just prospective parents and teachers but also funders. KIPP, whose network of charters now includes 224 schools and more than one hundred thousand students, even maintains a "Brand Guidelines" video on its website. The video explains to members of the extended KIPP community why it's so important for the network to maintain a strong brand, from using appropriate language and messaging down to featuring the right colors and fonts in brochures. The narrator compares KIPP to Target, asking viewers to imagine if the company looked and sounded different in every city. The KIPP website, T-shirts, written materials, stickers, the official Twitter account—even the network's phone greeting— are all "touch points," explains the narrator, using a term from the business world that refers to points of contact between buyers and sellers. "Every conversation that you have with someone about where you work is a touch point for KIPP's brand."[24]

Of course, corporate-style marketing requires a corporate-style budget. While KIPP and other CMOs maintain slick websites that feature professionally shot photographs and videos, the websites of autonomous charter schools and traditional public schools, by contrast, often have a DIY feel.[25] And schools without designated marketing personnel are unlikely to be able to follow the lead of CMOs as they extend their brands across YouTube, Instagram, and Twitter. Eventually, however, such investments may be necessary for survival.

Then there are the virtual charter schools, which may be the most aggressive advertisers of all. K12 Inc., the biggest player in the online schooling business, also dominates the selling of virtual schools, routinely airing TV ads during shows whose audiences tilt toward mothers of school-age children. One ad, titled "Uniquely Brilliant," features young students engaged in various self-directed learning projects, including robotics, under the watchful eye of a parent. In dozens of TV and online ads with titles like "Public

School at Home" and "Learning Happens Everywhere," K12 is presented as a superior alternative to traditional public schools.

Of course, K12's messaging—about custom-tailored education plans delivered by qualified instructors—has little to do with the reality of its online schools. Students graduate at a rate less than half that of traditional public schools. But no fine print needs to appear in the company's ads: edvertisers can make whatever claims they want.

Market Cannibalization

Carpe Diem Meridian charter school in Indianapolis had a problem. Student "count" day, the date on which the state measures school attendance in order to determine the amount of funding schools will receive, was looming, and Carpe Diem needed to recruit new students quickly. The solution: an ambitious marketing plan that involved blanketing the airwaves, targeting daycare centers and other sites where parents congregate, and hosting open houses to show off the school's tech-centric learning model. Then there were the gift cards. Anyone referring a student who enrolled at the school would receive a $100 gift card for use at a local grocery store. "People are more excited to do something where they get something out of it," the school's principal told a local education news site.[26]

Carpe Diem's marketing blitz ultimately fell short. Unable to attract enough students to remain viable, the school closed its doors in 2017, bringing a halt to the expansionary plans of a network that spread from Arizona to Indiana, Ohio, and Texas. Even grocery store gift cards, it turned out, weren't enough to win parents over to classrooms that bear a distinct resemblance to corporate call centers. The same computer-based model that "personalized" instruction for students was also intended to dramatically lower labor costs through class sizes of sixty or higher.[27]

Viewed through the eyes of a free-market advocate, the Carpe Diem story might well seem like a success: a school competing for "customers" and pulling out all the stops to win them. But education isn't just another consumer good, akin to sneakers or an iPhone, and one key way they differ is that the market for education is fixed. While Apple built a mass market for its products by convincing consumers to want something they had never had before, the customer base for education is limited by geography and the population of school-age children. In a competitive marketplace of schools, like Indiana's, that means edvertising is almost always aimed at convincing parents to leave one school for another, taking state education dollars with them.

This problem is particularly acute in urban areas where charter schools have proliferated even as the student population dwindles. In Detroit, for example, lax regulation and oversight have made it easy for operators to open new schools even amid a decline in the city's population. The result is a school-vs-school battle for potential recruits in which marketing plays an outsized role. At a hearing before the U.S. House Committee on Education and the Workforce, Detroit father Jonathan Clark described the process of choosing schools for his seven children as one filled with empty promises: "of after-school programs, dual enrollment, advanced math and reading, and state-of-the-art technology—but with no mechanism to ensure that we are given what we have been promised."[28] Research backs up Clark's claim. As one study of Detroit found, the mission statements of its schools were generally the same, regardless of the specific sales pitch being made.[29]

While Detroit owns the dubious honor of being the nation's

fastest-shrinking metropolis, it's not the only city faced with a diminishing student population. In Los Angeles, a dramatic drop in immigration, combined with a declining birth rate, means there are fewer school-age children in the city today. L.A. is already home to nearly three hundred charter schools enrolling roughly 140,000 students—the single largest concentration of charters in the United States.

Considering that there are no limits on the number of charters that can open, and considerable philanthropic heft and resources behind opening more, the competition for students will only heat up. Some of those charters may be excellent schools. But in a dog-eat-dog environment, that hardly matters. Rather than a rising tide lifting all boats, we're likely to see more marketing, more poaching, and more incentive for schools to do whatever it takes to hit their enrollment numbers.

Even school districts that have seen steady growth over the past decade are now looking at the demographic equivalent of a cliff's edge. In Denver, where student numbers have grown year after year, enrollment is projected to fall sharply as birth rates drop and the city's population changes. According to a Denver Public Schools enrollment report, 80 percent of the city's new residents since 2009 have been households without children.[30] This shift in Denver's demographics, and the shrinking of its student population, is occurring as the city restructures its education system along market lines, closing or replacing fifty traditional public schools while opening more than seventy charters.[31] A drop in the number of students means that schools must compete even harder for "customers," even if it means redirecting resources to marketing in a time of budget cuts and teacher layoffs.

According to one former Denver teacher, the business term

"market cannibalization" best describes this school-versus-school competition, fought via billboards, mailers, and ad campaigns. "That's what happens when you see a reduction in sales volume, sales revenue, or market share of one product as a result of the introduction of a new product by the same producer. In other words, you have too many options offering the same thing in too close of proximity, and it's detrimental to the core of the organization."[32] Her school, which served some of the highest-needs students in the city, was rationing paper and eliminating electives, even as it invested in yard signs aimed at attracting potential enrollees.

Zero-Sum Game

For Pennsylvania's Allentown School District, the start of a new school year also meant the launch of a new advertising campaign. In 2018, as it had done before, the school district in this former steel manufacturing hub spent $15,000 on radio ads, billboards, and promotional videos. But while $15,000 may seem like a drop in the bucket for a district with an annual budget of more than $300 million, that was money ultimately not spent on educational programs. District leaders bemoaned the fact that Allentown was forced to invest in marketing, even as the high school planetarium remained shuttered because the funds couldn't be found to reopen it, let alone revamp it into a facility aimed at inspiring future scientists. And yet as Superintendent Thomas Parker saw it, the district had no choice. As he told the local newspaper, "we know there are competitors in the marketplace and either we make sure we compete and keep our students in [the Allentown School District], or we'll be the victims of not doing so."[33]

Meanwhile, the schools in nearby Bethlehem were unveiling a new logo, part of a $75,000 marketing campaign aimed at keeping up with the private schools and charters that promote their product via brochures and billboards.[34] And many more schools now face competitive pressure from Pennsylvania's deep-pocketed virtual schools. According to a 2017 investigative report by the news organization PublicSource, twelve of the state's fourteen cyber schools spent a combined $21 million over a three-year period.[35] In addition to traditional marketing staples, like direct mail and bus ads, the online schools used an array of sophisticated digital tools, including paid internet searches and targeted Facebook ads that show up in the feeds of parents.

Most families, of course, aren't particularly interested in sending their children to virtual schools. But this relatively nascent segment of the public education ecosystem is already having an influence. In Pennsylvania, brick-and-mortar charter operators are devoting significant sums to advertising relative to the spending of the state's public school districts. In Allegheny County, for example, where the district now spends $15,000 per year to market its schools, a competing charter network, Propel Schools, spent $175,000 over a three-year period, appealing to parents via direct mail, paid advertising, and staffed shopping mall kiosks. Whether the source is state aid or local property tax revenue, taxpayer dollars are funding the advertising arms race. And as markets open up, traditional public schools will increasingly play this game.

Pennsylvania is not alone. In recent years, public school districts in Austin, Columbus, Denver, St. Louis, New York, and Los Angeles have all reported using public funds for advertising purposes. This is true even as they grapple with budget woes from declining enrollment and demographic shifts.

Future Forecast

As public education is redefined—from a public good to a matter of private choice—school marketing will further explode. And while widespread edvertising is a relatively recent phenomenon, indications of what the future holds are already apparent.

The Future Will Be Ad-Filled

New Orleans, with its nearly all-charter school system, offers a test case for how free-market principles in education beget school marketing. After Hurricane Katrina in 2014, the city became a laboratory for market-based education reform, and neighborhood schools no longer exist there as they do in most of the country. Instead, parents are required to choose a school, forcing the city's various charter schools to compete with each other for "customers." And that means marketing. On billboards, bus stop signs, even radio ads, the Big Easy's charter schools trumpet the language of "achievement," "excellence," and "success," while omitting details about school performance that often contradict the ads' upbeat claims. One recent study found that school marketing in the city is "skewed and inefficient"—the hallmark of a largely privatized system in which schools view one another as competitors.[36]

The competing claims, brands, and slogans in urban communities—where the logic of the education marketplace is most developed—have spawned a mini-industry, as parents turn to professional consultants to help them sort through the noise. While hiring personal advisors is nothing new among affluent parents trying to get their kids into elite private schools, school choice coaches are now popping up in cities where competition has produced confusion amid the cacophony.[37]

The Future Will Be Emotionally Manipulative

Research into the psychology of advertising has found that success-ful ad campaigns are far more likely to appeal to emotion than to reason. School marketing is no different. In one advertising tutorial for charter schools, a marketing firm coaches a school on how to amp up its messaging so it achieves maximum possible emotional impact: "The Only Thing We Don't Respect? Status Quo. Anna Lopez couldn't read last year. This year, she scored in the top 5% of the country. We're not betting Anna will change the world, we're making sure of it."[38]

But emotion need not only be inspirational. Fear can also be a powerful sales pitch to parents. In addition to ads that play on a general unease about the future, some schools highlight more direct threats to students. A Pennsylvania charter school, for instance, sent out promotional materials painting students at the local high school as drug users. The postcard refers to the arrest of a student and asks, "Why worry about this type of student at school? Come visit Arts Academy Charter School. Now enrolling grades 6–12."[39]

The Future Will Be Micro-Targeted

The spread of edvertising coincides with a dramatic evolution with-in marketing, namely the ability of marketers to precisely target potential consumers. Facebook knows where its users live, whether they are parents of school-age children and where those children attend school, and what school-related products parents are inter-ested in. All of this means that school sellers can aim messaging at highly specific demographics. Just as companies have used Face-book's ad parameters to target some groups and avoid others— ads for rental housing, for example, that aren't shown to African

Americans or mothers of high school students—schools could potentially do the same. Pinpointing audiences for recruitment will further stratify and segregate students. As education is increasingly "unbundled" into an assortment of products and services, highly personalized ads will inevitably follow.

The Future Will Have Deep Pockets

The ad that began airing in San Antonio at the end of the summer in 2018 was short and to the point. In English and Spanish, it made the case for change in the city's school system. San Antonio, intoned the narrator, needed more new, innovative schools that allowed teachers to cut through red tape and put kids ahead of the bureaucracy. The ad was part of an ambitious campaign called Keep Learning San Antonio, aimed at expanding charter schools in the city and restructuring the school district along free-market lines. By marketing standards, it was a smashing success. When the campaign concluded, the video had been viewed more than 4.8 million times—its message further amplified through local news reports.[40]

The ad was attributed to a Texas nonprofit called Families Empowered—a group that advocates for school choice, including in the form of taxpayer-funded school vouchers. But behind the glossy, professionally shot imagery were the deep pockets of the Walton family, heirs to the Walmart fortune, whose passion for the cause of school choice is rivaled perhaps only by the DeVos clan. The Walton name never appears in the ad, nor does it have to; unless they are explicitly political, edvertisements are not required to disclose who is paying for them.

As wealthy donors join the cause—of liberating school districts from red tape, teachers from unions, and education itself from brick-and-mortar schools—campaigns like Keep Learning San Antonio will proliferate.

The Future Will Tell You What You Want

When asked about the degree to which market research influenced the development of the iPad, Steve Jobs famously replied: "None. It's not the consumer's job to know what they want." In other words, Apple had set out not to respond to consumer preferences, but to shape what they wanted. The future of advertising, writes Niraj Dawar in the *Harvard Business Review*, will entail companies doing just that: "defining what customers are looking for and shaping their 'criteria for purchase.'"[41]

What does this mean for education marketing? The old approach to selling school, in which marketers set out to lure parents from one school to another, will soon become passé. Instead, edvertising 2.0 will be far more focused on redefining school, and reshaping parents' "purchasing criteria" in the process.

11

Teaching Gigs

"If you can't embrace a little wackiness at work, Fusion might not be for you," proclaims a since-removed page on the website for Fusion Academy, a fast-growing chain of for-profit private schools. The company boasts of its personalized approach, in which teachers work with individual students rather than teaching traditional classes. But what Fusion bills as a "revolutionary way to school" has also meant restructuring the teaching profession. Teachers at the company's sixty campuses earn around $30 an hour and are paid for just five minutes of prep time per week. Lesson planning, grading, and corresponding with parents is all uncompensated.[1] Health benefits are meager, retirement nonexistent, and turnover is sky high. Teaching, meet the gig economy.

For much of the twentieth century, teachers celebrated major gains in pay and status. But those steady improvements have largely ground to a halt during the past several decades. Adjusting for inflation, teacher pay stalled out in the late 1980s and began declining in 2009, even as wages for the average American worker continued to rise.[2] In 1990, the per capita income of American workers was $25,633. Just over a quarter century later, average pay had risen to $33,205.[3] Worker pay overall increased by roughly 30 percent; but for teachers, salaries were slipping.

Meanwhile, teacher job satisfaction has been on the decline as well. In 2013, the last year that MetLife conducted its *Survey of the American Teacher*, only 39 percent of teachers described themselves as very satisfied with their jobs, the lowest point in the poll's quarter-century history.[4] More recent studies have turned up still more ominous indicators, including that teachers are increasingly expressing their discontent by voting with their feet. According to the Department of Labor, teachers are quitting their profession at the highest rate since the government began collecting data.[5]

The middle-class status of teachers has been steadily eroding. While the teacher walkouts that began in the spring of 2018 have helped to shift public opinion in favor of raising teacher salaries, not everyone thinks that low pay and fewer benefits for teachers are a problem. For those seeking to restructure and de-professionalize teaching, the gig economy is a model. Think Uber for education. Think Fusion.

No Respect

The fight by teachers to be recognized as professionals dates back generations. In the earliest public schools, no standard for a qualified teacher existed, and would-be educators were frequently selected on minimal criteria, like their perceived ability to maintain order in the classroom. This interview from the mid-nineteenth century is a typical exchange:

Chairman: How old are you?

Candidate: I was eighteen years old the 27th day of last May.

Chairman: Where did you last attend school?

Candidate: At the Academy of S.

Chairman: Do you think you can make our big young-
sters mind?

Candidate: Yes, I think I can.

Chairman: Well, I am satisfied. I guess you will do for our
school.[6]

The candidate's lack of training was also typical. Teachers in the early days of public schooling generally possessed only marginally more formal education than their students, and frequently taught for just a few years—often during the interim between high school graduation and marriage. And with no clearly outlined profession-al skill set, teaching positions were often staffed through patron-age. As scholar and educator Ted Sizer once quipped, "The absence of laws around licensure and hiring led to a system in which some mayor's half-drunk illiterate uncle was hired to teach twelfth-grade English."[7]

The system was bad for students. But it was bad for teachers as well. Many teachers complained of being unprepared for the work, lacking adequate pay and respect, and being vulnerable to political intimidation vis-à-vis the content of their instruction.[8] Essentially working as what today we would call independent contractors, teachers could be hired or fired at will. Women, for instance, were regularly fired after they married or became pregnant.[9]

Across the end of the nineteenth century and beginning of the twentieth, policy makers worked to create professional training and licensure standards. Their aim was to improve the knowledge and skills of teachers by raising barriers to entry into the profession. Teachers, for their part, were supportive, because increasing professionalization made it easier to bargain for higher pay and better working conditions. A 1921 article lamenting the "exodus of teachers" reported that the salaries of stenographers, typewriters, and clerks were 50 percent to 100 percent larger than those of classroom educators.[10] By the end of the Great Depression, teachers were earning middle-class salaries.[11]

Yet some aspects of teaching would always complicate the degree to which the work would be viewed with esteem. Fields like law and medicine, for instance, display most of the characteristics associated with professions. Lawyers and doctors receive specialized training and master a complex body of knowledge. They control their own activity and organize their own work. They command significant pay and have established a culture of power and status.[12]

Teachers, by contrast, face real limits. Teaching is predominantly done by women, who have long held secondary status in American society.[13] Professions generally have higher status if they work with powerful clients, yet teachers work primarily with children. And unlike professions that can improve their standing by raising barriers to entry, teaching positions are created by state and local government in fulfillment of a guarantee to free and public education.

Then there is the perspective derived from what sociologist Dan Lortie has called the "apprenticeship of observation." Almost all Americans, by virtue of having attended school, have observed teaching for over a decade, leading to a widespread sense that "anyone can teach." In Lortie's words: "What child cannot, after all, do a reasonably accurate portrayal of a classroom teacher's actions?"[14] As a result of this seemingly everyday quality to teaching, the work is regularly viewed as important but easy—never mind what teachers do to prepare for class, or what is going on outside students' direct observation.

Unlike doctors, lawyers, or investment bankers, who have mastered esoteric subject matter that most Americans aren't familiar with, teachers generally possess ordinary content knowledge. And unlike other professionals, teachers actually transfer their knowledge to their clients. Thus, the things that teachers teach are, almost by definition, the things that every adult should know. In short, successful teachers render themselves unnecessary, and that has major consequences for their prestige.

The Way of the Dodo

Teacher professionalism, then, has been long-fought and hard-won. But many of their achievements look expensive and unnecessary to cost-cutters. Specialized training, for example, is an additional expense that raises the cost of public education. After all, when teachers invest in their professional education and acquire advanced degrees, they expect more pay. Yet teacher education can seem difficult to justify in terms of return on taxpayer investment. Thus, for those concerned about return on investment, teacher education has always seemed like a frill at best. An essay in the *Chronicle of Higher Education* summed up the critique: "A four- or even five-year education degree costs the same as other degrees, yet our field has failed to show that teachers who have these degrees are any more effective in the classroom than those licensed through alternative programs, or (in some cases) those who enter teaching with minimal preparation."[15]

As detailed in previous chapters, teacher licensure is a target of the crusade against regulation because it limits entry into the profession. Of course, doctors and lawyers are licensed too. In fact, they control licensure themselves—through the American Medical Association and the American Bar Association. But doctors and lawyers are generally more accepted as professionals than teachers are. Teachers, by contrast, face the popular opinion that anyone can teach. And if that is the case, then licensure only serves to increase costs. "Competition itself may be the most effective alternative to licensure," argued the authors of a report from the Koch-funded Mercatus Center. One affordable alternative to licensure, they noted, is "publicly posted customer feedback such as Yelp and Google reviews."[16]

Finally, measures that target unions make it harder for teachers to band together to demand higher pay and limit the burdens that can be placed on them. Following the lead of Wisconsin, states with Republican-dominated legislatures have enacted a raft of policies aimed at weakening teachers' unions. At the federal level, the Supreme Court's 2018 *Janus* decision that struck down the practice of collecting so-called agency fees may not have had the immediate cataclysmic impact on union membership that backers had hoped, but it is diminishing the ranks of union members.[17] And a flurry of follow-on lawsuits now working their way through the courts will try to force the unions to pay back these now-illegal fees to aggrieved former members. As teacher protests from West Virginia to Arizona made clear, organized rebellions do not require strong teachers' unions, which is why the next wave of anti-teacher legislation is aimed at punishing them for bringing "politics" into the classroom, including advocating for more school funding.[18]

Already, teaching is beginning to evolve, at least at the margins, as a new kind of job. At virtual schools, for example, teachers are responsible for vastly more students than could be crowded into a brick-and-mortar classroom, and they earn considerably less than their place-based counterparts. In some cases, if they work as "tutors" doing "on demand work," they earn as little as $20 an hour.

The endgame here is professional extinction. Teachers achieved white-collar status in the twentieth century and clung tenuously to it at the dawn of the twenty-first. Nor will teachers just drop a rung or two—to the status, say, of paraprofessionals. Instead, they will fall all the way out of the world of professionalism and into the gig economy. Say hello to your new TaskRabbits.

Lower Ed

No crystal ball is required to catch a glimpse of this future. Just head to a typical college or university campus.

Since the mid-1970s, the ranks of higher education have been thinned of full-time tenured and tenure-track professors. According to the American Association of University Professors (AAUP), over the past four decades the ranks of tenured faculty have declined by 26 percent, while the number of tenure-track faculty has dropped by half. Meanwhile, the number of part-time faculty has risen by 70 percent.[19] That means that when professors retire, they are increasingly likely to be replaced by someone in a teaching gig.

Whereas a majority of faculty members were once tenured or on a tenure-track, they are now vastly outnumbered by those with smaller salaries and less employment security. On campuses today, roughly three-quarters of positions are non-tenure-track. Among that sizable majority, the largest contingent is part-time faculty, who make up 40 percent of the labor force in higher education.[20]

Though second-class citizens on campus, full-time non-tenure-track faculty often have *some* measure of employment security— working on three-year contracts, for instance. While many, if not most, would prefer tenure-track jobs, their positions typically come with benefits.

Part-time faculty, on the other hand, are the true gig workers of higher education. Paid by the course, they rarely get benefits like health insurance and retirement plans. While college and university administrators have argued that such part-time labor is a commonsense way of addressing shifts in enrollment and demand for course offerings, it is also undeniably a cost-cutting strategy. A 2014 article in *University Business* magazine summed up the case in blunt terms: "Institutions of all types benefit from the fact that adjuncts—provided they don't become eligible for health benefits by working more than 30 hours a week—can be employed for a fraction of the investment needed for full-time faculty. In fact, many schools now include a large contingent of part-time faculty as routine business practice."[21]

Part-time adjunct faculty routinely shuttle themselves across multiple campuses each week, sharing offices with other part-timers if they're lucky enough to have access to one. Some teach as many as six classes each semester—two or three times what tenure-line faculty are required to teach.[22] The result is a high level of stress and burnout. And though some enjoy the increased flexibility, many report feeling vulnerable and expendable. As a blogger on the website *Inside Higher Ed* wrote: "Merely by taking the position as a contingent faculty, you are relegating yourself to: lower pay, lower prestige and a disposable status."[23]

According to the AAUP, the average salary for assistant professors—those just beginning their tenure-track careers—is $70,000. Full professors across all kinds of colleges and universities make an average of $120,000, while those at research universities make an average of $140,000 per year. Part-time faculty, by contrast, earn just a fraction of that, even when they are working the equivalent of full-time. The *Chronicle of Higher Education*, which collects salary data from adjuncts and the institutions that employ them, has found that most adjunct faculty earn between $3,000 and $4,000 per course.[24]

Those who can piece together a full-time teaching load of four classes each semester, then, would earn anywhere from $24,000 to $32,000 per year. Of course, fewer courses means getting by on even less. How much less? Economists at UC Berkeley's Labor Center found that one-quarter of part-time faculty are on public assistance.[25] Debra Leigh Scott, an adjunct professor in Temple University's Intellectual-Heritage program, put it in the starkest possible terms: "Suicide is my retirement plan." The statement raised eyebrows and generated plenty of handwringing. But Scott's career, cobbled together from an endless series of courses for little pay, is an all-too-typical adjunct trajectory.[26]

Of course, it isn't just the contingent faculty themselves who pay the price of this economic exploitation. Students are also impacted. As investments in public higher education have declined, the justification for relying on exploited adjuncts has only grown. Meanwhile, the costs of attending school have been shifted away from states and onto the students, who can expect to amass an average of $30,000 in student loans—even as they are being taught in huge classes by "gig" instructors.

As John Warner notes, while the "luxury" of full-time faculty is still afforded to the relatively small number of students who attend elite universities and select liberal arts colleges, the vast majority of undergraduate students will be taught by at least some instructors who are working without a safety net.[27] The cost of the relentless drive to cut costs, he notes, falls hardest on the students who are likely to need the most help—those attending non-selective four-year colleges and cash-strapped community colleges.

A Race to the Bottom

"Is this increasingly popular teaching job the Uber for teachers?" asked *eSchool News* in a recent story. For the online news site, which bills itself as a marketing solutions company serving the education technology industry, the answer was an emphatic "Yes." Just as apps like Uber, Lyft, and TaskRabbit have enabled users to sell their skills on their own schedules, proclaimed the authors, "this model has now come to the American education market."[28]

The writers went on to sing the praises of one of the fastest-growing segments of the gig education market: teaching English to students in China via videoconferencing. Services like 51Talk and VIPKid have exploded in popularity in recent years as more Chinese students seek to gain fluency in English. VIPKid, based in Beijing, was founded in 2013 and is currently valued at more than $3 billion. More than five hundred thousand Chinese students have signed on, as have some sixty thousand teachers from the United States and Canada.[29]

"Teach Chinese children from the comfort of your own home," is the sales pitch on VIPKid's website. Would-be tutors are required to provide the necessary technology and a quiet space from which to deliver their virtual services to students in China. The company provides Common Core–aligned lesson plans, communicates with parents, and even does the grading. Teachers enjoy "flexibility"—the time difference means that "school" typically begins around 5 a.m. for the mostly American workforce—and hourly wages start at $14 and top off at $22.

For a growing number of American teachers, signing on with VIPKid or a competitor company is likely a "side hustle": a way to supplement income at a time when rising costs, especially in urban areas, are eating into teacher pay. But the model of delivering pre-packaged content via videoconferencing also has the potential to upend the teaching profession more broadly. Virtual schools at least tend to pay their teachers a salary. The on-demand model, on the other hand, means that "providers" are paid only for the time they are actually teaching.

At Outschool, which bills itself as a marketplace for live online classes taught via video chat, teachers set the price per learner, starting with as little as $5 per course hour and averaging around $18 per course hour. CEO Amir Nathoo extolled the model's affordability in a recent interview titled "Can Outschool Bring the Gig Economy to K-12?" Free from the cost of facilities or travel, said Nathoo, Outschool can offer violin lessons for "$10 per hour compared to the typical $50 per hour cost of local classes."[30]

Of course, that cheap hourly rate also reflects another key difference between traditional K-12 teachers and their gig counterparts. The latter are not compensated as salaried employees, but rather as independent contractors who pay their own taxes and receive no benefits. And these online teachers aren't union members. Indeed, aside from when they happen to interact on online message boards, theirs is an existence without any colleagues at all.

While such TaskRabbit–style teaching and tutoring represents a particularly bleak vision for where the teaching profession is headed, the gig-work model of teaching is rapidly taking hold. As schools are increasingly subject to market logic, they are incentivized to hire teachers as cheaply as possible.

At Fusion Academy, for example, the key to profitability isn't the student tuition of $40,000–$60,000 a year, it's the use of hourly contracting as a model for paying teachers. Manhattan-based staff who are able to string together enough teaching time to be considered full-time earn less than $30,000 per year—roughly half of the starting salary for public school teachers in New York City. While that model may not be sustainable for teachers, who reported being encouraged by administrators to go on unemployment during the summer months, the company, which recently secured the backing of the private equity firm Leeds Equity Partners, has bold plans to open "more and more schools across the country."[31] Interestingly, the CEO of Fusion's management company got his start running National Heritage Academies, a chain of for-profit charter schools based in Michigan that enjoys close ties to the DeVos family.

Making teaching an on-demand job, akin to driving for Uber or Lyft, will only accelerate the redefinition of teaching already under way. Projects like Teach For America, now three decades old, have long presented teaching as short-term work. And several charter school chains proudly churn through young teachers who soon leave the profession. At Texas charter network YES Prep, for instance, teachers have an average of two and a half years of experience, compared with the fourteen years acquired by the average public school teacher.[32]

Do we really need teachers to view teaching as a lifelong calling? That was the question posed by charter school proponent Neerav Kingsland in 2018. Kingsland, who helped lay the groundwork for the all-charter system now in place in New Orleans, was making the case that students in the Big Easy benefit from having younger teachers who work long hours and leave the profession sooner than their peers in traditional public schools. "This model is delivering better results for children than the old talent model," writes Kingsland, whose group, The City Fund, seeks to bring a New Orleans–like "portfolio model" for schools to cities across the country.[33]

The problem with the argument that students benefit from teachers with less training or less experience is that it leads logically to the further de-professionalization of teaching. Some novices are likely exceptional, and some veterans are likely ineffective, but de-professionalizing teaching will only promote a race to the bottom. Imagine millions of novice teachers with no experience, churning through the schools every few years before they move on to other careers.

In this market-based future, there is little use for teachers who plan to work a lifetime, or even full-time. Families will change schools much more frequently, moving seamlessly between public and private, virtual and brick-and-mortar. Or they may choose to eschew "school" entirely, opting instead to purchase custom education "options" via an edu-debit card. To accommodate such movement, school staffing patterns will require a radical re-envisioning. Many schools won't be able to afford the luxury of keeping teachers on for a full year, let alone for an entire career. Like the adjuncts who increasingly staff colleges and universities, schooling in the unbundled era will require temp teachers willing to work on demand.

The outlines of this future can already be seen in the slick pitches of education staffing companies. "Find a Flexible Job as a Shared Economy Teacher," is the enticement in the "Shared Economy Jobs" section of JobMonkey.com, where education now has its own "niche." "Countless subject matter experts, just like you, are now able to build their own teaching business, grow their clientele, and earn a living doing what they love." Well, maybe not quite a living. After a few paragraphs of "everyone wins" salesmanship, some actual numbers appear. Teachers, claims the site, will make around $15 an hour.[34]

The flexible future is a win-win for schools and teachers, claims Brie Reynolds, director of online content for FlexJobs. "For schools and organizations that run such [virtual education] programs, hiring freelance talent can help them find people with excellent qualifications who might otherwise not be able to commit to a full-time or in-person position, but who are more than able to work part-time as a freelancer and often times from home."[35]

If there are downsides to gig teaching, you won't find them on these sites.

But one need only survey the ranks of second-class college instructors, the original shared-economy teachers, to discern the human cost of detaching the content of a teaching job from the structure of a profession. The fact that K-12 teachers stand to lose a great deal from the shift to gig work is also obvious from the status of the existing pool of temporary teachers who work as substitutes in the schools. While educator salaries may have stalled out and even declined in some states, pay for subs is orders of magnitude lower. At the bottom of the barrel is the state of Alabama, which reimburses local districts $35 per day for substitutes. Alaska is at the high-end of the scale. A certified teacher there can earn up to $125 a day, equivalent to an annual salary of $22,000, or roughly a third of what the average teacher earns.[36]

Have-Nots

As most adjuncts can attest, simply stringing together the equivalent number of working hours to total "full-time" isn't the same as having a full-time job. Even if they can manage to be paid for all of their working hours, and not just their hours inside classrooms, gig teachers will ultimately earn less per hour. That's because they will be teaching in a new world—one in which *anyone* can teach. With no claim on professional skill, teacher bargaining power will decline steeply.

But lower pay isn't the only downside of the Uberization of teaching. Teachers can also look forward to the heightened stress

of job insecurity that is a hallmark of gig work. Roughly 18 percent of teachers *already* hold down a second job; they're five times
as likely as other full-time workers to have a side job in addition
to their main work.[37] And all of those jobs are already taking a
psychic toll. A 2011 study found that teachers who work an additional job experience burnout at higher rates and have lower levels
of commitment to teaching.[38]

In a private Facebook group related to the Oklahoma teachers'
strike in 2018, an algebra teacher posted this message: "I coach 2
Sports, Uber, Lyft, drive a school bus route, drive for 'Party Bus
OKC,' and umpire little league . . . all to help pay bills (and miss a
lot of time at home with my 2 small girls to do it). I know I'm not
the only one who has to do this. What are your 'side-gigs'? Go."
His post received 1,300 responses.[39]

We began this chapter with a look back at just how hard-fought
the quest for professional status in teaching has been. Despite real
gains in prestige and pay, teachers have never overcome the widespread belief that their job is one that anyone can do. The push to
make teaching a gig rather than a profession is fueled in part by
this perception. What kind of status will teachers command when
anyone can teach?

Of course, teachers aren't the only ones who are going to be
affected by the transformation of their profession. What will the
impact on student learning be? Will teachers have pedagogical skill
and content knowledge? Or will they simply be adults who have
passed a basic criminal background check?

Additionally, as teachers shift to having a part-time presence—if
they have a physical presence at all—and become more alienated
from their labor, their relationships with students will severely
erode. Research shows that relationships between teachers and
students matter tremendously for student engagement, valuing of

learning, social and emotional health, and academic outcomes. Those relationships are built on regular contact and high levels of trust. But if teachers are gig workers, contact will be sporadic and ad hoc.

Not all students will be taught by the equivalent of TaskRabbit educators. In affluent communities, schools oriented around a stable teaching force and anchored in relationships will continue to be the norm. The structural shift to teaching as an on-demand service will have the most profound impact upon low-income students and students from historically marginalized groups, the same kinds of students who have already been disproportionately affected by the push to replace long-term teaching with "short careers by choice." In *The Fissured Workplace*, David Weil argues that the growth in gig work is being driven chiefly by firms focusing on their core businesses and outsourcing the rest of the work to contractors. Yet teaching is the core business of schools. If it is outsourced, what's left?

12

Education, à la Carte

When one hundred high school students at Brooklyn's Secondary School for Journalism staged a walkout to protest the use of a personalized learning platform backed by Facebook CEO Mark Zuckerberg, they wanted to make sure that the tech billionaire understood exactly why they were demonstrating. In a letter addressed to Zuckerberg, the students outlined a litany of grievances against the Summit Learning Platform, now used by nearly four hundred schools across the country. Among the students' complaints: Summit collects a vast array of personal information from them without their consent, then discloses it to other corporations. "What gives you this right, and why weren't we asked about this before you and Summit invaded our privacy in this way?" the students asked.

While Summit's promotional materials tout the platform as a way for students to "unlock the power within themselves to live fulfilled and successful lives," the Brooklyn high schoolers described their new, mostly online education experience as boring, isolating, and just plain bad. But at the heart of their protest against the adoption of new technology was an argument about the purpose of school. As seniors Akila Robinson and Kelly Hernandez wrote, "The entire program eliminates much of the human interaction, teacher support, and discussion and debate with our peers that we need in order to improve our critical thinking."[1]

The Factory Model

Pulling apart a public institution long central to American communities can be a hard sell, especially when accompanied by talk of budget cuts, school closures, and teacher layoffs. In response to public opposition, free-market advocates have made a strategic shift. They have presented their work as a quest not to unmake public schools, but to "personalize" them.

A vaguely defined term applied to everything from project-based schooling to computer-based instruction, "personalized learning" has attracted broad support. Who, after all, would be against either component of that two-word phrase? For proponents of dismantling public education, though, "personalized learning" means something very particular—a vehicle for unbundling education.

The problem, they argue, is that public schools are designed to strip young people of their individuality. Just as factories once stamped out widgets, these critics insist, so our public schools function today—a one-size-fits-all production process. Their preferred solution is a radical reimagining of education. Specifically, they favor breaking "school" into its component parts and putting each up for sale in an education marketplace. But they propose to do so in the name of personalization—in other words, for the good of young people. As New Hampshire's top education official put it, the aim is to "break down the system so each kid is treated as a unique entity."[2] They're ready to junk both the practices and the principles of public schooling.

To make their case, hard-line conservatives have worked to convince the public that its schools are organized in a hopelessly outdated manner. As Betsy DeVos and others have argued, America's public schools are the public-sector equivalent of bloated, industrial-era private companies. In fact, they have even gone so far as to claim that schools were originally modeled after factories—designed specifically to produce industrial labor.

This is a fabricated history. But it is also more than that. In holding up factories as models of inefficiency, DeVos is reading from a well-worn script with origins in mid-twentieth-century political theory. In articulating a critique of large firms, influential theorists argued that such companies were often irrational and almost always inefficient. The worst offenders of all were the biggest—vertically integrated organizations that controlled every stage of a production process. These massive corporations inevitably became bureaucracies and, as such, were managed through internal politics. Rather than being governed by information and market signals, they were led astray by personal interests that were divorced from the profit motive.

Even if these companies weren't plagued by internal politics, these political theorists surmised, they were hopelessly inefficient because they failed to specialize. Worse, such companies didn't even *recognize* their failures. Because all aspects of the business were mixed together above a single bottom line, very large corporations, particularly those that were vertically integrated, were unable to differentiate the profitable components of their businesses from the money losers. In such cases, the money-making segments ended up subsidizing the less profitable ones—a form of intra-organizational corporate welfare. These companies would be far better off, theorists conjectured, if they focused on their "core" business and contracted out any other services.[3]

In the 1980s, management consultants like Peter Drucker began to make the case for what he called "decentralization into autonomous units."[4] And by 1990, the practice of splitting a company into two or more separate businesses had become a relatively common occurrence, with firms spinning off their divisions at a rate of about fifty a year. As such practices became standard in the business world, calls for decentralization in the public sector grew louder as well. "Management lessons have been proven again and again in the last several decades," wrote IBM chairman Louis Gerstner in his 1995 book *Reinventing Education: Entrepreneurship in America's Schools.* "The issue is not just making schools more businesslike; rather, it is to run schools like other successful organizations."[5]

But what *is* the core business of schools? Classroom instruction is one core component, obviously. But beyond administering all aspects of the curriculum, schools also commonly run operations in the areas of transportation, catering, security, youth athletics, childcare, maintenance, bookkeeping, and more. In other words, as vertically integrated operations, schools violate all the core tenets of modern management consulting. Sheltered from market forces and protected by political arrangements, they could be ineffective and inefficient and still survive.

As privatization advocates like the Hoover Institution's Terry Moe argued, the solution to this problem was to be found in what he called "the contractual paradigm."[6] If schools could be broken into their component parts, they would have to be governed through some mechanism other than democratic politics and bureaucratic structures. Instead, they would function as contractors for an array of services that would be provided by specialists. Virtually every aspect of the work of schools, even curricular instruction, could be farmed out to private companies via performance contracting.

These 1990s-era critics didn't simply invoke the factory comparison because they believed that the designed function of classrooms was to churn out students as though they were widgets. Equally offensive to them was the endurance of bureaucratic governance structures in public education. Andrew Carnegie cornered the steel market in the late nineteenth century by building a vertically integrated monopoly. He owned the mines from which iron ore and coal were extracted, the railroads that transported them, the blast furnaces that produced coke, and the natural gas that powered those furnaces. But Carnegie Steel had long since fallen out of fashion as a corporate model. According to modern management theory, outsourcing was the key to success. By this same logic, the process of schooling should have been broken into its component parts. Instead of being centrally administered, it should have been outsourced to specialty companies.

The "factory model" metaphor was trotted out so often that it became casually accepted as historical fact. "Our K-12 system largely still adheres to the century-old, industrial-age factory model of education," the then secretary of education Arne Duncan claimed in a 2010 speech.[7] Similarly, the XQ Super School Project, underwritten by the extensive fortune of Laurene Powell Jobs, repeated the claim that public schools were relics of the past. "The world has gone from the Model T to the Tesla, from the typewriter to the touchscreen, from the switchboard to the smartphone," proclaimed one XQ talking point. "But in [high school] hallways and classrooms, very little has changed."[8]

This invented past, in which public schools were modeled on industrial-era factories, has been repeatedly debunked. It is well documented that the first high schools were created for young people whose families hadn't already sent them off to work, and that those schools often rivaled colleges and universities in prestige. Eventually, public demand for greater access led to the creation of more high schools, many of which grew quite large in size—perhaps even as large as factories. But at no point did policy makers collectively determine a model of any sort, much less one based on American industry.

It's understandable why the public has been willing to accept this bogus history. Nested inside state and municipal bureaucracies, public schools can often seem like the polar opposite of "personalized." And students are compelled to spend twelve years moving through required subjects—math, English, history, science—more or less at the same pace, and without particular regard for their talents and interests. School can be a drag.

But these are not problems resulting from a "factory model." Instead, the factory-like aspects of schooling are chiefly a product of the enormous scale of public education. Schools are already charged with doing the impossible—carrying out the work of human improvement in a country riven by racial, economic, and geographic inequity. The scope of such work further magnifies the challenge, particularly when the equal treatment of students is prized. After all, the "sameness" that libertarian-oriented conservatives disdain also reflects an egalitarian commitment, however imperfectly realized, to the ideal of education for all.

Ultimately, the simplistic analogy to factories isn't just historically inaccurate. It also allows its deployers to skip over the real problems of poverty and segregation by offering a seemingly commonsense solution. Address surface-level similarities between schools and industrial-era workplaces, they suggest, and public education will be fixed.

But if that diagnosis is wrong? In such a case, the prescription—breaking schools into their component parts and outsourcing as much as possible—might be a fatal one.

Unbundling

When Betsy DeVos and her allies talk about the future of education in the United States, they often refer to "unbundling." In this vision, schooling is akin to a cable company that has packaged together hundreds of channels. But in an unbundled world, each channel is a stand-alone commodity, allowing consumers to select what they want to watch, according to their specific interests. Just as TV viewers can pay for Netflix and opt out of, say, MSNBC, education "consumers" should be able to pick and choose from an assortment of learning-related products and services.

The current one-size-fits-all system is incapable of providing every student with a high-quality education because children aren't standardized, argues Doug Tuthill, head of the Florida school choice advocacy group Step Up For Students and a proponent of unbundling. Instead, families should be empowered to purchase from a selection of products and services, using the education equivalent of a health savings account. Writes Tuthill: "ESAs are how parents will pay the various education providers who collectively are providing their child a customized education."[9]

Unbundling is the logical extreme of what management consultants pushed for in the 1980s and 1990s. Its advocates make the case that by increasing marketplace competition, the weaker aspects of businesses are weeded out, enhancing the potential for profit among those remaining and better meeting consumer demand. Such an approach would represent a radical departure from the traditional organization of public education, which, as advocates of unbundling are quick to point out, allows for little customization. Instead of being able to pick and choose the pieces they want, families generally need to adopt the entire package.

In an unbundled world, the single process of education would no longer be controlled and run by a single provider. Instead, it could be split into its many component parts. As in the modern private sector, each of those aspects would be managed by specialist organizations, competing with each other in the free market—theoretically driving down price and increasing the number of consumer choices. Families would be able to select from an à la carte menu of courses, curricular units, and activities. The most wasteful parts of school would be eliminated, yielding significant savings. Students would ostensibly be more satisfied. Markets would irreversibly replace bureaucracies. And perhaps best of all, once it was broken into a million different pieces, the public education system could never be reassembled.

At the state level, conservative lawmakers have eagerly embraced unbundling policies. Fifteen states presently allow for some version of what is known as "course choice," in which parents and students can choose courses outside of what their schools and districts offer, with funding flowing to the respective provider.[10] In Wisconsin, school choice advocates want to allow students to take courses at any institution they choose, public or private, at a cost to their home school district. Other proposals go further. The controversial Learn Everywhere program in New Hampshire, for example, would require all schools to allow students to earn up to one-third of their credits toward graduation from a list of state-approved nonprofit and for-profit providers. But why limit students to selecting in-state options? Among the provisions of ALEC's 2014 Course Choice Program Act: letting students take courses from providers in other states.

The most ambitious attempt to codify unbundling into state policy occurred in Michigan in 2012, when Republicans sought to erase school district boundaries and allow students to spend their allotted school funding dollars however and wherever they liked. Proponents painted a bright picture of dynamic school choice in action—students no longer held hostage by buildings or school districts. "Any time, any place, any way, any pace," was the measure's official motto. But critics, including district leaders like Rob Glass, superintendent of schools in Bloomfield Hills, an upscale suburb of Detroit, warned that the aim of the legislation was to break Michigan's schools up into pieces, dilute public oversight, and sell off public property to private for-profit operators. "I've never considered myself a conspiracy theorist—until now," wrote Glass in a widely circulated letter to parents and local residents.[11]

Michiganders were unwilling to see their public education system "exploded and then re-marketed, in pieces," as teacher and writer Nancy Flanagan described the plan.[12] But the questions and concerns that dogged Michigan's version of school unbundling remain just as relevant, and unanswered, today. What are the implications of divorcing education from geographic place? How will students get anything like a coherent education in an on-demand, à la carte system?

Perhaps the most serious problem of all is the fact that when schooling is unbundled, the broader democratic community no longer has a say in how, and for what purpose, young people are educated. Proponents of unbundling make the case that young people and their parents know best. Education is a private matter, they argue—no more of concern to the broader community than what kind of car a family chooses to drive or what brand of sneakers they buy. Families are customers, and education is the product.

But this view represents a radical departure from the complex, often contradictory roles that Americans have historically expected schools to play—helping young people develop knowledge and skills, prepare for citizenship, fulfill their human potential, and discover their place in society and the world. As far back as the earliest days of public education in the United States, the role of schools in producing an educated citizenry was perceived as foundational to the survival of a democratic system. In the words of legal scholar Derek Black, "Public education was to be the fuel that makes democracy work and the only sure guarantee that those controlling government will preserve rights and liberties, rather than trample on them."[13] What happens to this broad, collective vision when education is unbundled and made a matter of private, individual choice?

In many communities, schools are at the very center of civic life. They function as gathering places, repositories of neighborhood tradition and identity, and an engine of local employment. That's why local residents, whether in small towns or big cities, have fought so hard against school closures. The shuttering of a vital community institution is often seen as a death knell for the community itself. In addition to the idea, and ideal, of school as a town or neighborhood center, there is the role that schools play as surrogate families—safe places where children spend their days while their own families work. As Harvard's Elizabeth City put it: "If there is not a physical place for school, where are the children and who is looking out for them?"[14]

Silicon School

On a chilly late November morning in 2018, the school district in tiny Wilder, Idaho, welcomed not one but two famous guests. Tim Cook, the CEO of Apple, had traveled from Silicon Valley;

Ivanka Trump, "first daughter" as well as President Trump's advisor on STEM and workforce development, had made the trek from Washington, DC. Both were in the far western part of the state to tout the same message: that personalized learning is the future of education.

In the quest to unbundle education, entrepreneurs in Silicon Valley are all too happy to assist. After all, public education is a potential goldmine—a honeypot of $500 billion that is refreshed each year with taxpayer dollars. But the savviest edupreneurs don't talk dollars and cents. Instead, they have learned to speak the language of personalized learning. As Ivanka Trump tweeted in advance of her trip to Idaho's aptly named Treasure Valley: "Visiting the Wilder School District with Tim Cook to learn firsthand how they are preparing America's future workforce using @apple technology to transform the learning environment and personalize students' educational experiences based on their unique needs and strengths!"[15]

If personalization and unbundling is the solution to the flaws of public education, then Silicon Valley is the natural place to go shopping. Why? Because technology is the seemingly self-evident way to address the impersonal nature of school.

Why is school impersonal? One reason has to do with the massive scale of the enterprise, which, when paired with the principle of equal treatment, leads to bureaucracy. There are 50 million students in American classrooms, who need to be kept safe all day and hopefully educated in some reasonable fashion. Classrooms, grade levels, schools, and districts are the organizational mechanisms that have evolved in response to this task. And in classic bureaucratic fashion, equal treatment is the aim (if not always the reality), meaning that students are treated more or less the same.

Another major challenge is the problem of cost. After all, although it is theoretically possible to achieve total personalization through one-on-one instruction for all students, it would come at astronomical cost. Teachers and staff are by far the most expensive part of education. Reducing class size by a factor of 20 would entail increasing spending by the same factor. As for providing each individual student with his or her own teacher, it would require per-pupil expenditures well above the average teacher's salary. Imagine trying to sell taxpayers on that.

Related to each of these problems is what teachers themselves are expected to know. As the key mediators in the learning process, teachers must possess a high degree of content knowledge and pedagogical skill. Yet if we customized education according to the specific interests of individual students, the things teachers might be expected to know would be virtually limitless. Instead, schools limit knowledge to the curriculum, divvy it up into subject areas, and further divide it by grade level. The result for the students is a learning experience that is in many ways the opposite of customized. As long as young people are educated in schools, this lack of personalization is seemingly inescapable.

But what if classrooms moved online and teachers were replaced by algorithms? Suddenly such challenges vanish. Rather than training several million teachers to work at any one time, only a few dozen appropriate learning algorithms would need to be written. Students would no longer need to be grouped, because they could each sit in front of their own screen, the algorithm assessing their answers to multiple choice questions, then following up with harder or easier questions accordingly. And the cost of all this would actually be lower than at present, because the role of teachers could be downsized to tech support, or even eliminated entirely.

When Ivanka Trump and Tim Cook made their visit to Idaho, they weren't just there to tout the promise of a tech-aided "school of the future," but to hold up Wilder as an exemplar of an education system that is shaking off its fusty, factory-age trappings. Since 2016, all of Wilder's students have been equipped with an iPad—part of an Apple program to provide technology to students in low-income districts. But that was just the beginning, as Superintendent Jeff Dillon explained it. Thanks to Apple, the district was transforming its education system to one based not on hours spent in the classroom, but on whether students had "mastered" various subjects. As Dillon predicted: "The plan will do away with regular class periods as students use their devices to guide their education and teachers become more like mentors."[16]

Not everyone on hand was buying the sales pitch, though. Six students walked out of Wilder High School to protest what they described as their school's excessive reliance on technology and their fear that days spent in front of a screen are not preparing them for life after graduation. "We came out to tell you guys what's really going on with our school," a student named Nadia told reporters. "We are not really learning anything. The teachers are not allowed to teach anything. We are learning on iPads all day and we have to wait at least a week or so to get a test unlocked. And a lot of kids have been falling behind and then they cover that up and say everyone's on target."[17]

Algorithms for All

Minneapolis parent Sarah Lahm recognizes a sales pitch when she sees one. So when Lahm, who blogs and writes about education in the Twin Cities and beyond, received a brochure offering parents at her kids' school an introduction to Dreambox, an online math program, she decided to dig a little deeper. The flowery prose touting the unique benefits of Dreambox—its ability to gain deep insights into student thinking and to identify "trajectories, pace and path to build competency and confidence"—came straight from the company's website. But there was plenty from Dreambox's own promotional materials that hadn't made it onto the parent mailer, including its promises of "detailed data mining" on the children who have no choice but to use its products.[18] The numbers that matter to Dreambox, a for-profit company that counts Netflix founder Reed Hastings as a major investor, aren't just student math scores.

In Minneapolis, as in a growing number of school districts, products like Dreambox are being sold not as a replacement for human interaction but as a supplement. Big budget shortfalls caused by declining enrollment and the increased cost of serving special education students and English language learners have meant teacher layoffs.[19] As Lahm points out, outsourcing some of the work to algorithmic assistants is a way for teachers to manage swelling class sizes.

As Audrey Watters has chronicled, the dream of a "teaching machine" that will free up teachers from some portion of their classroom work dates back decades. Indeed, today's versions of such machines, the algorithm-driven software that allows students to proceed through a predetermined data-driven learning path at their own pace, are the Silicon Valley descendants of 1970s-era "intelligent tutoring systems."[20] But while the concerted push to bring algorithms to all may have yet to produce measurable learning gains for students, the prospect of drastically scaling back the role, not to mention the cost, of teachers has investors salivating.

Tech-heavy charter school chains like Rocketship and Carpe Diem have already demonstrated what this future looks like. Students spend hours a day in corporate-style tech centers, monitored by a handful of teaching assistants. But why stop there? As personalized learning programs evolve to take over more and more of the work of teaching, even the diminished role of teacher as mentor or "guide on the side" may come to be seen as an unnecessary extravagance.

"The role of the teacher will never disappear," Milena Marinova, the director of artificial intelligence for the education multinational Pearson, told *Forbes* recently. Marinova's job entails plumbing the "terrabytes" of student data that Pearson has collected to create software that provides real-time feedback to users—just as a teacher would. But even that role will be rendered mostly irrelevant in the future that Pearson is hastening to deliver. Marinova explains, "When there is something highly complex and the student needs help, the human can interfere."[21] Otherwise, the algorithm will handle it.

In Marinova's quest to automate education, the model of good teaching comes from her own high school math teacher, who inspired her to become a mathematician. Would she have been so motivated by an AI educator? Of course, the replacement of flesh-and-blood teachers by personalized learning programs will not be universal. Students from privileged families will continue to be educated much as they always have been, with students and teachers coming together as communities of learners. Indeed, to the extent that the campaign for the automation of education has hit a wall, it has been in well-to-do communities like Cheshire, Connecticut, where parents revolted against the use of the online Summit Learning Platform.[22] It is the less-privileged students—like those in Idaho's Wilder School District or at the Brooklyn Secondary School for Journalism—who will spend their days largely on screens, save for the occasional "human interference."

The replacement of teachers by algorithms and online learning platforms also raises a profound question about the purpose of school. If teaching is the core business of public education and teachers are no longer required for that service to be delivered, are schools really necessary? The proliferation of education technology, coupled with the development of a school choice marketplace, means that students no longer need attend school at all. Instead, they can receive a customized education from products and services selected by their parents.

Step Up For Students' Doug Tuthill envisions a not-too-distant future when machine learning algorithms "help parents parse vast amounts of data, settling on the customized education options that have the highest probability of success for each individual child." The only obstacle to realizing this vision in his state is Florida's constitution, which—at least for the time being—still requires a uniform system of free public schools, overseen by elected school boards.[23]

In a 2013 interview, Betsy DeVos attributed her evangelism for digital learning to her own boredom as a high school student. "I can only imagine how much more boring it is today, when you check all of those new technologies at the door and go sit in rows of desks and listen to somebody talk at you for 30 or 40 minutes," she said.[24] The implication is that were students left—literally—to their own devices, they would be more engaged and more successful. Just how likely is that? In the best-case scenario, students pursuing their own unique interests might be more motivated. Completion rates, for example, could plausibly improve as students charted their own course of study, determined by what they care about. Still, much of school is social in nature and rooted in relationships. Move learning online, or outside schools entirely, and you risk destroying this sense of community. The unplanned experiment brought on by the 2020 coronavirus epidemic proved this beyond the shadow of a doubt. Remote learning, for millions of young people, was a sorry substitute for their shuttered schools.

DeVos and other proponents of an unbundled future paint a picture of limitless learning horizons, aided by technology and parent choice. But the algorithm-driven programs they hold up as empowering students and their parents are limited by design. In the schools they imagine, schooling is reduced to what can be coded in zeroes and ones.

CONCLUSION

Florida's current Republican governor had been in office barely a month when he signaled that his vision for the state's public education system entailed breaking it apart. "For me, if the taxpayer is paying for the education, it's public education," said Ron DeSantis. Where that money goes—to a district school, a charter, a homeschooling parent, or a private religious school—was a matter of little importance.[1]

As reporters for the *Tampa Bay Times* pointed out, DeSantis, who in the 2018 gubernatorial election beat an avowed supporter of public education by a mere thirty thousand votes, is enacting an agenda first envisioned by one of his predecessors. More than three decades ago, Jeb Bush rolled out an ambitious plan for private school vouchers, only to be stymied by the courts. This time around, however, the landscape appears far friendlier. With a Republican-dominated legislature and a newly conservative Supreme Court in place to brush aside constitutional objections, Florida seems poised to dismantle its public education system once and for all.[2]

Betsy DeVos was quick to agree. "If the taxpayer is paying for education, it's public education," she declared on Twitter. Days later, DeVos unveiled a proposed $5 billion federal program to fund Education Freedom Scholarships. Modeled on the neo-voucher programs enacted in more than a dozen states, her proposal openly encouraged state officials to defy their own laws by channeling public funds to private, mostly religious schools.

Soon after, DeVos announced that she would no longer enforce a federal law that prevents religious groups from providing federally funded educational services—like special education programming, tutoring, or mentoring—to private schools. The language in the Department of Education's advisory was dryly technical, but a momentous shift was well under way.

A Much-Delayed Alarm

Are you trying to scare people? That was the question that a senior scholar put to us after reading an early draft of this book. In a word, yes. The threat to public education, as we've laid out in the preceding chapters, is grave. A radical vision for unmaking the very idea of public schools has moved from the realm of ideological pipe dream to legitimate policy. Conservatives' faith in the individual and the market is nothing new; neither is their disdain for "government" schools or their loathing of unions. These positions have been remarkably consistent since the days of Goldwater. What has changed is the political context.

Yawning income disparities have translated into deep political inequality, conferring outsized influence to the deep-pocketed crusaders who reject the very idea of public schools. As the political ascent of Betsy DeVos so potently illustrates, once-fringe ideas now occupy centers of policy power, and threaten to consume a bedrock institution of our democracy. The unprecedented shutdown of schools across the country in response to the coronavirus pandemic, and the uncertainty around when—or even if—they'll reopen, has likewise given conservative groups an opportunity to push for an old vision. As a blog post on the conservative Reason Foundation's website put it: "The coronavirus pandemic has caused nearly all schools to close and has created a captive, nationwide audience of families interested in exploring alternative online platforms to keep their kids occupied and on track."[3]

Under the auspices of the official-sounding "National Coronavirus Recovery Commission," the influential conservative Heritage Foundation advised states to immediately restructure their K–12 public education systems, giving money directly to parents in the form of education savings accounts "to pay for any education-related service, product, or provider of choice." Also on the list: eliminating any certification requirements for teachers and "allowing anyone with a bachelor's degree to provide K–12 instruction online."[4] The Heritage proposal was both radical and familiar—the same policy proposals conservatives have pushed for decades, given new possibility by a global health emergency.

The movement of ideas like these from the margins toward the mainstream has been a long time coming. Hard-line conservatives have patiently moved their ideas forward, waiting for headwinds to die down and digging fallback trenches along the way. And in this steady march they have been unwittingly assisted by a bipartisan policy consensus—on test-based accountability, market-based reforms, and the weakening of teacher job protections—that have eased the way for the dismantling agenda.

Such policies, unleashed in the service of "fixing" public

education, won't be easy to contain. In an assessment of the charter school movement, for instance, two former assistant secretaries of education made a remarkable admission. "We wanted the infusions of capital and entrepreneurialism that accompany the profit motive, but we didn't take seriously enough the risk of profiteering," wrote Chester Finn Jr. and Bruno Manno in 2015.[5] Their public expression of contrition was all the more notable given that Finn and Manno had long been ardent champions of the free market. They had helped usher in a reality they were living to regret.

While much of the focus in this book has been on conservatives, Democrats have also played a significant role in redefining public education as a commodity to be fought over in a competitive marketplace rather than as a collective community good. Defending the Obama administration's education priorities, including "forcing competition on a public education monopoly," former Department of Education official Peter Cunningham claimed that "school choice is in our DNA."[6] The claim neatly encapsulates the hazardous ground that self-styled school reformers on the political left so often stand upon. After decades of hearing Democrats make the case for using market mechanisms to improve schools, the public is even less likely to discern the radical ideology at the heart of the dismantling agenda. What's the difference, after all, between the claim that charter schools are public because they're funded by taxpayer dollars—a standard talking point among pro-charter Democrats—and the argument made by the governor of Florida that "if the taxpayer is paying for the education, it's public education"?

Given this alignment between Republicans and Democrats, Americans have heard little over the past quarter century about education as a public good. Instead, schooling has come to be seen chiefly as a vehicle for getting ahead. The "public" aspect of public education—the part that benefits all of us, regardless of whether we have school-age children or any children at all—is increasingly forgotten. Instead, we are pitted against each other in a zero-sum game, in which one person's gain must come at the expense of someone else. Why *not* shop for a school that will give your children a leg up in life? Why *not* buy into an exclusive neighborhood with top-rated public schools that might as well be private? Why *not* push for school choice policies that allow for more school shopping?

As journalist Nikole Hannah-Jones points out, the erosion of America's commitment to public schools as a unifying and equalizing institution began just as the civil rights movement was gaining steam. "As black Americans became part of the public," writes Hannah-Jones, "white Americans began to pull away."[7] The same school vouchers that Betsy DeVos is peddling as a twenty-first-century tool for "customization," we may recall, originated as a way for white Southerners to resist school desegregation. Today, nearly seven decades after the Supreme Court ordered the end of dual school systems for black and white children, school segregation is on the rise once more. In sum, hard-line conservatives may be intent upon taking public education apart for good, but we haven't been doing much to ensure its survival.

Yet as we've seen with the recent teacher walkouts, and in the deep popular support they commanded, Americans can be roused into action. In state after state, residents pronounced themselves unwilling to give up on the idea of public education, strongly backing teachers in their calls for more investment in schools, and rebuking elected officials who refused to go along.

Popular sentiment has fueled political change, particularly in states where school funding has lagged and teacher pay is chronically low. By the spring of 2019, more than twenty governors had called for teacher pay increases.[8] States that saw strikes and walkouts, including Arizona, North Carolina, and West Virginia, also made substantial increases in school funding in the wake of the protests.[9] When voters across twelve Southern states were asked if they would support the "state adjusting the school funding system to ensure greater fairness among poor and wealthier communities," nearly 90 percent responded in the affirmative.[10]

Americans also rose up against the expansion of voucher programs. The overwhelming defeat of Arizona's universal school voucher proposal in 2018 was just the latest in a long string of losses for voucher proponents. And in states including Texas and Arkansas, conservative rural lawmakers have joined forces with urban Democrats to quash the expansion of DeVos-style school choice programs.[11] Unease with vouchers now appears to be widening to include charter schools, too, especially in places where the expansion of charters threatens traditional public schools.

Rising to the Challenge

The public schools make a particularly easy target for criticism. No other institution in American life includes so many of us—tens of millions each year—or strives to do so in such egalitarian fashion. That's an admirable aspiration. But sheer scale inevitably makes the system inconsistent in quality, even as it remains bureaucratic in its operation.

Additionally, no other public aim is as ambitious. Education, we might recall, is our collective effort to realize for all young people their full human potential, regardless of circumstance. By extension, it seeks to move our society toward ideals like truth and goodness, and to do so within the confines of a school. Impossible expectations, coupled with finite capacity, exposes public education to innumerable variants of the claim that it has fallen short.

Critiques of public schools, in short, are not likely to fade, even in the best of scenarios. Thus, as Americans line up in various configurations of support and opposition, the balance will be tipped toward change of some sort—even change that would dismantle this cornerstone of democratic life. In light of that, it is perhaps worth concluding this book by placing our hands on the other side of the scale—by restating the basic facts about schools' role as a driver of social progress.

Roughly two centuries ago, the first public schools began to emerge as an intentional effort to shore up the young republic. These "common schools," as they were known, brought American children together not merely to study, but to learn what it meant to be a full and equal participant in a democratic society. Prior to that time, Americans had educated their children in disparate fashion—at home, in private academies, with tutors, or in formal apprenticeships. The poorest attended pauper schools, if they attended school at all. The common schools, however, were open to everyone, and communities invested heavily in public education as a radical kind of experiment. As nineteenth-century reformer Horace Mann argued, it was the core mission of the public schools to bring different young people together—to consider not just "what one individual or family needs," but rather "what the whole community needs."[12]

As historians have documented, public education has repeatedly failed to live up to these principled ideals, particularly with regard to inclusion. For the first half of the nineteenth century, systemic bondage kept many Americans out of the schools; and even after the formal end of slavery, African Americans were denied anything that resembled equal access. Mexicans, whose border had shifted south, were regularly excluded from schools; the same was true for Native Americans who, similarly, found themselves strangers in a familiar land. Immigrants unable to pass for white often experienced schools as places of oppression. Catholics, Jews, and others often opted out of schools infused with the morality of Protestant Christianity.

Yet all of these groups fought to be included because they were determined to hold America to its promises. They believed that if the United States could live up to its ideals anywhere, it would be inside the schools. Over time, access expanded, as did the curriculum. The guarantee of primary education was extended to secondary schooling and, increasingly, to higher education. Funding for schools became both more substantial and more equitable. Expectations of care increased, as did the likelihood that students would receive appropriate kinds of support.

This belief in equitable access has extended broadly across the decades and across our differences. Each time public education has fallen short, Americans have used their voices and their votes to pull it toward its potential. This is not to paper over the work that has yet to be done. Segregation remains a plague on our schools; the fight for true equality of opportunity is an endless struggle; the quest for a balanced curriculum is all too often elusive. Confronting these shortcomings on the ground, and not merely as abstractions, is an exercise in heartbreak. Each failure is a breach of the social contract, a fractured promise, a dream deferred.

But we believe these shortfalls should be cause for redoubled effort—that the long march toward justice should be hastened, not abandoned. Unmaking the public education system might relieve us of that work, but it would hardly relieve us of our obligations.

In a 2018 speech, Betsy DeVos sounded a note of triumph. "This," she declared, "is our moment."[13] She may be right.

Yet the moment is not over. The best way to drive off a wolf is to band together and fight back.

ACKNOWLEDGMENTS

When we recorded the first episode of our podcast together in the spring of 2017, our expectations for the collaboration were summed up in the tagline we settled on: "Occasionally funny and periodically informative."

Three years and nearly one hundred episodes later, we find ourselves not just co-hosts, but co-authors. How did we get here? Some of it was dumb luck. We happen to get along, and we each possess different strengths. But the real secret has been a small army of supporters, who have shared with us their energy, their expertise, and their enthusiasm.

The roster of scholars who have joined us on the show is a veritable all-star team, and we have learned a great deal from all of them. We are particularly grateful to Derek Black, Mira Debs, Hunter Gehlbach, Ethan Hutt, Harvey Kantor, Tressie McMillan Cottom, Noliwe Rooks, Mike Rose, Carla Shedd, Marshall Steinbaum, Tina Trujillo, and Terrenda White, who have been ongoing sources of support as we seek to make sense of education policy in the twenty-first century.

We've also had incredible assistance from journalists, whose reporting is critical to understanding the policy landscape. People like Andrea Gabor, Anand Giridharadas, Dana Goldstein, Craig Harris, Christopher Leonard, Yawu Miller, and Audrey Watters are essential confederates in the pursuit of truth.

Then there are the educators. From California to Massachusetts, we have consistently found teachers willing to talk about their communities, their schools, and their experiences. These on-the-ground perspectives, along with exceptional reporting and first-rate scholarship, have helped us piece together a picture of the threats to public education and the possible future that awaits it.

The deepest gratitude, however, is to a final set of associates. At the end of the day, when we turn off our microphones or close our laptops, each of us has a partner to go home to. With each other, we've created work that we're proud of. But with each of them, we make a life. The final thanks, then, are to Katie and Russ, who likely listen to our podcast or will read this book only under duress, but whose love makes such things possible.

NOTES

Introduction

1. Matt Barnum, "Asked Whether She Is Using Crisis to Support Private School Choice, DeVos Says 'Yes, Absolutely,'" *Chalkbeat*, May 20, 2020, www.chalkbeat.org/2020/5/20/21265527/devos-using-coronavirus -to-boost-private-schools-says-yes-absolutely.

2. James Hohmann, "The Daily 202: Koch Network Laying Groundwork to Fundamentally Transform America's Education System," *Washington Post*, January 30, 2018.

3. Gordon Lafer, *The One Percent Solution* (Ithaca, NY: Cornell University Press, 2017), 152.

4. Melissa Quinn, "How Oklahoma Gov. Mary Fallin Wants to Change the Traditional Public Education Model," *Daily Signal*, March 14, 2016, www.dailysignal.com/2016/03/14/how-oklahoma-gov-mary-fallin-wants -to-change-the-traditional-public-education-model.

5. Allie Morris, "Sununu Taps Frank Edelblut for N.H. Education Commissioner," *Concord Monitor*, January 18, 2017, www.concordmonitor .com/Frank-edelblut-nominated-as-education-commissioner-7539551.

6. Valerie Strauss, "Betsy DeVos Claims Philosophy of Margaret 'Iron Lady' Thatcher as Her Own," *Washington Post*, July 20, 2017.

7. Matt Barnum, "To Back Up Claim That Schools Must Change,

DeVos Cites Made-Up Statistic about the Future of Work," *Chalkbeat*, November 21, 2017, www.chalkbeat.org/posts/us/2017/11/21/to-back-up -claim-that-schools-must-change-devos-cites-made-up-statistic-about-the -future-of-work.

8. Diane Ravitch, *Reign of Error* (New York: Vintage Books, 2013).

9. For more on this, see polling conducted by Phi Delta Kappa, which asks respondents to rate the overall quality of the nation's schools and that of their own children's schools.

10. Milton Friedman, "The Role of Government in Education," in *Economics and the Public Interest*, ed. Robert A. Solo (New Brunswick, NJ: Rutgers University Press, 1955).

11. U.S. Department of Education, "U.S. Secretary of Education Betsy DeVos Embarks on 'Rethink School' Tour," press release, October 2, 2018, www.ed.gov/news/press-releases/us-secretary-education-betsy-devos -embarks-%E2%80%9Crethink-school%E2%80%9D-tour.

12. Yvonne Wingett Sanchez and Rob O'Dell, "Arizona Voters Will Have a Say in School-Voucher Expansion, but Court Fight Looms," *AZ Central*, September 5, 2017.

Chapter 1: Private Values

1. National Center for Education Statistics, "Private School Enrollment," nces.ed.gov/programs/coe/indicator_cgc.asp.

2. Rebecca Klein, "Voucher Schools Championed by Betsy DeVos Can Teach Whatever They Want. Turns Out They Teach Lies," *HuffPost*, December 7, 2017.

3. See, for instance, Christopher A. Lubienski and Sarah Theule Lubienski, *The Public School Advantage: Why Public Schools Outperform Private Schools* (Chicago: University of Chicago Press, 2013).

4. Gallup, "Private Schools First, Public Schools Last in K-12 Ratings," August 21, 2017, news.gallup.com/poll/216404/private-schools-first-public -schools-last-ratings.aspx.

5. Stephen Worchel, Jerry Lee, and Akanbi Adewole, "Effects of Supply and Demand on Ratings of Object Value," *Journal of Personality and Social Psychology* 32, no. 5 (1975): 906–14.

6. Alex Zimmerman, "Betsy DeVos Is in New York City—and So Far, She's Only Touring Religious Private Schools," *Chalkbeat*, May 15, 2018, www.chalkbeat.org/posts/ny/2018/05/15/betsy-devos-is-in-new-york-city -and-so-far-shes-only-touring-private-schools.

7. Jennifer Miller, "Yiddish Isn't Enough," *New York Times*, November 21, 2014.

8. Jen Chung, "Betsy DeVos Visits Yeshivas, Not Public Schools, During First NYC Visit as Education Secretary," *Gothamist*, May 16, 2018.

9. In response to such claims, conservatives occasionally cite the characteristics of a "public good" identified by economists. For an example, see Corey DeAngelis, "Schooling Is Not a Public Good," Foundation for Economic Education, January 26, 2017, fee.org/articles/schooling-is-not -a-public-good. There, and elsewhere, conservative defenders of the free market assert that education does not meet this formal definition, and then proceed to ignore the substantive tension between what is good for *individuals* and what is good for the *collective whole*. Though we are familiar with this formal definition, we also appreciate the popular usage of "public good," which is more or less equivalent to "common good."

10. John Binder, "Americans Billed $60 Billion to Educate Illegal Aliens, Anchor Babies," *Breitbart*, December 4, 2019.

11. Jamie Ducharme, "Betsy DeVos Urges Ave Maria Grades to 'Embrace the Mess,'" *Time*, May 5, 2018, time.com/5266806/betsey-devos-ave-maria -transcript.

12. Derek Black, "Trump's 'Education Freedom' Plan Is an Attack on Public Schools. That's Un-American," *USA Today*, February 20, 2020.

13. National Center for Education Statistics, "Characteristics of Children's Families," May 2019, nces.ed.gov/programs/coe/indicator_cce.asp; National Center for Education Statistics, "Number and Percentage of Public School Students Eligible for Free or Reduced-Price Lunch, by State: Selected Years, 2000–01 through 2016–17," 2018, nces.ed.gov/programs/digest/d18 /tables/dt18_204.10.asp?current=yes.

14. Erin Richards, "Coronavirus School Closings: Ohio, Maryland, Michigan Become First States to Shut All K-12 Schools," *USA Today*, March 12, 2020.

15. U.S. Department of Education, "Prepared Remarks by Secretary DeVos to the Alfred E. Smith Foundation," press release, May 16, 2018, www.ed.gov/news/speeches/prepared-remarks-secretary-devos-alfred -e-smith-foundation.

16. Joseph Bast, "February 2002: The Year of School Vouchers," The Heartland Institute, February 1, 2002, www.heartland.org/publications -resources/publications/february-2002-the-year-of-school-vouchers.

17. Jeremy Pelzer, "Ohio Legislator Says America's Public Education System Is 'Socialism,' Should Be Privatized," March 19, 2014, www.cleveland .com/open/index.ssf/2014/03/ohio_lawmaker_americas_public.html.

18. Bill Bigelow, "The Koch Brothers Sneak into School," *HuffPost*, November 18, 2014.

19. Sam Blumenfeld, "The Meaning of Educational Freedom," *Practical Homeschooling* 33 (2000), www.home-school.com/Articles/the-meaning -of-educational-freedom.php.

20. "Statistics About Nonpublic Education in the United States," U.S. Department of Education, Office of Non-Public Education, www2.ed.gov /about/offices/list/oii/nonpublic/statistics.html.

21. Matthew Hennessey, "Homeschool for Freedom," *National Review*, May 14, 2016, www.nationalreview.com/2016/05/leftist-public-schools -homeschooling.

22. Hank Stephenson, "Rep. Paul Mosley on Lawmaker Cousins and Repealing Compulsory Education," *Arizona Capitol Times*, May 1, 2014.

23. American Legislative Exchange Council, "Resolution Support-ing Homeschooling Freedom," September 12, 2016, www.alec.org/model -policy/resolution-supporting-homeschooling-freedom.

24. Jane Mayer, *Dark Money: The Hidden History of the Billionaires Behind the Rise of the Radical Right* (New York: Doubleday, 2016).

25. Bryan Caplan, *The Case Against Education: Why the Education Sys-tem Is a Waste of Time and Money* (Princeton, NJ: Princeton University Press, 2018).

Chapter 2: Faith in Markets

1. U.S. Department of Education, "Prepared Remarks by U.S. Secretary of Education Betsy DeVos to the 2017 ASU GSV Summit," May 9, 2017, www.ed.gov/news/speeches/prepared-remarks-us-secretary-education -betsy-devos-2017-asu-gsv-summit.

2. "Jeb Bush Speech Text: Read the Former Florida Governor's Repub-lican Convention Remarks," *HuffPost*, August 30, 2012.

3. Israel Ortega, "Why Our Schools Need to Run Like Businesses," Heritage Foundation, September 8, 2008, www.heritage.org/education /commentary/why-our-schools-need-run-businesses.

4. Adam Smith, *An Inquiry into the Nature and Causes of the Wealth of Nations* (London: W. Strahan and T. Cadell, 1776).

5. Sheldon Richman, "The Free Market Is a Beautiful Thing," *Rea-son*, April 14, 2013, reason.com/archives/2013/04/14/the-free-market-is -a-beautiful-thing.

6. Milton Friedman, "Epilogue: School Vouchers Turn 50, but the Fight Is Just Beginning," in Robert C. Enlow and Lenore T. Ealy, eds., *Liberty and Learning: Milton Friedman's Voucher Idea at Fifty* (Washington, DC: Cato Institute, 2006), 156.

7. Myron Lieberman, "Free-Market Strategy and Tactics in K-12 Edu-cation," in Enlow and Ealy, *Liberty and Learning*, 83.

8. Andrew Coulson, "A Critique of Pure Friedman: An Empirical Reas-sessment of 'The Role of Government in Education,'" in Enlow and Ealy, *Liberty and Learning*, 118.

9. Thomas D. Snyder, ed. *120 Years of American Education: A Statistical Portrait*, U.S. National Center for Education Statistics, nces.ed.gov /pubs93/93442.pdf.

10. Nancy MacLean, *Democracy in Chains: The Deep History of the Radical Right's Stealth Plan for America* (New York: Viking), 2017.

11. Richard Nixon, Special Message to the Congress on Education Reform, The American Presidency Project, March 3, 1970, www.presidency .ucsb.edu/documents/special-message-the-congress-education-reform.

12. Terry Moe in Emily Esfahani Smith, "Profile in School Reform: Terry Moe," *Defining Ideas*, April 15, 2011, www.hoover.org/research/profile -school-reform-terry-moe.

13. Denis P. Doyle and Chester E. Finn Jr., *Educational Quality and Family Choice: Toward a Statewide Public School Voucher Plan* (Washington, DC: National Institute of Education), 1983.

14. Robert Pear, "Reagan Proposes Vouchers to Give Poor a Choice of Schools," *New York Times*, November 14, 1985.

15. Eleanor Byman, "School Vouchers a 'Cruel Hoax,'" *Chicago Tribune*, December 12, 1985.

16. Jeffrey R. Henig, *Rethinking School Choice: Limits of the Market Metaphor* (Princeton, NJ: Princeton University Press, 1993), 67.

17. Ember Reichgott Junge, *Zero Chance of Passage: The Pioneering Charter School Story*, (Edina, MN: Beaver's Pond Press, 2012), 85.

18. Angela G. Smith, "Public School Choice and Open Enrollment: Implications for Education, Desegregation, and Equity," *Nebraska Law Review* 74, no. 2 (1995): 277, digitalcommons.unl.edu/nlr/vol74/iss2/2.

19. Ted Kolderie, *Beyond Choice to New Public Schools: Withdrawing the Exclusive Franchise in Public Education* (Washington, DC: Progressive Policy Institute), 1990.

20. Anna David, *Public-Private Partnerships: The Private Sector and Innovation in Education*, The Reason Foundation, Policy Study No. 142, July 1992, p. 12.

21. Junge, *Zero Chance of Passage*, 178.

22. Bill Clinton, "Democratic Leadership Council Keynote Address," May 6, 1991, www.c-span.org/video/?17869-1/democratic-leadership-coun cil-keynote-address.

23. John E. Chubb and Terry M. Moe, "America's Public Schools: Choice Is a Panacea," *Brookings Review* 8, no. 3 (1990): 4.

24. John J. Miller, "Eight Books That Changed America," *Philanthropy Roundtable*, July/August, 2002.

25. Chubb and Moe, "America's Public Schools," 9.

26. Moe in Smith, "Profile in School Reform."

27. Quoted in John E. Coons et al., "The Pro-Voucher Left and the Pro-Equity Right," *Annals of the American Academy of Political and Social Science* 98, no. 114 (2000): 98–114.

28. Friedman, "Epilogue," 156.

29. Joseph Bast, "February 2002: The Year of School Vouchers," The Heartland Institute, February 2, 2002, www.heartland.org/publications-resources/publications/february-2002-the-year-of-school-vouchers.

30. Bruce Murphy, "The Legacy of Annette Polly Williams," *Urban Milwaukee*, November 11, 2014, urbanmilwaukee.com/2014/11/11/murphys-law-the-legacy-of-annette-polly-williams.

31. Robert Pondiscio, "Florida's Opportunity to 'Go Big or Go Home' on School Choice," *Flypaper*, February 6, 2019, edexcellence.net/articles/floridas-opportunity-to-go-big-or-go-home-on-school-choice.

Chapter 3: The Cost-Cutting Crusade

1. Deven Carlson, "Not Just a 'Red State Revolt': The Story Behind the Oklahoma Teacher Walkout," *Brown Center Chalkboard*, Brookings Institution, April 12, 2018, www.brookings.edu/blog/brown-center-chalkboard/2018/04/12/oklahoma-teacher-walkouts-backstory.

2. Gene Perry, "Oklahoma Continues to Lead the U.S. in Deepest Cuts for Education," *Oklahoma Policy Institute*, October 16, 2014, okpolicy.org/oklahoma-continues-lead-u-s-deepest-cuts-education.

3. Teaching: Respect but Dwindling Appeal. The 50th Annual PDK Poll of the Public's Attitudes Toward the Public Schools (PDK International, Arlington, VA: 2018), pdkpoll.org/assets/downloads/pdkpoll50_2018.pdf.

4. Quoted in Matt Barnum, "Why the School Spending Graph Betsy DeVos Is Sharing Doesn't Mean What She Says It Does," *Chalkbeat*, April 13, 2018, www.chalkbeat.org/posts/us/2018/04/13/why-the-school-spending-graph-betsy-devos-is-sharing-doesnt-mean-what-she-says-it-does.

5. Bill Gates, "Flip the Curve: Student Achievement vs. School Budgets," *Huffington Post*, March 1, 2011.

6. "Total and Current Expenditures per Pupil in Public Elementary and Secondary Schools: Selected Years, 1919–20 through 2006–07," *Digest of Education Statistics*, National Center for Education Statistics, 2009, nces.ed.gov/programs/digest/d09/tables/dt09_182.asp.

7. Jay Chambers, Thomas B. Parrish, and Jenifer J. Harr, *What Are We Spending on Special Education Services in the United States, 1999–2000?*, U.S. Department of Education, 2000, www.air.org/sites/default/files/SEEP1-What-Are-We-Spending-On.pdf.

8. Nick Niedzwiadek, "NYC Special Ed 'Crisis' Draws Attention of State Education Officials," *Politico*, March 2, 2020.

9. Robert A. Margo, *Race and Schooling in the South, 1880–1950: An Economic History* (Chicago: University of Chicago Press, 1990).

10. See, for instance: Bruce D. Baker, Matthew Di Carlo, and Mark Weber, *The Adequacy and Fairness of State School Finance Systems* (Washington, DC & New Brunswick, NJ: Albert Shanker Institute & Rutgers Graduate School of Education, 2019), schoolfinancedata.org/wp-content/uploads /2020/02/SFID_AnnualReport_2020.pdf; C. Kirabo Jackson, *Does School Spending Matter? The New Literature on an Old Question* (Cambridge, MA: National Bureau of Economic Research, 2018).

11. Matthew M. Chingos and Grover J. Whitehurst, "Class Size: What Research Says and What It Means for State Policy," Brookings, May 11, 2011, www.brookings.edu/research/class-size-what-research-says-and-what -it-means-for-state-policy.

12. Bruce D. Baker, *Educational Inequality and School Finance* (Cambridge, MA: Harvard Education Press, 2018), 43.

13. "Outside Jobs for Regular, Full-Time Public School Teachers," National Center for Education Statistics, nces.ed.gov/pubs2018 /2018137_TeacherJobs.pdf.

14. Sylvia Allegretto and Lawrence Mishel, *The Teacher Pay Penalty Has Hit a New High*, Economic Policy Institute, September 5, 2018, www.epi .org/publication/teacher-pay-gap-2018.

15. Motoko Rich, "Why Don't More Men Go into Teaching?," *New York Times*, September 6, 2014.

16. "Presidential Debate in Baltimore (Reagan-Anderson)," The American Presidency Project, September 21, 1980, www.presidency.ucsb.edu/ws /index.php?pid=29407.

17. Paul Blustein, "Recent Budget Battles Leave the Basic Tenets of Welfare State Intact," *Wall Street Journal*, October 21, 1985.

18. Robert Gebeloff, "The Numbers That Explain Why Teachers Are in Revolt," *New York Times*, June 4, 2018.

19. John Miller, "Fifty Flowers Bloom: Conservative Think Tanks— Mini–Heritage Foundations—At the State Level," *National Review*, November 19, 2007, pp. 42–44.

20. "2017 Public Elementary-Secondary Education Finance Data," U.S. Census Bureau, www.census.gov/data/tables/2017/econ/school-finances /secondary-education-finance.html.

21. Cato Institute, "Cracking the Books," www.cato.org/cracking -books.

22. Jennifer Berkshire, "Winning Battles on Education," *Progressive*, June 1, 2018, progressive.org/magazine/winning-battles-on-education.

23. Dana Goldstein and Ben Casselman, "Teachers Find Public Support

as Campaign for Higher Pay Goes to Voters," *New York Times*, May 31, 2018.

24. Matthew DeFour, "As Scott Walker Campaigns for a Third Term, Poll Finds Shifting Political Landscape," *Wisconsin Political Journal*, March 6, 2018, host.madison.com/wsj/news/local/govt-and-politics/as-scott-walker -campaigns-for-a-third-term-poll-finds/article_350e3e03-429b-558c-b95d -ec1e0c77c523.html.

25. Theda Skocpol and Alexander Hertel-Fernandez, "The Koch Network and Republican Party Extremism," *Perspectives on Politics* 14, no. 3 (2016): 695.

26. "New Study Blows a Hole in Conservative Doctrine," editorial, *Kansas City Star*, March 16, 2018, www.kansascity.com/latest-news /article205595439.html.

27. Baker, *Educational Inequality and School Finance*.

28. Julien Lafortune, Jesse Rothstein, and Diane Whitmore Schanzenbach, *School Finance Reform and the Distribution of Student Achievement*, NBER Working Paper No. 22011, July 2016, www.nber.org/papers /w22011.

29. Kirabo Jackson, Rucker Johnson, and Claudia Persico, "The Effects of School Spending on Education and Economic Outcomes: Evidence from School Finance Reforms," *Quarterly Journal of Economics* 131, no. 1 (2016): 157–218.

30. Chad Livengood, "Education Reform Group Forges Voucher-Like Plan for Michigan," *Detroit News*, April 19, 2013, www.pressreader.com /usa/the-detroit-news/20130419/281479273900295.

31. Clare Lombardo, "White House Proposes Merging Education and Labor Departments," NPR, June 21, 2018, www.npr.org/sections/ed/2018 /06/21/622189097/white-house-proposes-merging-education-and-labor -departments.

32. Bryan Caplan, "The World Might Be Better Off Without College for Everyone," *The Atlantic*, January/February 2018.

33. James Hohmann, "Koch Network Laying Groundwork to Fundamentally Transform America's Education System," *Washington Post*, January 30, 2018.

34. Quoted in Emily Esfahani Smith, "Profile in School Reform: Terry Moe," *Defining Ideas*, April 15, 2011, www.hoover.org/research/profile -school-reform-terry-moe.

35. Inez Feltscher, *Report Card on American Education: Ranking State K-12 Performance, Progress and Reform*, American Legislative Exchange Council, 2018, www.alecreportcard.org/publication/report-card-on-ameri can-education-22nd-edition.

36. Jenny Abamu, "The Data Tells All: Teacher Salaries Have Been Declining for Years," *EdSurge*, April 5, 2018, www.edsurge.com/news /2018-04-05-the-data-tells-all-teacher-salaries-have-been-declining-for -years.

37. Gordon Lafer, *The One Percent Solution: How Corporations Are Remaking America One State at a Time* (Ithaca, NY: Cornell University Press, 2017), p. 152.

Chapter 4: The War on Labor

1. Elizabeth Catte, Emily Hilliard, and Jessica Salfia, eds., *55 Strong: Inside the West Virginia Teachers' Strike* (Cleveland, OH: Belt Publishing, 2018), 31.

2. Alexia Fernández Campbell, "The Bizarre Right-Wing Campaign to Discredit Striking Arizona Teachers," *Vox*, April 27, 2018.

3. Josh Weishart, "The 2019 WV Teacher Strike: Educational Equality and Liberty," joshuaweishart.com, February 19, 2019, joshuaweishart.com /the-2019-wv-teacher-strike.

4. Dana Goldstein, *The Teacher Wars: A History of America's Most Embattled Profession* (New York: Doubleday, 2014), 69.

5. Jon Shelton, *Teacher Strike! Public Education and the Making of a New American Political Order* (Urbana: University of Illinois Press, 2017), 32.

6. Joseph E. Slater, *Public Workers: Government Employee Unions, the Law, and the State: 1900–1962* (Ithaca, NY: Cornell University Press, 2004), 189.

7. Marjorie Murphy, *Blackboard Unions: The AFT and the NEA, 1900–1980* (Ithaca, NY: Cornell University Press, 1992), 209.

8. Terry M. Moe, "The Staggering Power of the Teachers' Unions," *Hoover Digest*, July 13, 2011, www.hoover.org/research/staggering-power -teachers-unions.

9. Jon Shelton, *Teacher Strike!*

10. Leo Casey, "Why Teachers' Unions and Due Process Matter," *Bridging Differences* (blog), *Education Week*, September 25, 2014, blogs.edweek .org/edweek/Bridging-Differences/2014/09/today_leo_casey_of_the.html.

11. Goldstein, *The Teacher Wars*, 5.

12. Colleen Wilson, "White Plains Teachers Flooded with Emails from DeVos-Funded Mackinac Prg Post-Janus," *Rockland/Westchester Journal News*, June 28, 2018, www.lohud.com/story/news/education/2018/06/28 /teachers-emails-mackinac/743033002.

13. Bloomberg, "Group Funded by Conservative Billionaires Launches

Anti-Union Campaign Following Supreme Court Ruling," *Los Angeles Times*, June 28, 2018.

14. Moshe Marvit, "For 60 Years, This Powerful Conservative Group Has Worked to Crush Labor," *The Nation*, July 15, 2018.

15. Robert Barnes and Anne Marimow, "Supreme Court Rules Against Public Unions Collecting Fees from Nonmembers," *Washington Post*, June 27, 2018.

16. Barry Goldwater, *Conscience of a Conservative* (1960; repr., Princeton, NJ: Princeton University Press, 2007), 54.

17. Lee Edwards, "Barry M. Goldwater: The Most Consequential Loser in American Politics," Heritage Foundation, July 3, 2014, www.heritage .org/political-process/report/barry-m-goldwater-the-most-consequential -loser-american-politics.

18. Thomas Dye and Harmon Zeigler, *The Irony of Democracy: An Uncommon Introduction to American Politics* (Boston: Wadsworth Cengage Learning, 2009), 200.

19. Alexander Hertel-Fernandez, "How ALEC Helped Undermine Public Unions," *Washington Post*, December 17, 2014.

20. Goldwater, *Conscience of a Conservative*, 51–52.

21. Rick Perlstein, *Before the Storm: Barry Goldwater and the Unmaking of the American Consensus* (New York: PublicAffairs, 2009), 38.

22. Robert Bruno and Steven Ashby, *A Fight for the Soul of Public Education* (Ithaca, NY: Cornell University Press, 2016), 252.

23. Dave Umhoefer, "For Unions in Wisconsin, a Fast and Hard Fall since Act 10," *Milwaukee Journal Sentinel,* November 11, 2016, projects .jsonline.com/news/2016/11/27/for-unions-in-wisconsin-fast-and-hard-fall -since-act-10.html.

24. Theda Skocpol and Alexander Hertel-Fernandez, "The Koch Network and Republican Party Extremism," *Perspectives on Politics* 14, no. 3 (2016): 681–99.

25. Noam Scheiber, "Supreme Court Labor Decision Wasn't Just a Loss for Unions," *New York Times*, July 1, 2018.

26. James Feigenbaum, Alexander Hertel-Fernandez, and Vanessa Williamson, "From the Bargaining Table to the Ballot Box: Political Effects of Right to Work Laws," National Bureau of Economic Research Working Paper, January 2018, www.nber.org/papers/w24259.

27. Carl Bernstein, *A Woman in Charge: The Life of Hillary Rodham Clinton* (New York: Alfred A. Knopf, 2007), 169.

28. White House, Office of the Press Secretary, "Remarks of the President to the United States Hispanic Chamber of Commerce," March 10,

2009, obamawhitehouse.archives.gov/the-press-office/remarks-president-united-states-hispanic-chamber-commerce.

29. William G. Howell, "Results of President Obama's Race to the Top," *Education Next* 15, no. 4 (2015), www.educationnext.org/results-president-obama-race-to-the-top-reform.

30. Terry M. Moe, "The Staggering Power of the Teachers' Unions," *Hoover Digest*, July 13, 2011, www.hoover.org/research/staggering-power-teachers-unions.

31. Peter Schweizer, "The Dance of the Lemons," *Hoover Digest*, January 30, 1999, www.hoover.org/research/dance-lemons.

32. Richard Kahlenberg, "How Due Process Protects Teachers and Students," *American Educator*, Summer 2015, www.aft.org/ae/summer2015/kahlenberg.

33. Emily Badger, "Why a California Judge Just Ruled That Teacher Tenure Is Bad for Students," *Washington Post*, June 10, 2014.

34. Derek Black, "New Jersey Supreme Court Ends Challenge to Teacher Tenure Laws," *Education Law Prof Blog*, December 18, 2018, lawprofessors.typepad.com/education_law.

35. Emmanuel Felton, "Have Obama's Education Policies Weakened the Democratic Party?," *Hechinger Report*, July 26, 2016, hechingerreport.org/have-obamas-education-policies-weakened-the-democratic-party.

36. Valerie Strauss, "Remember the 2018 Teachers Strikes in Republican-Led States? Now Legislators in Three States Are Trying to Retaliate," *Washington Post*, February 1, 2019.

37. Bureau of Labor Statistics, U.S. Department of Labor, "The Economics Daily: 20 Major Work Stoppages in 2018 Involving 485,000 Workers," www.bls.gov/opub/ted/2019/20-major-work-stoppages-in-2018-involving-485000-workers.htm.

38. Gallup, "Labor Unions," news.gallup.com/poll/12751/labor-unions.aspx.

39. Ipsos, "Most Americans Believe Teachers Have a Big Impact, But Are Paid Unfairly," September 12, 2018, www.ipsos.com/en-us/news-polls/Views-on-American-Teachers.

40. Alexander Hertel-Fernandez, "Polling the Teacher Walkouts: Strong Support for the Teachers, Unions, and Future Labor Action," *On Labor*, February 19, 2019, onlabor.org/polling-the-teacher-walkouts-strong-support-for-the-teachers-unions-and-future-labor-action.

41. James Hohmann, "Koch Network Poised to Scale up Efforts to Remake K-12 Education with a Pilot Project in Five States," *Washington Post*, January 29, 2018.

Chapter 5: Neo-Vouchers

1. Michael D. Shear, "For Trump and DeVos, a Florida Private School Is a Model for Choice," *New York Times*, March 3, 2017.

2. See, for instance, "Pierce v. Society of Sisters," *Oyez*, www.oyez.org /cases/1900-1940/268us510.

3. Samuel Windsor Brown, *The Secularization of American Education* (New York: Teachers College Press, 1912), 1.

4. Kyle Duncan, "Secularism's Laws: State Blaine Amendments and Religious Persecution," *Fordham Law Review* 72, no. 3 (2003): 496.

5. "Public Isn't Clamoring for School Vouchers," ABC News/Washington Post Poll, October 9, 2000, abcnews.go.com/images/pdf/832a2 SchoolVouchers.pdf; Washington Post/ABC News Poll, April 17, 2011, www.washingtonpost.com/wp-srv/politics/polls/postpoll_04172011.html; Martin R. West, Michael B. Henderson, Paul E. Peterson, and Samuel Barrows, *The 2017 EdNext Poll on School Reform*, www.educationnext.org /2017-ednext-poll-school-reform-public-opinion-school-choice-common -core-higher-ed.

6. Mark Walsh, "Tax Credits Pass Muster in Arizona," *Education Week*, February 3, 1999, web.archive.org/web/20040920171252/http:// www.edweek.org/ew/vol-18/21ariz.h18.

7. *Arizona Christian School Tuition Organization v. Winn.* 563 U.S. 125 (2011).

8. Quoted in Matt Barnum, "The Rise of Tax Credits," *Chalkbeat*, September 18, 2017, www.chalkbeat.org/posts/us/2017/09/18/the-rise-of-tax -credits-how-arizona-created-an-alternative-to-school-vouchers-and-why -theyre-spreading.

9. West et al., *2017 EdNext Poll on School Reform*.

10. Alia Beard Rau, "Arizona Private-School Families Cash In on State's Tax-Credit Program," *Arizona Republic*, July 26, 2015.

11. Leslie Postal, "Florida Private Schools Get Nearly $1 Billion in State Scholarships with Little Oversight, Sentinel Finds," *Orlando Sentinel*, October 17, 2017.

12. Arianna Prothero, "'There Is No Oversight': Private-School Vouchers Can Leave Parents on Their Own," *Education Week*, November 14, 2017, www3.edweek.org/ew/articles/2017/11/15/there-is-no-oversight-private -school-vouchers-can.html.

13. Leslie Postal and Annie Martin, "Anti-LGBT Florida Schools Getting School Vouchers," *Orlando Sentinel*, January 23, 2020.

14. Prothero, "'There Is No Oversight.'"

15. Gus Garcia-Roberts, "McKay Scholarship Program Sparks a Cottage Industry of Fraud and Chaos," *Miami New Times*, June 23, 2011.

16. Quoted in Matt Barnum, "The Rise of Tax Credits."

17. Carl Davis, *State Tax Subsidies for Private K-12 Education*, Institute on Taxation and Economic Policy, October 2016.

18. Ty Tagami, "School Superintendents Say Georgia's Tax Credit Program Is Profitable for the Rich," *Atlanta Journal-Constitution*, May 17, 2017; full report: Sasha Pudelski and Carl Davis, *Public Loss Private Gain: How School Voucher Tax Shelters Undermine Education*, AASA: The School Superintendents Association, May 2017, www.aasa.org/vouchertaxshelter.

19. Michelle Reese, "Rigged Privilege: Private School Tax Credits Rife with Abuse," *East Valley Tribune*, August 1, 2009, www.eastvalleytribune .com/news/private-school-tax-credits-rife-with-abuse/article_7debd2e5 -d000-5aed-b813-a0d252377755.html.

20. Reese, "Rigged Privilege."

21. Leslie Postal, Beth Kassab, and Annie Martin, "Private Schools' Curriculum Downplays Slavery, Says Humans and Dinosaurs Lived Together," *Orlando Sentinel*, June 1, 2018.

22. Rebecca Klein, "Voucher Schools Championed by Betsy DeVos Can Teach Whatever They Want. Turns Out They Teach Lies," *HuffPost*, December 7, 2017.

23. Rebecca Klein, "Inside the Voucher Schools that Teach L. Ron Hubbard, but Say They're Not Scientologist," *HuffPost*, December 11, 2017.

24. Postal, Kassab, and Martin, "Private Schools' Curriculum Downplays Slavery."

25. "Prepared Remarks by Secretary DeVos to the Alfred E. Smith Foundation," May 16, 2018, content.govdelivery.com/accounts/USED/bulletins /1f07a66.

26. Klein, "Voucher Schools Championed by Betsy DeVos."

27. Lindsey M. Burke, *The Education Debit Card: What Arizona Parents Purchase with Education Savings Accounts*, Friedman Foundation for Educational Choice, August 2013, www.edchoice.org/wp-content/uploads /2013/08/2013-8-Education-Debit-Card-WEB-NEW.pdf.

28. Rob O'Dell and Yvonne Wingett Sanchez, "Oversight of ESA School-Voucher Program 'Almost a Sham,'" *Arizona Republic*, June 22, 2017.

29. Dana Goldstein, "Arizona Frees Money for Private Schools, Buoyed by Trump's Voucher Push," *New York Times*, April 7, 2017.

30. Laurie Roberts, "Arizona Voters Said 'Hell No' to Prop. 305, Ducey's School Voucher Plan. But Will He Listen?," *Arizona Republic*, November 6, 2018.

31. Rob O'Dell and Yvette Wingette Sanchez, "Group Will Ask Arizona Voters to Ban Expansion of State's School Voucher Program," *Arizona Republic*, February 20, 2020.

32. Rob O'Dell and Nick Penzenstadler, "You Elected Them to Write New Laws. They're Letting Corporations Do It Instead," *USA Today*, June 19, 2019.

33. Alexander Hertel-Fernandez, Caroline Tervo, Theda Skocpol, "How the Koch Brothers Built the Most Powerful Rightwing Group You've Never Heard Of," *The Guardian*, September 26, 2018.

34. Amy Howe, "Argument Analysis: Justices Divided in Montana School-Choice Case," *SCOTUSblog*, January 22, 2020, scotusblog.com /2020/01/argument-analysis-justices-divided-in-montana-school-choice -case.

Chapter 6: The Pursuit of Profit

1. Doug Livingston, "School's Out for White Hat," *Alliance Review*, August 7, 2018, www.the-review.com/news/20180807/schools-out-for -white-hat-pioneering-for-profit-company-exits-ohio-charter-scene.

2. Patrick O'Donnell, "The 95% 'Fees' That Charter Schools Pay White Hat Go Before the Ohio Supreme Court Today," *Cleveland Plain Dealer*, September 23, 2014.

3. Karla Scoon Reid, "Millionaire Industrialist Touts 'White Hat' Firm to Build Charter Model," *Education Week*, May 22, 2002, www.edweek .org/ew/articles/2002/05/22/37whitehat.h21.html.

4. "Pioneering Ohio Charter Operator Sells Off Assets," *Education Week*, August 13, 2018, www.edweek.org/ew/articles/2018/08/11 /pioneering-ohio-charter-school-operator-sells_ap.html.

5. James P. Stucker and George R. Hall, *The Performance Contracting Concept in Education*, RAND Corporation, 1971.

6. Marjorie L. Rapp, *Case Studies in Educational Performance Contracting: Gilroy, California*, RAND Corporation, 1971, www.rand.org /pubs/reports/R900z5.html.

7. Michael Carpenter, A.W. Chalfant, and George R. Hall, *Case Studies in Educational Performance Contracting: Texarkana, Arkansas; Liberty-Eylau, Texas*, RAND Corporation, 1971, www.rand.org/pubs /reports/R900z3.html.

8. Donald M. Levine, "Major Problems in Performance Contracting for Education," in Donald M. Levine, ed., *Performance Contracting in Education—An Appraisal* (Englewood Cliffs, NJ: Educational Technology Publications, 1972), 32.

9. Robert Poole, "Ronald Reagan and the Privatization Revolution,"

Reason Foundation, June 8, 2004, reason.org/commentary/ronald-reagan -and-the-privatiz.

10. Christina Nifong, "Hartford's Bid to Privatize Its Public Schools Gets Tardy Slip," *Christian Science Monitor*, December 27, 1994, www .csmonitor.com/1995/0027/27014.html.

11. Robert Poole, "Ronald Reagan and the Privatization Revolution," *Reason Foundation*, June 8, 2004, reason.org/commentary/ronald-reagan -and-the-privatiz.

12. David Osborne and Ted Gaebler, *Reinventing Government: How the Entrepreneurial Spirit Is Transforming the Public Sector* (New York: Penguin Books, 1993), 93.

13. Osborne and Gaebler, *Reinventing Government*, 45.

14. John S. Friedman, "Big Business Goes to School," *The Nation*, February 17, 1992, p. 190.

15. Samuel E. Abrams, *Education and the Commercial Mindset* (Cambridge, MA: Harvard University Press, 2016).

16. Emily Hanford, "The Story of the University of Phoenix," American Radio Works, americanradioworks.publicradio.org/features/tomorrows -college/phoenix/story-of-university-of-phoenix.html.

17. John Sperling, *Rebel with a Cause* (New York: John Wiley and Sons, 2000).

18. James Coleman and Richard Vedder, *For-Profit Education in the United States: A Primer*, Center for College Affordability and Productivity, 2008, pp. 26–27.

19. A.J. Angulo, *Diploma Mills: How For-Profit Colleges Stiffed Students, Taxpayers, and the American Dream* (Baltimore, MD: Johns Hopkins University Press, 2016), xv.

20. U.S. Senate, Health, Education, Labor and Pensions Committee, executive summary of *For Profit Higher Education: The Failure to Safeguard the Federal Investment and Ensure Student Success* (Washington, DC: U.S. Government Publishing Office, 2012), www.help.senate.gov/imo /media/for_profit_report/ExecutiveSummary.pdf.

21. U.S. Senate, executive summary of *For Profit Higher Education*.

22. Tressie McMillan Cottom, *Lower Ed: The Troubling Rise of For-Profit Colleges in the New Economy* (New York: The New Press, 2018).

23. Mark Binelli, "Michigan Gambled on Charter Schools. Its Children Lost," *New York Times*, September 5, 2017.

24. Stephanie Saul, "Profits and Questions at Online Charter Schools," *New York Times*, December 12, 2011.

25. Interview with Stephen Dyer, January 4, 2018.

26. Kyra Gurney, "How the Political Clout of a Charter School Mega Company Could Be at Risk in Florida," *Miami Herald*, October 25, 2016.

27. Denise Smith Amos, "Charter School Industry Donations Prompt Questions," *Florida Times-Union*, August 2, 2016.

28. "Charter Schools Are Big Business. Who's Making Money off Public Education?," *Arizona Republic*, August 22, 2018.

29. Craig Harris, "Charter Board Vote Allows Eddie Farnsworth, School Operator and Lawmaker, to Make Millions," *Arizona Republic*, September 2018.

30. E.J. Montini, "Charter School Corruption Will Go Unchecked in Arizona," *Arizona Republic*, August 18, 2018.

31. Craig Harris, "Charter Reform? Bill to Rein in Charter Operators Has Big Exemptions for Major Players," *Arizona Republic*, February 1, 2019.

32. Craig Harris, "Arizona Charter School Founder Makes Millions Building His Own Schools," *Arizona Republic*, July 11, 2018.

33. Sean Sullivan and Emma Brown, "Trump Pitches $20 Billion Education Plan at Ohio Charter School That Received Poor Marks from State," *Washington Post*, September 8, 2016.

34. In John O'Connor, "Q&A: Charter Schools USA CEO Jonathon Hage," StateImpact Florida, September 29, 2011, stateimpact.npr.org /florida/2011/09/29/q-a-charter-school-usa-ceo-jonathon-hage.

35. Auditor of State, *Community School Facility Procurement*, Public Interest Report, State of Ohio, 2019, ohioauditor.gov/auditsearch/Reports /2019/Community_School_Facility_Procurement_Public_Interest_Report .pdf.

36. Craig Harris, "Arizona Charter School Founder Makes Millions Building His Own Schools."

37. Stanford University Center for Research on Education Outcomes, *Charter Management Organizations 2017*, Stanford, CA, credo.stanford .edu/sites/g/files/sbiybj6481/f/cmo_final.pdf.

38. Oliver Hart, Andrei Shleifer, and Robert W. Vishny, "The Proper Scope of Government: Theory and an Application to Prisons," NBER Working Paper No. 5744, September 1996, www.nber.org/papers/w5744.

Chapter 7: Virtual Learning

1. "Ohio Budget Expands Digital Learning Opportunities for Students; National Digital Learning Experts, Former Governors Bush and Wise, Laud State Action," press release, July 1, 2011, www.prweb.com/releases/2011 /7/prweb8617792.htm.

2. James Pogue, "The GOP's Biggest Charter School Experiment Just Imploded," *Mother Jones*, March/April 2018, www.motherjones .com/politics/2018/01/the-gops-biggest-charter-school-experiment-just -imploded.

3. Alex Molnar et al., *Virtual Schools in the U.S. 2019* (Boulder, CO: National Education Policy Center, 2019). Retrieved from nepc.colorado.edu /publication/virtual-schools-annual-2019.

4. Carl F. Kaestle, "Public Education in the Old Northwest: 'Necessary to Good Government and the Happiness of Mankind,'" *Indiana Magazine of History* 84, no. 1 (1988): 60–74.

5. Marshall Cushing, *The Story of Our Own Post Office* (Boston: A.M. Thayer & Company, 1893), 47–67; Daniel Calhoun Roper, *The United States Post Office* (New York: Funk & Wagnalls, 1917), 1001–10.

6. H.F. Bergmann, "The Silent University: The Society to Encourage Studies at Home, 1873–1897," *New England Quarterly* 74, no. 3 (2001): 447–77.

7. Joseph F. Kett, *Pursuit of Knowledge Under Difficulties: From Self-Improvement to Adult Education in America* (Stanford, CA: Stanford University Press, 1994).

8. *American Federationist* 12 (1905): 9.

9. Tom Clark, *Virtual Schools: Trends and Issues* (Phoenix, AZ: West-Ed, 2001), 21.

10. Matthew Wicks, quoted in Kathryn Winograd, "ABCs of the Virtual High School," *Technology Source*, March/April 2002.

11. Katherine Mackey and Michael B. Horn, *Florida Virtual School: Building the First Statewide, Internet-Based Public High School*, Innosight Institute, 2009, p. 2.

12. Mackey and Horn, *Florida Virtual School*, 14.

13. Clark, *Virtual Schools*.

14. "Current Expenditures per Pupil in Average Daily Attendance in Public Elementary and Secondary Schools, by State or Jurisdiction: Selected Years, 1959–60 through 2006–07," *Digest of Education Statistics*, National Center for Education Statistics, 2009, nces.ed.gov/programs/digest/d09 /tables/dt09_186.asp.

15. Joseph R. Freidhoff, *Michigan's K-12 Virtual Learning Effectiveness Report, 2013–2014*, Lansing: Michigan Virtual Learning Institute, 2015, media.mivu.org/institute/pdf/er_2014.pdf.

16. Bill Tucker, "Laboratories of Reform: Virtual High Schools and Innovation in Public Education," Education Sector, 2007, p. 6, charter-schoolcenter.ed.gov/resource/laboratories-reform-virtual-high-schools-and -innovation-public-education.

17. Pat Kossan, "As Class Sizes Grow, Experts Differ on Best Use of State Education Funding," *Arizona Republic*, May 17, 2009.

18. See, for instance, Eric A. Hanushek, "The Economic Value of Higher Teacher Quality," NBER Working Paper Series, National Bureau of Economic Research, Cambridge, MA, www.nber.org/papers/w16606.

19. Terry Moe, "Liberating Learning," Center on the American Experiment, January 2010, p. 6.

20. Alex Molnar, ed., *Virtual Schools Report 2017*, National Education Policy Center, Boulder, CO, 2017, nepc.colorado.edu/publication/virtual-schoolsannual-2017.

21. Stephanie Saul, "Profits and Questions at Online Charter Schools," *New York Times*, December 12, 2011.

22. Gary Miron, Christopher Shank, and Caryn Davidson, *Full-Time Virtual and Blended Schools: Enrollment, Student Characteristics, and Performance*, National Education Policy Center, Boulder, CO, 2018, nepc.colorado.edu/publication/virtual-schoolsannual-2018.

23. Center for Research on Education Outcomes, Online Charter School Study, Stanford University, 2015, credo.stanford.edu/sites/g/files/sbiybj6481/f/online_charter_study_final.pdf.

24. Jenny Abamu, "Researchers Push Back as Betsy DeVos, ALEC Advance Virtual School Expansion," *EdSurge*, July 18, 2017, www.edsurge.com/news/2017-07-18-researchers-push-back-as-betsy-devos-alec-advance-virtual-school-expansion.

25. Saul, "Profits and Questions at Online Charter Schools."

26. Dierdre Fernandes, "System for Virtual Virginia Academy Flawed, Critics Say," *Virginian-Pilot*, February 21, 2011, pilotonline.com/news/government/politics/virginia/article_cf00e659-dc67-5473-9eae-f48d7748e405.html.

27. National Alliance for Public Charter Schools, *A Call to Action to Improve the Quality of Full-Time Virtual Charter Public Schools*, June 2016, www.publiccharters.org/sites/default/files/migrated/wp-content/uploads/2016/06/Virtuals-FINAL-06202016-1.pdf?x87663.

28. Kimberly Hefling, "DeVos Champions Online Charter Schools, but the Results Are Poor," *Politico*, October 8, 2017.

29. Megan Guza, "Former PA Cyber CEO Nick Trombetta Gets 20 Months in Prison for Tax Fraud," *Pittsburgh Tribune-Review*, July 24, 2018.

30. Elizabeth Hardison, "Poor School Districts Are Funding the State's Cyber Charter Schools, Research Shows. That Wasn't Always the Case," *Pennsylvania Capital Star*, August 20, 2019.

31. Abamu, "Researchers Push Back."

32. John Chubb and Terry Moe, "Virtual Schools," *Education Next*, Winter 2009, p. 52.

33. Aaron Pallas, "The Good, Evasive and Very Bad Answers Betsy DeVos Gave to Questions from Democrats About Education," *Washington Post*, February 1, 2017.

34. Mathematica Policy Research, Center on Reinventing Public Education, and Center for Research on Education Outcomes, "Online Charter School Students Falling Behind Their Peers," press release, October 27, 2015, credo.stanford.edu/sites/g/files/sbiybj6481/f/online_press_release.pdf.

35. Miron, Shank, and Davidson, *Full-Time Virtual and Blended Schools*.

36. Stephanie Wang, "Indiana Virtual Charter Schools Linked to a Decline in Student Test Scores, a New Study Shows," *Chalkbeat*, March 9, 2020, chalkbeat.org/posts/in/2020/03/09/indiana-virtual-charter-schools -linked-to-a-decline-in-student-test-scores-a-new-study-shows.

37. Motoko Rich, "Online School Enriches Affiliated Companies If Not Its Students," *New York Times*, May 18, 2016.

38. Stephanie Saul, "Profits and Questions at Online Charter Schools," *New York Times*, December 12, 2011.

39. Letter from Ohio Department of Education to Representative Sherrod Brown, February 5, 2018, brown.senate.gov/download/doe-letter-ecot.

40. Stephanie Wang, "In a Damning Audit, Indiana Calls on Two Virtual Schools to Repay $85 Million in Misspent State Funds," *Chalkbeat*, February 12, 2020, chalkbeat.org/posts/in/2020/02/12/in-a-damning-audit -indiana-calls-on-two-virtual-schools-to-repay-85-million-in-misspent -state-funds.

41. Saul, "Profits and Questions at Online Charter Schools."

42. News Corp, "News Corporation to Acquire Education Technology Company Wireless Generation," press release, November 22, 2010, www .newscorp.com/news/news_464.html.

43. Miron, Shank, and Davidson, *Full-Time Virtual and Blended Schools*.

44. Kate Murphy, "For-Profit Charter Schools Would Be Banned Under California Bill Heading to the Governor," *Mercury News*, August 23, 2018, www.mercurynews.com/2018/08/23/for-profit-charter-schools-would-be -banned-under-california-bill-heading-to-the-governor.

Chapter 8: The End of Regulation

1. From the introduction to Regulatory Studies on the Cato Institute website, www.cato.org/research/regulatory-studies.

2. Judith Serrin and William Serrin, eds., *Muckraking: The Journalism That Changed America* (New York: The New Press, 2002), 4–6.

3. Tracy Steffes, *School, Society, and State: A New Education to Govern Modern America, 1890–1940* (Chicago: University of Chicago Press, 2012).

4. Nancy Beadie, "The Federal Role in Education and the Rise of Social Science Research," *Review of Research in Education* 1, no. 1 (2016): 4.

5. Project, "Education and the Law: State Interests and Individual Rights," *Michigan Law Review* 74 (1976): 1379.

6. David Tyack and Thomas James, "State Government and American Public Education, *History of Education Quarterly* 26, no. 1 (1986): 54.

7. William D. Guthrie, "Public Service Commissions," in *Legal Phases of Corporate Financing, Reorganization, and Regulation* (New York: Macmillan, 1917), 350.

8. Milton Friedman, "The Goldwater View of Economics," *New York Times*, October 11, 1964.

9. Robert A. Kagan, *Regulating Business, Regulating Schools: The Problem of Regulatory Unreasonableness*, Project Report No. 81-A14, Stanford University, Institute for Research on Educational Finance and Governance, 1981, p. 15.

10. Martha Derthick and Paul J. Quirk, *The Politics of Deregulation* (Washington, DC: Brookings Institution Press, 1985), 8.

11. William H. Clune, III, *The Deregulation Critique of the Federal Role in Education*, National Institute of Education, Washington, DC, 1982, p. 1.

12. Ronald Reagan, "Radio Address to the Nation on Proposed Natural Gas Deregulation Legislation," February 26, 1983, *The American Presidency Project*, www.presidency.ucsb.edu/ws/?pid=40982.

13. Between 1963 and 1974, state legislatures passed 73 laws promoting accountability.

14. For more, see David Labaree, "On the Nature of Teaching and Teacher Education: Difficult Practices That Look Easy," *Journal of Teacher Education* 51, no. 3 (2000): 228–33.

15. Ken Zeichner, "Reflections of a University-Based Teacher Educator on the Future of College- and University-Based Teacher Education," *Journal of Teacher Education* 57, no. 3 (2006): 328.

16. For more on Teach For America, see Jack Schneider, *Excellence for All: How a New Breed of Reformers Is Transforming America's Public Schools* (Nashville, TN: Vanderbilt University Press, 2011).

17. Richard Cano, "Thousands of Untrained Teachers Are Leading Arizona's Public School Classrooms," *Arizona Republic*, August 22, 2018.

18. Doug Tuthill, "Less School Regs, More School Choice," *redefinED*, September 12, 2018. www.redefinedonline.org/2018/09/tuthill-on-regulations.

19. Michael Q. McShane, Jenn Hatfield, and Elizabeth English, *The Paperwork Pile-Up: Measuring the Burden of Charter School Applications*, American Enterprise Institute, May 19, 2015, www.aei.org/research -products/report/the-paperwork-pile-up-measuring-the-burden-of-charter -school-applications.

20. John Fensterwald, "California's Charter Schools Soon to Enter an Uneasy Era," *EdSource*, September 10, 2019, edsource.org/2019/californias -charter-schools-face-uncertain-future-under-a-new-state-law/617320.

21. "Opposition to SCR Policy 406," Excellent Schools PA, March 22, 2018, excellentschoolspa.org/wp-content/uploads/2018/03/3_22-ESPA -Opposition-to-SRC-Policy-406.pdf.

22. Jeanne Allen and Patrick Korten, "Charter Schools Are Being Stifled by Regulatory Overload," *Washington Examiner*, March 26, 2018.

23. Joseph Bast, Lindsey M. Burke, Andrew J. Coulson, Robert Enlow, Kara Kerwin, and Herbert J. Walberg, "Choosing to Learn," *National Review*, March 12, 2014, www.nationalreview.com/2014/03/choosing -learn-joseph-bast-lindsey-m-burke-andrew-j-coulson-robert-enlow-kara -kerwin.

24. Paul T. Hill, *Enforcement and Informal Pressure in the Management of Federal Categorical Programs in Education* (Santa Monica, CA: The RAND Corporation, 1979).

25. Annie Waldman, "DeVos Has Scuttled More Than 1,200 Civil Rights Probes Inherited from Obama," ProPublica, June 21, 2018, www .propublica.org/article/devos-has-scuttled-more-than-1-200-civil-rights -probes-inherited-from-obama.

26. U.S. Department of Education, "Secretary DeVos Announces Regulatory Reset to Protect Students, Taxpayers, Higher Ed Institutions," press release, June 14, 2017, www.ed.gov/news/press-releases/secretary -devos-announces-regulatory-reset-protect-students-taxpayers-higher-ed -institutions.

27. Terry W. Hartle, "Comments on Gainful Employment," American Council on Education, September 13, 2018, www.acenet.edu/Documents /Comments-Gainful-Employment-2018.pdf.

28. Erica L. Green, "Education Department Says It Will Scale Back Civil Rights Investigations," *New York Times*, June 16, 2017.

29. Gloria Stewner-Manzanares, "The Bilingual Education Act: Twenty Years Later," *New Focus* 6 (1988), ncela.ed.gov/files/rcd/BE021037 /Fall88_6.pdf.

30. Janet R. Beales, *Special Education: Expenditures and Obligations*, Reason Foundation, Policy Study No. 161 (1993), reason.org/wp-content /uploads/files/5bba489f654fc1f7ac773f817b4745f4.pdf.

31. Gary Miron, "Charters Should Be Expected to Serve All Kinds of

Students," *Education Next* 14, no. 4 (2014), educationnext.org/charters
-expected-serve-kinds-students.

32. Peter Balonon-Rosen, "Education Secretary DeVos Visits Catholic
Voucher School in Indy," *State Impact*, May 23, 2017, indianapublicmedia
.org/stateimpact/2017/05/23/education-secretary-devos-visits-indy-catholic
-voucher-school.

33. For more on these cases and others, see the prize-winning work of
journalist Craig Harris and his *Arizona Republic* colleagues, reported in a
five-part series called "The Charter Gamble."

34. Craig Harris, Anne Ryman, Alden Woods, and Justin Price, "The
Rise of Big Charters in Arizona Was Fueled by Powerful Friends," *Arizona
Republic*, December 16, 2018.

35. Chris Jones and Nadia Pflaum, "Beyond the Books: A \$5 Million
Question at American Preparatory Academy," KUTV, November 15, 2018,
kutv.com/news/beyond-the-books/beyond-the-books-a-5-million-question
-at-american-preparatory-academy.

36. Susan H. Fuhrman and Richard F. Elmore, *Ruling Out Rules: The
Evolution of Deregulation in State Education Policy* (New Brunswick, NJ:
Consortium for Policy Research in Education, 1995).

37. Fuhrman and Elmore, *Ruling Out Rules*, 19–20.

38. Clune, *The Deregulation Critique of the Federal Role in Education*,
63.

Chapter 9: Don't Forget to Leave Us a Review

1. Quoted in Carol Burris, "Trump and DeVos Love 'Education Savings
Accounts.' You Should Know How They Really Work," *Washington Post*,
February 12, 2018.

2. William Cronon, *Nature's Metropolis: Chicago and the Great West*
(New York: W.W. Norton, 1992).

3. Carl Bialik, "Let's Rate the Ranking Systems of Film Reviews," *Wall
Street Journal*, January 23, 2009.

4. Pete Wells, "The Art of Complaining," *New York Times*, February 6,
2019.

5. Georgios Askalidis, Su Jung Kim, and Edward C. Malthouse,
"Understanding and Overcoming Biases in Online Review Systems," *Decision Support Systems* 97 (2017): 23–30.

6. Elizabeth Dwoskin and Craig Timberg, "How Merchants Use Facebook to Flood Amazon with Fake Reviews," *Washington Post*, April 23,
2018.

7. Saeideh Bakhshi, Partha Kanuparthy, and Eric Gilbert, "Demographics, Weather and Online Reviews: A Study of Restaurant Recommen-

dations," Proceedings of the 23rd International World Conference, April 2014, dx.doi.org/10.1145/2566486.2568021.

8. Jonathan Oosting, "Jeb Bush Pushes A-F Grades for Michigan Schools," *Detroit News*, September 24, 2018.

9. "Florida's Intuitive Letter Grades Produce Results," *EdNext Podcast*, October 5, 2016, www.educationnext.org/floridas-intuitive-letter-grades -produce-results-forum-jeb-bush-accountability.

10. Eva-Marie Ayala and Holly K. Hacker, "A-F Outrage Spurs Lawmaker's Move to Kill Texas' New School Grading Plan," *Dallas News*, January 6, 2017.

11. Jack Schneider, *Beyond Test Scores: A Better Way to Measure School Quality* (Cambridge, MA: Harvard University Press, 2017).

12. Kevin Mahnken, "Power Is Knowledge: New Study Finds That Wealthy, Educated Families Are Using School Ratings to Self-Segregate," *The 74*, February 5, 2019, www.the74million.org/power-is-knowledge-new -study-finds-that-wealthy-educated-families-are-using-school-ratings-to -self-segregate.

13. Matt Barnum, "Eight Years Ago, the L.A. Times Published Teachers' Ratings. New Research Tells Us What Happened Next," *Chalkbeat*, August 5, 2018, chalkbeat.org/posts/us/2018/08/05/l-a-times-teacher -ratings-research.

14. Cited in Natalie Maemura and Rachel Van Gelder, "To Rate or Not to Rate: Students' Thoughts on Rate My Teacher," *Verde Magazine*, October 9, 2014, verdemagazine.com/to-rate-or-not-to-rate-students-thoughts -on-rate-my-teacher.

15. Travis Kalanick, "The Future of Work: Independence and Flexibility," *Pacific Standard*, October 15, 2015, psmag.com/economics/the-future -of-work-independence-and-flexibility.

16. Matthew A. Kraft and Allison F. Gilmour, "Revisiting the Widget Effect: Teacher Evaluation Reforms and the Distribution of Teacher Effectiveness," *Educational Researcher* 46, no. 5 (2017): 234–49.

17. Lior Jacob Strahilevitz, "Less Regulation, More Reputation," in Hassan Masum and Mark Tovey, eds., *The Reputation Society* (Cambridge, MA: MIT Press, 2011), 71.

18. Josh Dzieza, "The Rating Game: How Uber and Its Peers Turned Us into Horrible Bosses," *Recode*, October 28, 2015, www.recode.net/2015 /10/28/11620138/the-rating-game-how-uber-and-its-peers-turned-us-into -horrible-bosses.

Chapter 10: Selling School

1. Jennifer Robinson and Keri Miksza, "Wild West of Education: Virtual Schools Simply Indiana's Latest Effort to Siphon Money away from

Public Districts," *Journal Gazette*, June 12, 2018, www.journalgazette.net /opinion/columns/20180612/wild-west-of-education.

2. "Creating First-Rate Education in Indiana: An Address by Governor Mitch Daniels," May 4, 2011, American Enterprise Institute, www.aei.org /events/creating-first-rate-education-in-indiana.

3. Federal Trade Commission, "Truth in Advertising," www.ftc.gov /news-events/media-resources/truth-advertising.

4. Heather Vogell, "For-Profit Schools Reward Students for Referrals and Facebook Endorsements," ProPublica, October 6, 2017, www .propublica.org/article/for-profit-schools-reward-students-for-referrals-and -facebook-endorsements.

5. William Daughtrey, William Hester, and Kevin Weatherill, *Tuition Trends in Independent Day Schools*, NAIS Research, 2016, www.nais.org /Articles/Documents/Member/TuitionTrends_Final.pdf.

6. Quoted in Daughtrey, Hester, and Weatherill, *Tuition Trends in Independent Day Schools*.

7. Daughtrey, Hester, and Weatherill, *Tuition Trends in Independent Day Schools*.

8. National Business Officers Association, *Independent School Financial Sustainability Report*, 2010, factsmgt.com/wp-content/uploads /Independent-School-Financial-Sustainability-2010.pdf.

9. "Number, Highest Degree, and Years of Full-Time Teaching Experience of Teachers in Public and Private Elementary and Secondary Schools, by Selected Teacher Characteristics," *Digest of Education Statistics*, National Center for Education Statistics, 2015, nces.ed.gov/programs/digest /d15/tables/dt15_209.20.asp.

10. Quoted in Christopher Lubienski, "Marketing Schools: Consumer Goods and Competitive Incentives for Consumer Information," *Education and Urban Society* 40, no. 1 (2007): 118–41.

11. Catherine DiMartino and Sarah Butler Jessen, *Selling School: The Marketing of Public Education* (New York: Teachers College Press, 2018).

12. *The Brian Lehrer Show*, "Eva Moskowitz," March 24, 2015, www .wnyc.org/story/the-brian-lehrer-show-2015-03-24.

13. DiMartino and Jessen, *Selling School*.

14. Marc Bain, "More U.S. School Kids Than Ever Are Wearing Uniforms This Fall," *Quartz*, September 11, 2018, qz.com/quartzy/1382336 /school-uniforms-are-rapidly-on-the-rise-at-us-public-schools.

15. St. Mark's School, *Handbook, 2016–2017*, www.stmarksschool.org /uploaded/photos/Admission/PDFs/SMHandbook201617.pdf.

16. Christina Veiga, "Success Academy Graduates 16 Students at Its Inaugural Commencement," *Chalkbeat*, June 7, 2018, www.chalkbeat.org/posts

/ny/2018/06/07/success-academy-graduates-16-students-at-its-inaugural
-commencement.

17. Greg Toppo, "Charter Schools' 'Thorny' Problem: Few Students Go on to Earn College Degrees, *USA Today*, March 14, 2017.

18. Cynthia McCabe, "Exploitative Charter School Lotteries Not Required by Law," *NEA Today*, January 20, 2011, neatoday.org/2011/01 /20/exploitative-charter-school-lotteries-not-required-by-law.

19. "Truth in Edvertising," *Have You Heard* podcast, 2018, soundcloud .com/haveyouheardpodcast/truth-in-edvertising.

20. Penny Davis, *How to Market Your Charter School Like a PR Pro: Using Earned Media*, National Charter Schools Institute, August 2007, nationalcharterschools.org/product/market-charter-school-like-pr-pro -using-earned-media.

21. Stephanie Hacke and Mary Niederberger, "PA Charter Schools Spend Millions of Public Dollars in Advertising to Attract Students," *PublicSource*, August 29, 2017, projects.publicsource.org/chartereffect /stories/pennsylvania-charter-schools-spend-millions-of-public-dollars-in -advertising-to-attract-students.html.

22. The ad is no longer available online but ran on ZipRecruiter and oth-er sites. For similar ads, see this search: https://www.ziprecruiter.com/Jobs /Media-Advertising/-in-Tucson,AZ.

23. Kreative Webworks, Inc., "Charter School Marketing," www .charterschoolmarketing.com.

24. KIPP Foundation, "KIPP Brand Guidelines," vimeo.com/107304223.

25. DiMartino and Jessen, *Selling School*.

26. Hayleigh Colombo, "Charter School Offered $100 Reward to Anyone Who Referred Students Who Enrolled," *Chalkbeat*, January 29, 2015, www .chalkbeat.org/posts/in/2015/01/29/charter-school-offered-100-reward-to -anyone-who-referred-students-who-enrolled.

27. Dylan Peers McCoy, "Carpe Meridian Loses Its Charter," *Indianap-olis Star*, June 8, 2017.

28. Testimony of Jonathan Clark, U.S. House of Representatives, Educa-tion and the Workforce Committee, June 13, 2018, edworkforce.house.gov /uploadedfiles/testimony_j_clark_6.13.18.pdf.

29. Christopher Lubienski and Jin Lee, "Competitive Incentives and the Education Market: How Charter Schools Define Themselves in Metropoli-tan Detroit," *Peabody Journal of Education* 91, no. 1 (2016): 64–80.

30. Andrew Kenney, "Denver's Student Population Expected to Shrink in 2019 After More Than a Decade of Growth," *Denverite*, December 8, 2017, denverite.com/2017/12/08/denver-student-population-shrinking.

31. David Osborne, "A 21st Century School System in the Mile High

City," Progressive Policy Institute, 2016, files.eric.ed.gov/fulltext/ED570147
.pdf.

32. Jennifer Berkshire, "When Schools Eat Schools," *Have You Heard*,
July 13, 2016, haveyouheardblog.com/when-schools-eat-schools.

33. Jacqueline Palochko, "Bethlehem Area Introduces New Logo with
Nod to the Past and Future," *Morning Call*, August 22, 2018, www.mcall
.com/news/education/mc-nws-bethlehem-area-new-logo-20180822-story
.html.

34. Palochko, "Bethlehem Area Introduces New Logo."

35. Hacke and Niederberger, "PA Charter Schools Spend Millions of
Public Dollars in Advertising to Attract Students."

36. J. Celeste Lay, "How Uneven Marketing of Schools in New Orleans
Is Turning Education into a Commodity," Scholars Strategy Network,
November 7, 2017, scholars.org/brief/how-uneven-marketing-schools-new
-orleans-turning-education-commodity.

37. Heidi Glenn, "Confused by Your Public School Choices? Hire a
Coach," NPR, November 27, 2017.

38. Kennedy Spencer, "Inspire & Impact: Results Through Marketing,
Charter School Tools," www.charterschooltools.org/tools/InspireImpact
Presentation.pdf.

39. Sara Satullo, "Outrage Over Charter School Ad That Portrays Liberty High Kids as Druggies," August 21, 2016, www.lehighvalleylive.com
/bethlehem/index.ssf/2016/08/why_worry_about_this_type_of_s.html.

40. Colleen Dippel, "Helping Texas Families Find the Best Schools,"
Walton Family Foundation, August 9, 2016, www.waltonfamilyfoundation
.org/stories/k-12-education/helping-texas-families-find-the-best
-schools.

41. Niraj Dawar, "When Marketing Is Strategy," *Harvard Business
Review*, December 2013, hbr.org/2013/12/when-marketing-is-strategy.

Chapter 11: Teaching Gigs

1. Cale Guthrie Weissman, "This DeVos-Style School Turned Teachers
into Economy Workers," *Fast Company*, April 26, 2018.

2. "Table 211.50. Estimated Average Annual Salary of Teachers in Public Elementary and Secondary Schools: Selected Years, 1959–60 through
2015–16," *Digest of Education Statistics*, National Center for Education
Statistics, nces.ed.gov/programs/digest/d16/tables/dt16_211.50.asp.

3. U.S. Census Bureau, "Total CPS Population and Per Capita Income,"
Historical Income Tables: People, www.census.gov/data/tables/time-series

/demo/income-poverty/historical-income-people.html.

4. Dana Markow, Lara Macia, and Helen Lee, *MetLife Survey of the American Teacher: Challenges for School Leadership*, 2013, www.metlife .com/content/dam/microsites/about/corporate-profile/MetLife-Teacher -Survey-2012.pdf.

5. Michelle Hackman and Eric Morath, "Teachers Quit Jobs at Highest Rate on Record," *Wall Street Journal*, December 28, 2018.

6. Michael Sedlak, "Let Us Go and Buy a Schoolmaster," in Donald Warren, ed., *American Teachers: Histories of a Profession at Work* (New York: Macmillan, 1989).

7. Quoted in John Taylor Gatto, "School on a Hill," *Harper's Magazine*, September, 2001.

8. Warren, *American Teachers*; Jack Schneider, "Marching Forward, Marching in Circles: A History of Problems and Dilemmas in Teacher Preparation," *Journal of Teacher Education* 69, no. 4 (2018): 330–40.

9. See, for instance, T.W. Goodrich, "Should Married Teachers Be Fired?," *School Executives Magazine* 52, no. 6 (1932).

10. "The Exodus of Teachers," *School and Society* 13 (1921): 97–99.

11. See Sedlak, "Let Us Go and Buy a Schoolmaster."

12. For more, see Andrew Abbott, *The System of Professions: An Essay on the Division of Expert Labor* (Chicago: University of Chicago Press, 1988); Amitai Etzioni, ed. *The Semi-Professions and Their Organization: Teachers, Nurses, Social Workers* (New York: Free Press, 1969); Keith M. Macdonald, *The Sociology of the Professions* (London: Sage, 1995).

13. "Teacher Trends," National Center for Education Statistics, nces.ed .gov/fastfacts/display.asp?id=28.

14. Dan Lortie, *Schoolteacher* (Chicago: University of Chicago Press, 1975), 62.

15. Leah Wasburn-Moses, "A Fix for Teacher Education: The Three-Year Degree," *Chronicle of Higher Education*, July 29, 2013, www.chronicle .com/article/A-Fix-for-Teacher-Education-/140565.

16. Patrick McLaughlin, Matthew D. Mitchell, and Andrew M. Baxter, *The State of Occupational Licensure in Illinois*, Mercatus Center, June 19, 2017, www.mercatus.org/publications/state-occupational-licensure-illinois.

17. Mike Antonucci, "Union Report: One Year Later, It's Clear—the Janus Effect Is Not Yet What Either Side Had Hoped For, or Feared," *The74*, June 25, 2019, www.the74million.org/article/union-report-one-year -later-its-clear-the-janus-effect-is-not-yet-what-either-side-had-hoped-for -or-feared.

18. Sarah Jones, "Arizona Lawmakers Are Looking to Stifle Teachers' Political Speech," *New York Magazine*, January 2, 2019.

19. John Barnshaw, "Facilitating Institutional Achievement Through Enhanced Benchmarking," *Academe*, March–April 2016, American Association of University Professors, www.aaup.org/sites/default/files /FacilitatingInstitutionalImprovementMA16.pdf.

20. "Trends in the Academic Labor Force, 1975–2015," AAUP, www .aaup.org/sites/default/files/Academic_Labor_Force_Trends_1975-2015 .pdf.

21. Mark Rowh, "Optimizing Adjuncts in Higher Ed," *University Business*, December 4, 2014, www.universitybusiness.com/optimizing-adjuncts -in-higher-ed.

22. Phyllis Korkki, "Adjunct Professors Step Up Their Efforts to Increase Pay," *New York Times*, April 5, 2018.

23. Piss Poor Prof, "Can You Afford to Adjunct?," *Inside Higher Ed*, June 15, 2009, www.insidehighered.com/advice/2009/06/15/can-you-afford -adjunct.

24. Lee Hall, "I Am an Adjunct Professor Who Teaches Five Classes. I Earn Less Than a Pet Sitter," *The Guardian*, June 22, 2015.

25. Ken Jacobs, Ian Eve Perry, and Jenifer MacGillvary, "The High Public Cost of Low Wages," UC Berkeley Labor Center, April 13, 2015, labor-center.berkeley.edu/the-high-public-cost-of-low-wages.

26. Stacey Patton, "'Suicide Is My Retirement Plan,'" *Chronicle Vitae*, November 25, 2014, chroniclevitae.com/news/818-suicide-is-my-retirement -plan.

27. John Warner, *Why Can't They Write?* (Baltimore: Johns Hopkins University Press, 2018), 119.

28. Karina Godoy, Rebecca Crutchfield, and Sarah Griego, "Is This Increasingly Popular Teaching Job the Uber for Teachers?," *eSchool News*, May 3, 2017, www.eschoolnews.com/2017/05/03/teaching-job-uber-tea chers.

29. Sam Meredith, "Chinese Unicorn VIPKid Says It's Focused on Maintaining Quality in the Face of 'Rapid Growth,'" CNBC, November 28, 2018, www.cnbc.com/2018/11/28/rapid-growth-in-education-tech-risks -harming-the-learning-experience-vipkid-ceo-says.html.

30. Rick Hess, "Straight Up Conversation: Can Outschool Bring the Gig Economy to K-12?," *Education Week*, October 3, 2019, blogs .edweek.org/edweek/rick_hess_straight_up/2019/10/straight_up _conversation_outschool_ceo_amir_nathoo.html?cmp=soc-edit-tw.

31. Leeds Equity Partners, "Leeds Equity Partners Completes Investment in Fusion Education Group," press release, November 21, 2017,

www.prnewswire.com/news-releases/leeds-equity-partners-completes
-investment-in-fusion-education-group-300560575.html.

32. Motoko Rich, "At Charter Schools, Short Careers by Choice," *New York Times*, August 26, 2013.

33. Neerav Kingsland, "New Orleans, the New Yorker, and the Perils of Flawed Comparisons," *Relinquishment* (blog), August 14, 2018, relinquishment.org/2018/08/14/new-orleans-the-new-yorker-and-the-perils-of-flawed-comparisons.

34. Job Monkey, "Find a Flexible Job as a Shared Economy Teacher," www.jobmonkey.com/shared-economy/teaching-tutoring-jobs.

35. Quoted in Autumn A. Arnett, "The Gig Economy Is Making Waves in Education," *Education Dive*, August 4, 2016, www.educationdive.com/news/the-gig-economy-is-making-waves-in-education/423791.

36. National Education Association, "Status of Substitute Teachers: A State-by-State Summary," 2000–2001, www.nea.org/home/14813.htm.

37. Alexia Fernandez Campbell, "'I Feel Mentally Numb': More Teachers Are Working Part-Time Jobs to Pay the Bills," *Vox*, April 4, 2018.

38. Lori A. Brown and Michael E. Roloff, "Extra-Role Time, Burnout, and Commitment: The Power of Promises Kept," *Business Communication Quarterly* 74, no. 4 (2011): 450–74.

39. Campbell, "'I Feel Mentally Numb.'"

Chapter 12: Education, à la Carte

1. Valerie Strauss, "Students Protest Zuckerberg-Backed Digital Learning Program and Ask Him: 'What Gives You This Right?'" *Washington Post*, November 17, 2018.

2. Allie Morris, "Sununu Taps Frank Edelblut for N.H. Education Commissioner," *Concord Monitor*, January 18, 2017, www.concordmonitor.com/Frank-edelblut-nominated-as-education-commissioner-7539551.

3. See, for instance, Terry M. Moe, "The New Economics of Organization," *American Journal of Political Science* 28, no. 4 (1984): 739–77.

4. Peter F. Drucker, "The Coming of the New Organization," *Harvard Business Review*, January 1988, hbr.org/1988/01/the-coming-of-the-new-organization.

5. Louis V. Gerstner Jr. et al., *Reinventing Education: Entrepreneurship in America's Schools* (New York: Plume, 1995), 15.

6. Terry M. Moe, "The New Economics of Organization": 750.

7. "The New Normal: Doing More with Less—Secretary Arne Duncan's Remarks at the American Enterprise Institute," U.S. Department of

Education, November 17, 2010, www.ed.gov/news/speeches/new-normal
-doing-more-less-secretary-arne-duncans-remarks-american-enterprise
-institut.

8. "Build Momentum for High School Transformation," XQ Super School, xqsuperschool.org/future-of-work/part1.

9. Doug Tuthill, "More Money for Florida Education? What It Needs Is More Customization," *redefinED*, August 30, 2018. www.redefinedonline.org/2018/08/more-money-for-florida-education-what-it-needs-is-more-customization.

10. Liana Loewus and Andrew Ujifusa, "Course Choice: A Different Way to Expand School Choice?," *Education Week*, April 4, 2017, www.edweek.org/ew/articles/2017/04/05/course-choice-a-different-way-to-expand.html.

11. "Rob Glass, Michigan Superintendent, Asks Parents to Oppose 'Ideologically-Driven' Education Bills," *Huffington Post*, November 29, 2012.

12. Nancy Flanagan, "What's the Matter with Michigan?," *Education Week*, November 24, 2012, blogs.edweek.org/teachers/teacher_in_a_strange_land/2012/11/whats_the_matter_with_michigan.html.

13. Derek Black, "Fight for Federal Right to Education Takes a New Turn," *Education Law Prof Blog*, December 11, 2018, lawprofessors.typepad.com/education_law/2018/12/fight-for-federal-right-to-education-takes-a-new-turn.html.

14. Elizabeth City, "Will Unbundling Provide the Best Education for All?" *Phi Delta Kappan* 92, no. 3 (2010): 63.

15. Clark Corbin, "Ivanka Trump and Apple CEO Visit Wilder Schools," *Idaho Ed News*, November 27, 2018, www.idahoednews.org/news/ivanka-trump-and-apple-ceo-visit-wilder-schools.

16. Nate Poppino, "Ivanka Trump and Apple's CEO Visit the Treasure Valley," *Idaho Statesman*, November 27, 2018, www.idahostatesman.com/news/politics-government/state-politics/article222224730.html.

17. Corbin, "Ivanka Trump and Apple CEO Visit Wilder Schools."

18. Sarah Lahm, "Dreambox or Data Mining Nightmare?," *Bright Light Small City*, December 31, 2018, www.brightlightsmallcity.com/dreambox-or-data-mining-nightmare.

19. Kelly Smith, "Twin Cities Schools Cutting Teacher, Staff Jobs as They Face Massive Shortfalls," *Star Tribune*, April 27, 2018, www.startribune.com/twin-cities-schools-cutting-200-teacher-school-staff-jobs-as-they-face-massive-shortfalls/481115711.

20. Audrey Watters, "What Is 'Adaptive Technology'?," *Hack Education*, September 9, 2014, hackeducation.com/2014/09/09/adaptive-learning.

21. Parmy Olson, "Building Brains: How Pearson Plans to Automate Education with AI," *Forbes*, August 29, 2018.

22. Nick Tabor, "Mark Zuckerberg Is Trying to Transform Education. This Town Fought Back," October 11, 2018.

23. Tuthill, "More Money for Florida Education?"

24. "Interview with Betsy DeVos, the Reformer," *Philanthropy*, Spring 2013, www.philanthropyroundtable.org/philanthropy-magazine/article/spring-2013-interview-with-betsy-devos-the-reformer.

Conclusion

1. Jeffrey S. Solochek, "Gradebook Podcast: Is Private Education Public When Taxpayers Fund It? An Expert's View," *Tampa Bay Times*, February 21, 2019.

2. Emily L. Mahoney and Jeffrey S. Solochek, "Ron DeSantis and GOP Poised to Redefine Florida Public Education," *Tampa Bay Times*, March 4, 2019.

3. Christian Barnard, "What Will Happen to the Education System When the Coronavirus Pandemic Is Over?" Reason Foundation, April 24, 2020, reason.org/commentary/what-will-happen-to-the-education-system-when-the-coronavirus-pandemic-is-over.

4. "Saving Lives and Livelihoods: Recommendations for Recovery," Heritage Foundation, April 20, 2020, p. 5, thf_media.s3.amazonaws.com/2020/NCRCreport_phase1and2_recs%5B1%5D.pdf

5. Chester Finn Jr. and Bruno V. Manno, "Charter Schools: Taking Stock," *EdNext*, August, 27, 2015, www.educationnext.org/charter-schools-taking-stock.

6. Peter Cunningham, "Beware of NAEP Theories and Look for Courage in American Education," *EdPost*, April 20, 2018, educationpost.org/beware-of-naep-theories-and-look-for-courage-in-american-education.

7. Nikole Hannah-Jones, "Have We Lost Sight of the Promise of Public Schools?," *New York Times Magazine*, February 21, 2017.

8. "These Governors Are Calling for Teacher Pay Raises," *Education Week*, March 6, 2019, www.edweek.org/ew/section/multimedia/these-governors-are-calling-for-teacher-pay.html?cmp=soc-edit-tw.

9. Michael Leachman and Eric Figueroa, "K-12 School Funding Up in Most 2018 Teacher-Protest States, but Still Well Below Decade Ago," Center on Budget and Policy Priorities, March 6, 2019, www.cbpp.org/sites/default/files/atoms/files/3-6-19sfp.pdf.

10. Denisa R. Superville, "Public Schools in the South Need More

Investments, Poll of Region's Voters Finds," *Education Week*, January 30, 2018, blogs.edweek.org/edweek/District_Dossier/2018/01/new_report_makes_urgent_call_on_education_in_the_south.html.

11. Julie Chang, "How Rural Lawmakers Killed School Choice Legislation in Texas," *Statesman*, November 8, 2017, www.statesman.com/NEWS/20171108/How-rural-lawmakers-killed-school-choice-legislation-in-Texas.

12. Horace Mann, *Tenth Annual Report of the First Secretary of the Massachusetts Board of Education* (Boston: Dutton and Wentworth, 1849).

13. "Prepared Remarks by Secretary DeVos to the Alfred E. Smith Foundation," U.S. Department of Education, May 16, 2018, www.ed.gov/news/speeches/prepared-remarks-secretary-devos-alfred-e-smith-foundation.

INDEX

Abeka, 73
Academica, 93
Accelerated Christian Academy, 73
Accelerated Christian Education
    (curriculum), 73
ACCEL Schools, 81, 95–96
accountability: bipartisan consen-
    sus on, 209–11; consumer choice
    and, 69–72, 74–78, 86–87,
    91–97, 139–40, 198–99; online
    reviews and, 138–40, 144–46;
    profit motive as substitute for,
    79–99
Act 10 (Wisconsin), 36, 54
Adamson Act, 120
adjunctification, 180–82, 186–88
admissions policies and figures,
    159–62. See also charter
    schools; private schools; regula-
    tions
Advanced Placement courses,
    104–5
advertising. See marketing
AFT (American Federation of
    Teachers), 46, 48

AI (artificial intelligence), 204. See
    also algorithms
Airbnb, 14, 149
Alabama, 106, 187
Albert Shanker Institute, 49
ALEC (American Legislative
    Exchange Council), xvii, 12, 20,
    34, 42–43, 52, 77, 94, 111–12,
    125–26, 135, 144–45, 197
algorithms, 41–42, 104, 109–13,
    191–96, 200–206. See also
    personalization (of learning);
    teachers
Alito, Samuel, 51
Allen, Jeanne, 94, 129
Allentown, 168
"Alternative Certification Act"
    (ALEC model legislation), 126
Amazon, 28, 39, 42, 140–43
American Association of Univer-
    sity Professors, 180
American Bar Association, 178
American Council on Education,
    132

American Enterprise Institute, 127, 155

American Federation for Children, 25, 97

American Leadership Academy, 96–97

American Medical Association, 178

Americans for Prosperity, 35, 37, 54

America Online, 104

Amtrak, 83

Angulo, A.J., 89

Anthony, Susan B., 46

anxiety, xvii, 49, 158, 171

Apollo Education Group, 88

Apple, 200–202

apprenticeships of observation, 125, 177, 187–88. *See also* professionalization (of teachers); teachers

Arizona, xxi, 11–12, 26, 42–45, 59, 66–76, 87–88, 92–94, 96–97, 107, 135–36, 212

Arizona Academies of Math and Science, 163

Arizona Capital Times, 12

Arizona Christian School Tuition Organization, 71

Arizona Department of Education, 126

Arizona Empowerment Scholarship Account program, 75

Arizona Republic, 77, 93–94

Arizona State University / Global Silicon Valley Summit, 14–15

Arizona Tax Research Association, 107

Arkansas, 55, 106

Arnn, Larry, 9–10

Ashby, Steven, 53

The Atlantic, 13

attribution problems (in consumer ratings), 147–48

austerity, 36–37, 45, 48–50. *See also* Great Recession

Ave Maria University, 7

Avenues: The World School, 98–99

Baker, Bruce, 31

Baltimore, 98–99

Barker, George, 110

Barnett, Lou, 20

Bast, Joseph, 9, 25

Baumol, William, 31

Baumol's Cost Disease, 31

Beckham, Jonathan, 140

Before the Storm (Perlstein), 122

Benjamin Franklin Charter Schools, 135

Bennett, William, xvi, 20, 88, 108, 150

big pharma, 91–95, 155–56

The Big Short (film), 35

Bilingual Education Act, 133

Birkin bags, 2–3

Black, Derek, 8, 57, 199

Blaine, James G., 63–65

Blaine Amendments, 63–65, 67–68, 74, 78

blended learning, 101, 107–8

Bloomfield Hills, 198

Bob Jones University, 73

Boies, David, 57

Bolick, Clint, 72

Borrower Defense to Repayment rule, 132

Bradley Foundation, 23, 50

branding. *See* marketing

Brennan, David, 79–80, 93

Brenner, Andrew, 9

Briarcliffe College, 88

Brookings Institution, 122, 131

Brooklyn Secondary School for Journalism, 190–91, 204

Brown v. Board of Education, 18–19, 130

Bruno, Bob, 53

bureaucracies, 8, 16, 20, 84–86, 91, 118, 150, 172, 192–97. *See also* regulations

Burke, Lindsey, 75

Bush, George W., 4, 69

Bush, Jeb, 15, 93, 100–101, 117, 144, 207

Bush v. Gore, 57

Business Roundtable, 52
Byman, Eleanor, 21

California, 60, 111, 116–17, 128
Caplan, Bryan, 13, 41
Carnegie, Andrew, 194
Carpe Diem Meridian charter
    school, 165, 203–4
The Case Against Education
    (Caplan), 13
Casey, Leo, 49
CASSA (Cleveland Arts and Social
    Sciences Academy), 95
casualization (of higher ed), 180–82
Catholicism, 64, 74, 214
Cato Institute, 18, 35, 118–19
Center for College Affordability
    and Productivity, 89
Center for Education Reform
    (CER), 94, 129
Center for Public Integrity, 77
charter schools: as alternative to
    traditional publics, 10, 165–68;
    caps on, 127–28; creation of,
    21–22; Democratic support for,
    11, 22–23, 55, 57–58, 97; for-
    profit versions of, 92–97, 185,
    203–4; management companies
    and, 80–81, 91–95, 116–17,
    136, 163–64; marketing and,
    154–55, 159–65; religious
    instruction and, 92; teacher cer-
    tification and, 126–29; union-
    ization and, 45, 57–59. *See also
    specific schools and manage-
    ment companies*
Charter Schools USA, 93, 96
cheating scandals, 82, 128
Chicago Teachers Federation
    (CTF), 46
Chicago Tribune, 21
Children's Health Insurance Pro-
    gram (CHIP), 34
China, 183–84
choice. *See* charter schools;
    neo-vouchers; private schools;
    voucher programs

Christensen, Clayton, 101
Christian Science Monitor, 83
Chronicle of Higher Education,
    178, 182
Chubb, John, 23, 85, 112
citizenship, 6–7, 34–43, 123, 148,
    180, 198–99, 212–13
Citizens United decision, xiv–xv
City, Elizabeth, 199–200
The City Fund, 185
civil rights, 129–32
Civil Rights Act (1964), 130
Clark, Jonathan, 166
class, 25–26, 39, 46, 55, 68,
    119–21, 156–57, 177. *See also*
    poverty
class size, 30, 33, 36, 38, 58–61,
    86, 98–99, 106–7, 109–12,
    156–57, 165–66
Clayton Act, 120
Clean Air Act, 122
Clean Water Act, 122
Clearwater Academy Interna-
    tional, 73
Cleveland, 58
Cleveland Scholarship and Tutor-
    ing Program, 24
Clinton, Bill, 23, 55, 85, 97, 123
Clinton, Hillary, 54–55, 95
Club for Growth, 35
Clune, William H., 137
CMOs (charter management orga-
    nizations). *See* charter schools;
    school management companies
Cohen, Philip N., 32
collective bargaining, 36, 46–48,
    50–54. *See also* privatization;
    teachers; unions
college-going, 2, 158, 161
Colorado, 63. *See also* Denver
Common Core standards, 57, 183
common good (education as), xvi–
    xix, 4–7, 43, 146–48, 213–15,
    221n9
common school movement, 213–15
Commonwealth Charter Academy,
    162

competition (among schools),
    162–65. *See also* market forces;
    marketing; per-pupil funding
compulsory schooling, 10–12,
    120–21
Connections Academy, 110, 116
Conscience of a Conservative
    (Goldwater), 51
Conservative Caucus of State Leg-
    islators, 34, 52
consumerism, 14–18, 63–65,
    74–78, 86–87, 91–97, 139–40,
    198–99
Cook, Tim, 199–202
coronavirus pandemic, xiii–xiv,
    8, 209
correspondence schools, 101–4
costs (of public education), 110;
    class size and, 30, 33, 38, 43,
    200–201; equity concerns and,
    7, 17, 22–29, 39, 56–57, 61, 88,
    132–36, 195; Great Recession
    and, 35–37; regulations and,
    29, 121–23, 132–36; student
    outcomes and, 37–42; teacher
    pay and, 27–29, 31–33, 41–42,
    178–87. *See also* privatization;
    special education; teachers
Cottom, Tressie McMillan, 90–91
Coulson, Andrew, 18
"Course Choice Program Act"
    (ALEC model legislation), 197
Creamer, Damian, 135
credence goods, 146–48
credentialing, 90–91, 103, 120–21,
    123–26
credit recovery programs, 108–9
Cunningham, Peter, 210

Dallas News, 144–45
Daniels, Mitch, 155
Dark Money (Mayer), xiv, 12–13
data mining, 190–91, 202–3
Davis, Carl, 71
Dawar, Niraj, 173
D.C. Opportunity Scholarship
    Program, 24
DeAngelis, Corey, 221n9

debit cards, 74–78, 186
debt burden (of students), 88–91
decentralization, 193
Deerfield Academy, 158
democracy, 16–18, 198. *See also*
    citizenship; market forces
Democracy in Chains
    (MacLean), xiv
democratic governance: market-
    based evasions of, xviii–xix;
    public education and, xix
Democratic Party, 210; charter
    schools and, 11, 22–23, 55–58,
    97; New Democrats and, 22–23,
    83–84, 97
Denver, 129, 167–68
Department of Defense, 81, 88
Department of Education, 34, 41
deprofessionalization (of teaching).
    See gig economy; teachers
deregulation. *See* regulations
DeSantis, Ron, 207
desegregation, 18–19, 51, 129–30
Detroit, 58, 166–67, 198
Detroit Federation of Teachers,
    58
DeVos, Betsy, 50; coronavirus
    opportunism and, xiii–xiv, 8;
    factory-model myth and, 192;
    homeschooling and, 12; lob-
    bying groups founded by, 25,
    50, 111; Michigan politics and,
    92–93; privatization agenda of,
    xvii, 6–10, 14–15, 62–65, 74,
    113–14, 118–19, 139, 192, 196,
    205–9, 211, 215; regulatory
    rollback and, 28–29, 131–32;
    "Rethink School" tour of,
    xx; teacher certification and,
    127–28; voucher programs and,
    xv–xvi, 4–7, 76, 207–8
Digital Learning Now!, 100, 105
Dillon, Jeff, 202
DiMartino, Catherine, 162
Diploma Mills (Angulo), 89
direct mailers, 159–60
dismantling (of public education),
    xiv, 7, 11, 21, 38, 43–45, 101,

118–19, 125, 137, 140, 191, 208. *See also* privatization
DLC (Democratic Leadership Council), 22–23
Dorsett Educational Systems, 82
Dreambox, 202–3
dropout rates, 103, 135, 161
Drucker, Peter, 193
Ducey, Doug, 136
Duncan, Arne, 4, 55, 194
Dye, Thomas, 52
Dzieza, Josh, 152

EAI (Education Alternatives, Inc.), 83–84
East Valley Tribune, 72
Economic Policy Institute, 32
EdChoice, 25–26
Edelblut, Frank, xvi
Edison Project/EdisonLearning, 85–87, 98, 116
Education and Workforce Development Task Force (ALEC), 111
The Education Debit Card (Friedman Foundation), 75
Education for All Handicapped Children Act, 29, 130
Education Freedom Scholarships, 208
education savings accounts (ESAs), xvi, 20–21, 45, 74–78, 196, 209
Education Week, 70
edvertising, 155–57. *See also* marketing
Edwards, Lee, 51
efficiency (of markets), 17–19. *See also* market forces; privatization
Electronic Classroom of Tomorrow (ECOT), 94–96, 100–101, 114–15, 117
Electronic High School, 104–5
Elementary and Secondary Education Act (1965), 21, 130
emergency certifications, 126
Endangered Species Act, 74
Endicott, Katie, 44
English language learners, 203
enslavement, 213–14

Equal Educational Opportunities Act, 130, 133
equity, 7, 17, 22–29, 39, 56–57, 61, 88, 132–36, 195, 214
eSchool News, 183
Espinoza v. Montana Department of Revenue, 77
Excellent Schools PA, 128–29
experience goods, 146–48

Facebook, 115, 169, 171–72, 188, 190–91
factory model myth, xvii, 191–96
Fallin, Mary, xvi
families. *See* accountability; consumerism; marketing
Families Empowered, 172
Farley, Steve, 68
Farnsworth, Eddie, 93–94, 135
fear, xvii, 49, 158, 171. *See also* positional goods
Federal Communications Commission, 103
Federal Meat Inspection Act, 119
Federal Trade Commission, 120, 155
"Fed Up Friday," 44
Felton, Emmanuel, 58
51Talk, 183
financial aid (as for-profit driver), 87–88
Finn, Chester, Jr., 20, 85, 210
The Fissured Workplace (Weil), 189
Flanagan, Nancy, 198
FlexJobs, 186
Florida, 24, 26, 30, 42, 69–75, 92, 105–6, 205, 210
Florida Virtual School (FLVS), 105
Flurie, Maurice, 162
Food and Drug Administration, 95, 155
Forbes, 204
Fordham Law Review, 65
for-profit colleges, 87–91, 132, 180–82
Foundation for Excellence in Education, 69, 100
Foxx, Virginia, 41

Franks, Trent, 66
fraud and self-dealing (in public
    expenditure), 71–72, 75–76, 88,
    93–99, 115–16, 127–29, 132,
    136–37, 143
freedom (personal), 5, 7, 10–13,
    132, 149–50. *See also* privatiza-
    tion
Freedom Foundation, 50, 59
Friedman, Milton, xviii–xix,
    17–20, 24–26, 122
Friedman Foundation, 75, 129
Fusion Academy, 174–75, 184–85

Gaebler, Ted, 84
Gainful Employment regulations,
    132
Garcia-Roberts, Gus, 70
Gates, Bill, 28–29, 126
gay students, 69–70, 73
Georgia, 42
Gerstner, Louis, 193
GI Bill, 88
gig economy, 138, 149, 152–53,
    174–75, 180–89
Gilroy, California, 81–82
Ginsburg, Ruth Bader, 77
Glass, Rob, 198
Goldstein, Dana, 46, 49
Goldwater, Barry, 19–20, 51–54,
    66, 121–23, 208
Goldwater Institute, 72
Golle, John, 83
González, Mary, 145
government: bureaucracy and, 8,
    16, 20, 84–86, 91, 118, 150,
    172, 192–97; market interfer-
    ence of, 14–21, 63–65, 74–78,
    82–84, 86–87, 91–97, 139–40,
    194, 198–99, 210; monopoly
    of, 16, 82–84, 194, 210;
    neo-vouchers' undermining of,
    62–72; performance contract-
    ing and, 81–82, 86–87, 193–94,
    196–99; profit motive as sub-
    stitute for, 79–99; Progressive
    Era and, 119–21; starvation
    of, 33–35; tyranny and, 5–10,

14–15, 19; undermining of,
    208–12. *See also* accountability;
    privatization; public education
graduation rates, 113
Great Depression, 7, 18, 50, 177
Great Recession, 35, 53, 55
GreatSchools.org, 139, 145–46

Hage, Jonathan, 93, 96
Hannah-Jones, Nikole, 211
Hart, Oliver, 98
Harvard Business Review, 173
Hawaii, 104
Hawaii E-School, 105
Heartland Institute, 9, 25
Heritage Foundation, xvi, 16, 20,
    34–35, 51, 129, 209
Hermès, 3
Hernandez, Kelly, 191
Hertel-Fernandez, Alexander, 36
higher education, 87–88, 180–82.
    See also for-profit colleges
Higher Education Act, 131
High-Tech Institute, 88
Hill, Paul, 131
Hillsdale College, 9–10
homeschooling, 10–11
homosexuality, 69–70, 73
Hoover Institution, 19, 56, 129,
    193
Howe, William, 56
Hubbard, L. Ron, 73
Huizenga, J.C., 92
Hurricane Katrina, 170
HY Processing, 71

IDEA (Individuals with Disabilities
    Education Act), 29, 70, 130
Illinois, 67
Illinois Virtual High School, 104
India, 113
Indiana, 77, 92, 115, 134, 154
Indianapolis, 58
inequality, 8, 43, 49, 208. *See also*
    class; poverty
Institute for Professional Develop-
    ment, 87
Institute on Taxation and Eco-

nomic Policy, 71
International Correspondence
   School, 102
invisible hand, 16–17
Invisible Hands (Phillips-Fein), 9
ITT Technical Institute, 88–90
Ivy Academia Charter School, 160
Ivy Prep Academy, 160

James, Thomas, 121
Janus v. AFSCME, 50–51, 54, 59,
   179
Jessen, Sarah Butler, 162
JobMonkey.com, 186
Jobs, Laurene Powell, 194
Jobs, Steve, 173
Johnson, Lyndon, 19, 122

K12 Inc., 88, 96, 108, 110,
   112–17, 164–65
Kaestle, Carl, 102
Kagan, Robert, 122
Kahlenberg, Richard, 56
Kalanick, Travis, 149
Kansas, 37, 126
Kansas Policy Institute, 126
Kavanaugh, Brett, 77–78
Keating-Owen Child Labor Act,
   120
Keegan, Lisa Graham, 71
Keep Learning San Antonio
   (campaign), 172–73
Kennedy, John F., 47
Kentucky, 44
Kingsland, Neerav, 185
KIPP Schools, 163–64
Klein, Rebecca, 73
Koch brothers, xiv–xv, 9, 12–13,
   35–37, 42, 50, 54, 77, 89
Kolderie, Ted, 21–22
Korten, Patrick, 129
Kreative Webworks, 163

Lafer, Gordon, xv
Lager, William, 94–95, 101, 115
Lahm, Sarah, 202–3
Lau v. Nichols, 133
League of Women Voters, 21

Learn Everywhere, 197
"Learning Happens Everywhere"
   (ad), 165
Leeds Equity Partners, 185
Lehrer, Brian, 159
Leona Group, 92
Lesko, Debbie, 76
Levine, Donald M., 82
libertarianism, 5, 7–13. *See also*
   privatization
licensure. *See* professionalization
   (of teachers)
lobbying, 25, 50, 91–95, 110–11.
   See also marketing
Lockheed Martin, 81
Lortie, Dan, 32, 177
Los Angeles, 167
Los Angeles Times, 146
luxury goods, 156–59
Lyft, 183

Mackinac Center for Public policy,
   50
MacLean, Nancy, xiv
Maine, 104
Mann, Horace, 213
Manno, Bruno, 210
Marinova, Milena, 204
market forces: anticommunism
   and, 51–52; beneficiaries of,
   62–78; consumer-citizens and,
   14–18, 63–65, 69–72, 74–78,
   86–87, 91–97, 139–40, 198–99;
   Democratic support for, 11,
   22–23, 55–58, 97; deregulation
   and, 134–36; DeVos's advocacy
   for, 14–15; freedom of choice
   and, 5, 10–13, 16; gig workers
   and, 174–75; marketing and,
   154–55, 162–65; per-pupil
   funding and, 23, 26, 39, 98,
   104–10, 165–68, 201; profit
   motive and, 79–99, 104–8;
   school improvement and, 15–16,
   21–25, 209–10; virtual schools
   and, 105–12
marketing: importance of, to private schools, 2–3, 156–59;

marketing (*continued*): lobbying as, 91–95, 110–11, 116–17; per-pupil funding and, 23, 26, 39, 98, 104–10, 165–69, 201; positional goods and, 156–62; privatization's hegemony and, 170–73; rating systems and, 138–43; traditional public school budgets and, 168–69; truth-in-advertising and, 95–97, 155–58

Marvit, Moshe, 51

Massachusetts, 10, 128

Mayer, Jane, xiv, 12–13

McGinley, Jeri, 36

"The Meaning of Educational Freedom" (article), 11

Medicare and Medicaid, 34

Mendez v. Westminster, 130

Mercatus Center, 179

Mercury News, 116–17

merit pay, xix, 55

Miami New Times, 70

Michelin restaurant guide, 141–42, 151

Michigan, 39–40, 52–55, 92, 106, 109–10, 126, 198. *See also* Detroit

Michigan Connections Academy, 110

Michigan Education Association, 53

Michigan Virtual Charter Academy, 110, 114

Michigan Virtual School, 106

microtargeting, 171–72

Milken, Michael, 108

Miller, John J., 23

Milwaukee, 23–24

Milwaukee Parental Choice Program, 23–25

Minnesota, 21–22, 57, 84, 92, 202–3

Miron, Gary, 92, 134

mission statements, 166–67

Mississippi, 75

Missouri, 77

Missouri College, 88

Moe, Terry, 19, 23–24, 42, 48, 85, 107, 112, 193

money laundering, 66–68. *See also* private schools; tax-credit scholarship programs

monopoly (by government), 16, 82–84, 194, 210

Montana, 77–78

Montini, E.J., 94

moral panics, 49

Moskowitz, Eva, 159, 162

Mosley, Paul, 12

Murdoch, Rupert, 115

Nathoo, Amir, 184

National Alliance for Public Charter Schools, 161–62

National Charter Schools Institute, 162

National Conservation Commission, 119

National Coronavirus Recovery Commission, 209

National Education Policy Center, 66–67, 114, 116

National Heritage Academies, 92, 97, 185

National Institute of Education, 20

National Institute on Money in State Politics, 110

National Labor Relations Act (NLRA), 46–47

National Park Service, 120

National Review, 11, 23, 129

National Right to Work Foundation, 51, 59

National Teachers Association, 46

A Nation at Risk (report), xviii

NEA (National Education Association), 46, 48–49, 52

neoliberalism, xix, 125

neo-vouchers, 26, 40, 62–72, 74–78, 208

Nevada, 26, 75, 113

New Deal, 7, 51–52, 84

New Democrats, 83–84, 97. *See also* Democratic Party

New Hampshire, 191–92, 197

New Jersey, 57
New Mexico, 126
New Orleans, 129, 170, 185
New Schools Venture Fund, 145
New York (state), 57, 60
New York City, 47, 49, 185
New York Daily News, 141
New York Times, 109–10, 114, 122, 142
Niche.com, 145
Nixon, Richard, 19
No Child Left Behind Act (NCLB), 4, 57
no excuses discipline policies, 160
Noonan, Tommy, 143
North Carolina, 60–61, 75, 212
Northwest Ordinance, 102

Obama, Barack, 4, 55, 57–58, 131–32, 210
Occupational Safety and Health Act, 122
Ocean Hill-Brownsville strike, 49
Office for Civil Rights (in ED), 131
Ohio, 24, 77, 79–80, 92, 94–95, 100, 111, 113, 116
Oklahoma, 27, 42–44, 59, 113, 188
Olin Foundation, 23
Olson, Justin, 107
123TaxCredit.com, 68
online learning, 75, 104–5. *See also* algorithms; personalization (of learning); virtual schools
online reputation systems, 149–53. *See also* rating systems
Oregon, 104
Organic Act, 120
Orlando Sentinel, 69, 73–74
Osborne, David, 84
Outschool, 184
outsourcing. *See* performance contracting

Packard, Ron, 93, 96
Parker, Thomas, 168
Pearson, 204

Peer Assistance and Review, 150–51
Pell Grants, 88
Pennsylvania, 111
Pennsylvania Cyber Charter School, 111
performance contracting, 81–82, 86–87, 193–94, 196–99
Perlstein, Rick, 122
per-pupil funding, 23, 26, 39, 98, 104–10, 165–68, 198, 200–201
personalization (of learning), 109–10, 165–66, 191–96, 200–206
Peterson, Paul, 24
Philadelphia Federation of Teachers, 57–58
Phillips, Tim, 54
Phillips Academy, 1
Phillips-Fein, Kim, 9
Pioneer Institute, 128
Politics, Markets, and America's Schools (Chubb and Moe), 23, 86
Poole, Robert, 83–84
Pope, Art, 60
portfolio districts, 129, 185
positional goods, 148, 156–59
poverty, 8, 38, 144, 195
Practical Homeschooling, 11
Preparatory Charter School, 160
President's Commission on Privatization (Reagan), 83
Primavera online school, 135
private schools: admissions freedom and, 134–36; college attendance and, 2; curricula of, 73–74; descriptions of, 1–3; freedom from regulations of, 69–72; gig economy and, 174–75; management companies and, 80–87, 115–17, 163–64, 185; marketing and, 2–3, 156–59; neo-vouchers and, 62–65; prestige markers of, 159–62; regulatory rollback and, xvi; religious, xvii, 3–7, 24–25, 62–65, 73–74;

private schools (*continued*): scarcity and, 2–3, 124, 148; state oversight and, 68–76; teacher certification and, 1–2; tuition constraints and, 1–2, 89–90, 98–99, 156–57; vouchers and, xv–xvi, 18–19, 24–25, 62–65. *See also* tax-credit scholarship programs; voucher programs

privatization: anti-tax agendas and, xv, xvi; arguments against, 98–99; consumerism and, 14–18, 69–72, 74–78, 86–87, 91–97, 139–40, 198–99; coronavirus and, xiii–xiv; customer reviews and, 139–40; Democratic Party's adoption of, 22–23, 83–87; economic anxiety and, xvii; education as a private good and, xviii–xix, 4–7; fraud and self-dealing as a consequence of, 71–76, 88, 93–99, 115–16, 127–29, 132, 136–37, 143; gig economy and, 174–75; ideological roots of, xxi–xxii, 1–13, 18–21; lobbying and, 91–95; marketing and, 154–55, 170–73; popular resistance to, xxi, 65; profit motive and, 79–99, 104–8; regulatory rollback and, xvi, 118–19, 129–32; scarcity and, 2–3, 124, 148; workforce preparation and, 38–39, 41

professionalization (of teachers), 123–26, 175–80, 186–89

profit motive, 79–99, 113–16, 192, 210

Progressive Era, 119–21

Proposition 305 (Arizona), 76

Protestantism, 64–65, 214

psychology (of advertising), 171

public education: accountability and, 4–5, 69–72, 74–78, 86–87, 91–97, 138–46, 198–99, 209–11; bureaucracies of, 8, 16, 20, 84–86, 91, 118, 150, 172, 192–97; as a common good, xvi, xviii–xix, 4–7, 43, 146–48, 213–15, 221n9; complexity of, 146–48; compulsory attendance and, 10–12, 120–21; costs of, 27–31, 98–99, 104–8, 132–36, 165–66; democratic governance of, xix, 6–7; dismantling of, xiv, 7, 11, 21, 38, 43–45, 101, 118–19, 125, 137, 140, 191, 208; equity goals and, 7, 17, 22–29, 39, 56–57, 61, 88, 132–36, 195, 214; fixed revenues of, 80–81, 86, 98–99, 110; government tyranny and, 7–10, 14–15; higher education sector and, 87–88, 180–82, 186; physical infrastructure of, 43; purposes of, 16–17, 38–39; rating systems and, 138–41, 144–46, 150–53; regulations of, xvi, 118–19, 132–36; scale of, 195, 212–13; state budget and, xv, 35–37; tax support for, 6, 19, 27–31, 33–42; unbundling of, xiv, 14–15, 76–77, 191–92, 196–202; wraparound services associated with, 8, 30, 60–61, 120–21, 193, 204–5. *See also* charter schools; private schools; privatization; virtual schools; voucher programs

Public Loss Private Gain (report), 71–72

public/private partnerships, 84

"Public School at Home" (ad), 165

public schools. *See* charter schools; traditional public schools

PublicSource, 169

Pure Food and Drug Act, 119

race, 18–19, 24–26, 29, 48, 74, 90–91, 129–30, 145–46, 156, 195, 211, 213–14

Race to the Top program, 55–56

radio, 103

RAND Corporation, 81

RateMyTeachers.com, 139, 149, 151–52

rating systems, 138–46, 150–53, 179

Reagan, Ronald, xvi, xvii, xviii, 19–21, 33–35, 63, 83–84, 123

Reason, 17

Reason Foundation, 22, 83, 134, 209

#RedforEd, 45

regulations: charter schools' evasion of, 91–95, 126–29; civil rights enforcement and, 129–32; conservative calumny regarding, xvi, xix, 118–19, 121–23, 132–36; costs of, 132–37; higher education and, 87–88; marketing and, 95–97, 155–56; neo-vouchers' skirting of, 68–72; origins of, 119–21; rating systems and, 139–40; teacher licensure and, 2, 59, 109, 120–29, 175–80, 185–89; test scores and, 4, 100–101; virtual schools' evasion of, 105, 110–11, 116–17

regulatory capture, 93–95, 124

regulatory creep, 129

Reinventing Education (Gerstner), 193

Reinventing Government (Osborne and Gaebler), 84

Report Card on American Education (ALEC, 2018), 42, 94

report cards, 144–45

Republican Party, 37, 79, 92, 94–95

reputational rating systems. *See* rating systems

"Rethink School" tour, xx

Reuther, Walter, 52–53

Revenue Act, 120

ReviewMeta, 143

reviews (by customers). *See* rating systems

Reynolds, Brie, 186

Rhee, Michelle, 56

rights (of students), 123–24, 129–36. *See also* civil rights

right-to-work laws, 51, 53–55

risk assumption, 89–91

Robinson, Akila, 191

Rocketship charter schools, 203–4

Roe, Thomas, 34

"The Role of Government in Education" (Friedman), 18

Roosevelt, Franklin D., 19, 51

San Antonio, 172

Sanders, Bernie, 10

San Jose State University, 87

Sasse, Ben, 12

scarcity, 2–3, 124, 148

Schmidt, Benno, 85

school boards, 6–7, 86–87

school choice. *See* charter schools; market forces; neo-vouchers; privatization; virtual schools; voucher programs

Schooldigger.com, 145

School Funding Reform for Wisconsin, 36

school management companies, 80–81, 83–87, 115–17, 163–64, 185. *See also* charter schools; private schools; profit motive

School Superintendents Association, 71–72

School Tuition Organizations, 68. *See also* tax-credit scholarship programs

school uniforms, 160

Scientology, 73

Scott, Debra Leigh, 182

segregation, 18–19, 129–30, 195, 213–14

self-dealing, 71–72

Selling School (Jessen and DiMartino), 162

seniority (for teachers), 48

Sherman Antitrust Act, 120

Skocpol, Theda, 36

slavery. *See* enslavement

Smiley Terminals, 138–40

Smith, Adam, 16

Snyder, Rick, 110

social and emotional learning, 148, 188–89

socialism, 7–10, 51–53
Social Security, 33–34
Society to Encourage Studies at Home, 102
Sotomayor, Sonia, 77
Soviet Union, 9
special education, 29, 69–70, 133–35
Sperling, John, 87–88
starve the beast discourse, 33–35, 43, 68
state constitutions, 27–28, 62–65, 205; school spending and, 34
State Policy Network, 34
Stepman, Inez, 111
Step Up For Students, 70, 140, 196, 205
St. Mark's School, 161
Strahilevitz, Lior, 151
student loans, 88–91
student surveys, 151–53
substitute teachers, 186–87
Success Academy, 159–61, 163–64
Summit Learning Platform, 190–91, 204
supervision (of students and teachers), 103, 109, 113–14, 120, 150. *See also* gig economy; teachers
Supreme Court, 6, 18–19, 63, 65–66, 77, 133, 179, 207–8, 211. *See also specific decisions*
Survey of the American Teacher (MetLife), 175

Tampa Bay Times, 207
TaskRabbit, 149, 180, 183–84, 189
Tax Credit Scholarship Program (Florida), 24, 62–63
tax-credit scholarship programs, xv–xvi, xvi, 20–21, 26, 66–72, 77–78, 208
tax cuts, 35–37
taxpayer rights: educational costs and, 27–33, 35–38, 207; fixed revenues and, 80–81, 86, 98–99, 110; private religious schools and, 62–65; regulations' costs

and, 121–23, 132–36; return on investment discourses and, 39–42; state oversight of expenditures and, 62–63, 67–72; truth-in-advertising and, 95–97
Taylor, Lori, 37
TDR Learning Academy, 73
teacher education programs, 125, 176–78. *See also* credentialing; regulations
teachers: advanced degrees and, 158; algorithmic replacements for, 41–42, 104, 109–13, 191–96, 200–206; certification and professionalization and, 2, 59, 123–26, 175–80, 185–89; cost-cutting's effects on, 81–82, 86, 98–99, 106–7, 114–15; evaluations of, 56, 107, 139–40, 146, 150–53; gender of, 32–33, 125, 130–31, 176–77; as gig workers, 149, 152–53, 174–75, 183–87; labor actions of, xxi, 27–28, 36, 43, 45–47, 58–61, 112–13, 175, 179, 188, 211; licensing requirements for, 2, 59, 109, 120–21, 123–26, 175–80, 185–89; mentoring of students and, 38, 40, 103, 109, 113–14, 188–89, 191; online reviews of, 138–40; pay for, xix, 27–28, 31–33, 41–42, 46–50, 55, 108–10, 174–78, 183–89, 200–201, 211; public support for, xxi, 27–28, 43, 211; shortages of, 101–2, 126; side hustles of, 183–84, 186–89; unionization and, xv, 46–50. *See also* unions
The Teacher Wars (Goldstein), 46
Teach For America, 125, 185
technology. *See* algorithms; data mining; personalization (of learning); Summit Learning Platform; virtual schools
television, 103
Tennessee, 75, 112
test scores: cheating scandals

and, 82; consumer ratings
and, 144–46; as contractual
outcome, 129; as measures of
school quality, 2, 4–5, 56,
81–82, 86, 97, 100–101, 114;
teacher evaluations and, 56–57,
107
Texarkana public schools, 81–82
Texas, 144–45
Thatcher, Margaret, xvii, 82–83
Thirer, Irene, 141
Ticknor, Anna Eliot, 102
Title I, 21, 130
Title IX, 131
Title VI, 130
traditional public schools: building conditions and, 43, 108–9;
charters as competitors to,
162–68; complexity of, 146–48;
coronavirus relief funds and,
xiii; curriculum standards and,
73–74; dismantling agenda and,
xiv, 7, 11, 21, 38, 43–45, 101,
118–19, 125, 137, 140, 191,
208; factory-model myth and,
xvii, 191–96; as "government
schools," 7–8, 10, 80, 82, 84;
management companies and,
83–84; marketing pressures
and, 156, 168–69; voucher
programs and, xiv–xv. See also
neo-vouchers; public education;
voucher programs
transgender students, 131
Treu, Rolf, 56
Trinity Lutheran Church of
Columbia, Inc. v. Comer, 77–78
Trombetta, Nick, 111
Trump, Donald, xiii, 7–8, 10, 41,
54, 95, 118
Trump, Ivanka, 199–202
Trump University, 88
Tuition Assistance Funds (DoD),
88
tuition rates, 1–2, 89–90, 98–99,
156–57. See also neo-vouchers;
tax-credit scholarship programs;
voucher programs

Tuthill, Doug, 126, 196, 205
tutoring, 75, 183–87
Tyack, David, 121
tyranny, 5–6

UAW (United Auto Workers),
52–53
Uber, 14, 138–39, 149–50, 152,
175, 183
unbundling, 76–77, 191–92,
196–202, 214–15
unions: charter schools and, 45,
209; conservative war on, 43,
50–54; as Democratic Party
constituency, xvii; Democratic
Party support and, 52–58; gig
economy and, 174–75; licensure
requirements and, 124–26;
origins of, 46–50; public support for, 60; racial tensions and,
48–49; teachers' membership
in, xv, 179; Thatcher's assault
on, 82–83; virtual learning as
undermining, 101, 112–13;
vouchers' undermining of,
63–65; wildcat labor actions
and, 58–61, 112–13, 179
"Uniquely Brilliant" (ad), 164
United Federation of Teachers
(UFT), 47
United Teachers Los Angeles
(UTLA), 58
University Business, 181
University of Phoenix, 87–88
University of Southernmost Flor-
ida, 88
University Prep Charter, 160
Urdan, Trace, 88
USA Today, 77
USDA (U.S. Department of Agri-
culture), 141–42
U.S. Post Office, 83, 102
Utah, 104–6, 136

value-added movement, 107, 146
The Vanishing American Adult
(Sasse), 12
Vedder, Richard, 89

Vergara v. California, 56–57
Veritas Preparatory Charter
  School, 160
VIPKid, 183
Virginia, 106
virtual schools, 104–8, 135,
  154–55, 169, 179–80, 183–87,
  191–96, 199–207; ALEC's support for, 111–12; as alternative
  to traditional publics, 10; marketing of, 164–65; nonunion
  workforces of, 112–13; quality of, 113–16; regulation of,
  116–17
Voinovich, George, 79
voucher programs: billionaire
  support for, xiv–xv, 12–13,
  172; civil rights issues and,
  134–36; desegregation orders
  and, 18–19, 211; inception
  of, xv–xvi, xviii–xix, 18–19;
  marginalized students as beneficiaries of, 20–26, 68, 72, 75;
  marketing and, 154–55; Milwaukee experience and, 23–25;
  private religious schools and,
  xvii, 2, 24–25; profit motive
  and, 79–80; public rejections of,
  21, 76–77; Reagan's support for,
  20; targeted at the affluent, 77;
  teacher qualifications and, 126.
  See also neo-vouchers

Walker, Scott, 25, 36, 53
Warner, John, 182
Washington, DC, 106, 128
Washington Post, 140, 143

Watters, Audrey, 203
Way, Glenn, 97, 135
The Wealth of Nations (Smith), 16
Weil, David, 189
Weishart, Joshua, 45
Wells, Pete, 142
Welner, Kevin, 66
Westinghouse Learning Corpora-
  tion, 81
West Virginia, 27, 44–45, 59, 126,
  212
Westwood College, 88
Weyrich, Paul, 20
Whitefield Academy, 71
White Hat Management, 80, 93
Whittle, Chris, 85–87, 98, 116
Wilder School District, 200–202,
  204
Williams, Annette, 25
Wisconsin, 25–26, 36, 42, 47,
  54–55, 77, 103, 126, 179, 197.
  See also Milwaukee
workforce development, 38–39,
  41, 111, 200–201

XQ Super School Project, 194

Yarbrough, Steve, 71
Yelp, 139–40, 142–43, 151, 153,
  179
YES Prep, 185

Zagat, Nina and Tim, 142
Zeichner, Ken, 125
Zeigler, Harmon, 52
Zuckerberg, Mark, 190–91

ABOUT THE AUTHORS

Jack Schneider is the author of three previous books and an award-winning scholar. He is a host of the education podcast *Have You Heard* and lives in Massachusetts.

Jennifer Berkshire is a freelance journalist and a host of the education podcast *Have You Heard*. She lives in Massachusetts.

PUBLISHING IN THE PUBLIC INTEREST

Thank you for reading this book published by The New Press. The New Press is a nonprofit, public interest publisher. New Press books and authors play a crucial role in sparking conversations about the key political and social issues of our day.

We hope you enjoyed this book and that you will stay in touch with The New Press. Here are a few ways to stay up to date with our books, events, and the issues we cover:

- Sign up at www.thenewpress.com/subscribe to receive updates on New Press authors and issues and to be notified about local events
- Like us on Facebook: www.facebook.com/newpress-books
- Follow us on Twitter: www.twitter.com/thenewpress
- Follow us on Instagram: www.instagram/thenewpress

Please consider buying New Press books for yourself; for friends and family; or to donate to schools, libraries, community centers, prison libraries, and other organizations involved with the issues our authors write about.

The New Press is a 501(c)(3) nonprofit organization. You can also support our work with a tax-deductible gift by visiting www.thenewpress.com/donate.